Journeying

Journeying

Children Responding to Literature

Edited by

Kathleen E. Holland
Amherst-Pelham School District

Rachael A. Hungerford
Lycoming College

Shirley B. Ernst
Eastern Connecticut State University

HEINEMANN
Portsmouth, NH

Heinemann
A division of Reed Publishing (USA) Inc.
361 Hanover Street
Portsmouth, NH 03801
Offices and agents throughout the world

The authors and publisher are grateful to the following for permission to reprint previously published material:

Pages 6–23, 73–74, 83–84: Rosenblatt, L. M. (1982). The literary transaction: Evocation and response. *Theory into Practice, 21*(4), 268–277. Copyright © 1982 The College of Education, The Ohio State University. Reprinted by permission of the author and publisher.

Page 58: Excerpts from Allen, J. S., Girard, M., & Kristo, J. V. (1991). Read aloud: Prime time instruction. *New England Reading Journal 27*(1), 2–13. Copyright © 1991. Reprinted by permission of the New England Reading Association.

Page 72: From Ahlberg, Allen & Janet (1986). *The Jolly Postman or Other People's Letters*. Reprinted by permission of Little, Brown and Company, Boston, and William Heinemann Ltd, London.

Page 116: Two illustrations by Nancy Winslow Parker from *Bugs* by Nancy Winslow Parker and Joan Richards Wright. Copyright © 1987 by Nancy Winslow Parker. Reprinted by permission of Greenwillow Books, a division of William Morrow & Company, Inc.

Pages 151, 152: "April" and "August" reprinted by permission of Amy A. McClure: *Sunrises and Songs,* copyright © 1990. Published by Heinemann, a division of Reed Publishing (USA) Inc., Portsmouth, NH.

Every effort has been made to contact copyright holders for permission to reprint borrowed material where necessary, but if any oversights have occurred, we would be happy to rectify them in future printings of this work.

Library of Congress Cataloging-in-Publication Data
Journeying : children responding to literature / edited by Kathleen E.
  Holland, Rachael A. Hungerford, Shirley B. Ernst.
    p. cm.
    Includes bibliographical references and index.
    ISBN 0-435-08758-4
    1. Literature—Study and teaching (Elementary)—United States.
2. Children—United States—Books and reading. 3. Reader-response criticism—United States. I. Holland, Kathleen E. II. Hungerford, Rachael A. III. Ernst, Shirley B.
LB1575.5.U5J68 1993
372.65′0973—dc20
        93–12655
        CIP

Printed on acid-free paper.
Production by Ocean Publication Services
Cover Design by Julie Hahn
Design by Katherine Harvey

Printed in the United States of America
93 94 95 96 97   9 8 7 6 5 4 3 2 1

Contents

Contributors

Margaret Anzul, Ph.D., is a school librarian at Kings Road Middle School in Madison, New Jersey.

Bernice Cullinan, Ph.D., is a professor emeritus at New York University in New York City, New York.

Maryann Downing, Ph.D., is a member of the Adjunct Faculty of New York University in New York City and a teacher at the Fieldston School in Riverdale, New York.

Brian Edmiston, Ph.D., is an assistant professor at the University of Wisconsin–Madison in Madison, Wisconsin.

Ann Egan-Robertson, M.Ed., is a reading teacher at the Mosier Elementary School in South Hadley, Massachusetts.

Shirley B. Ernst, Ph.D., is an associate professor at Eastern Connecticut State University in Willimantic, Connecticut.

Lee Galda, Ph.D., is a professor at the University of Georgia in Athens, Georgia.

Joanne M. Golden, Ph.D., is a professor at the University of Delaware in Newark, Delaware.

Elaine Handloff, M.S., is a teacher at the Independence School in Newark, Delaware.

Kathleen E. Holland, Ph.D., is a language arts resource teacher in the Amherst-Pelham School District in Amherst, Massachusetts.

Rachael A. Hungerford, Ed.D., is an assistant professor at Lycoming College in Williamsport, Pennsylvania.

Deborah G. Jacque, M.Ed., is a kindergarten teacher in the Amherst-Pelham School District in Amherst, Massachusetts.

Barbara Kiefer, Ph.D., is an assistant professor at Teachers College at Columbia University in New York City, New York.

Janice V. Kristo, Ph.D., is an associate professor at the University of Maine at Orono in Orono, Maine.

Susan Lehr, Ph.D., is an associate professor at Skidmore College in Saratoga Springs, New York.

Amy A. McClure, Ph.D., is an associate professor at Ohio Wesleyan University in Columbus, Ohio.

Leslie A. Shaw, M.Ed., is an English teacher at the Franklin County Vocational-Technical High School in Turners Falls, New York.

Kathy G. Short, Ph.D., is an associate professor at the University of Arizona at Tuscon in Tuscon, Arizona.

Lynda Hobson Weston, Ph.D., is an assistant professor at Ashland College in Ashland, Ohio.

Jo-Anne Wilson Keenan, Ed.D., is a first-grade teacher at Pottinger Elementary School in Springfield, Massachusetts.

Judy A. Yocom, Ph.D., is a resource teacher at the American School of Paris in Paris France.

Acknowledgments

We, the editors, wish to express our heartfelt gratitude to all the contributors to this book, who fervently supported this three-year project. Their belief that it was both timely and needed was a constant impetus to our work. We also thank our editors, Dawn Boyer and Nancy Sheridan of Heinemann Educational Books and Marilyn Rash of Ocean Publication Services for their outstanding belief in this project from the start and their counsel on all aspects of this work. And, finally, we especially thank our husbands and significant others for their constant love, belief, and patience during the preparation of this book.

K.E.H.

R.A.H.

S. B. E.

Introduction:
Mapping the Journey

Kathleen E. Holland, Rachael A. Hungerford, & Shirley B. Ernst

The genesis of this book was the 1989 convention of the National Council of Teachers of English, where the fiftieth anniversary of the publication of Louise Rosenblatt's book, *Literature as Exploration* was celebrated. She received many tributes, and there was much discussion of the impact of Rosenblatt's transactional theory of reader response on research and pedagogy, but one aspect was missing. There was no discussion of children's responses to literature.

BEGINNING THE JOURNEY

Study of children's responses to literature is a relatively young area of research and pedagogy. Until 1979, all research into reader response had been conducted among adolescents and adults as it was believed that children were not experienced enough to respond adequately to literature. Also, "real" literature was considered to be in the curricular domain of high schools and universities. However, in 1979, this situation began to change because Janet Hickman completed pioneering research that investigated developmental aspects of children's responses to literature.

Hickman's research was pioneering for a number of reasons. First, she presented children's literature as legitimate literary work. Hickman believed that the literature shared with children in elementary and middle school classrooms is as valuable as the literature they encounter in high school and college. She asserted that children's literature is the foundation upon which subsequent literary experiences are built. In children's literature, children first experience traditional literary elements of character, plot, setting, and theme. Also, children's literature has its own genres for children to explore: picture books, poetry, information books, folk and fairy tales, science fiction, fantasy, historical fiction, realistic fiction, and biography.

Moreover, Hickman discovered that children respond to literature in their own unique ways. Children demonstrate a broader range of responses than has been documented among adolescents and adults. While the latter groups usually respond in verbal and written modes, Hickman found that children are capable of verbal, artistic, dramatic, and written responses.

Hickman also discerned three developmental levels in childhood—early, middle, and late—with characteristic responses distinct to but not limited to each. Early childhood is the time from birth to primary grades. Middle childhood is the period from primary to intermediate grades. Late childhood is the time from intermediate through middle or junior high school.

Hickman used ethnographic methodology. For an extended period of time, she was a participant-observer in three elementary classrooms (K–1, 2–3, 4–5) where teachers used literature as the basis for their language arts program. Thus, Hickman was able to describe elementary students interacting with books in a literature-based reading program. For the first time, researchers and educators were able to read an account of how elementary literature-based reading programs work.

Hickman asserted the importance of Rosenblatt's transactional theory of reader response to elementary educators and children's literature researchers. Because of the predominance of basal reading programs in elementary schools and the focus on the skills children need to learn to read, no one had seriously considered the need for a literary theory that elementary teachers could use as a basis of their practices when helping students accomplish literacy. Hickman presented Rosenblatt's literary theory as a crucial element of literature-based reading programs.

Finally, Hickman recognized the importance of the teacher in creating contexts for responses among children. Teachers can help or constrain the aesthetic and/or efferent responses of their students by the settings they create. A key component of these responses is the degree to which teachers allow choices of books and response modes. In the classrooms Hickman researched, children were allowed to choose their own reading materials from among large classroom libraries or from among books with thematic similarities that were selected by the teacher to be used for in-depth discussion groups. Teachers were not only the creators of "communities of readers," as Susan Helpler later found, but also creators of communities of responders who shared their unique verbal, artistic, dramatic, and/or written interpretations of the literature they heard read aloud or read themselves.

JOURNEYING IN THE PRESENT

Other children's literature researchers and elementary and middle school educators have explored different facets of children's responses to literature. The anchor for these later studies has been Rosenblatt's transactional theory of reader response. This book is a forum that allows many of these researchers and educators to present their findings on children's responses to literature. While this book does not pretend to be an exhaustive collection of the research completed since 1979, it offers a sampling of the kinds of investigations that have been completed in this area.

The researchers who contributed to this book are like Hickman in three ways. First, their research methodology continues to be ethnographic. Second, they deeply explore the variety of children's responses—verbal, artistic, dramatic, and written. Finally, they investigate the role of the teacher in providing contexts for aesthetic and efferent responses and in allowing children to choose their own literature and response modes.

However, the researchers in this book have moved beyond Hickman's research to new directions. Whereas Hickman advocated the importance of Rosenblatt's transactional theory within the new concept of literature-based elementary classroom reading programs, these researchers have seen the acceptance and proliferation of such programs within the whole language movement. Their call for elementary and middle school teachers to learn about Rosenblatt's theory is not a response to basal reading programs; rather, their intention is to point to the need for teachers to ensure that literacy and literary theory work collaboratively within whole language classrooms.

These researchers have viewed with alarm the "basalization" of children's literature. While Hickman redefined children's literature as legitimate literary work that children could respond to in their own ways, these researchers present legitimate ways of using original children's literature in the classrooms to foster children's responses. These strategies take into consideration how children uniquely accomplish their own literary development through response modes, such as oral language, art and media, drama, and written expression.

These researchers seem less concerned than Hickman with the developmental aspects of children's responses to literature. Rather, they explore response modes, teachers' influences on children's responses, contexts for children's responses, and various children's literature genres.

Their journeying begins with a speech by Louise Rosenblatt given to elementary and middle school educators, literary academics, and education researchers at the 1982 Children's Literature Conference at The Ohio State University. Her speech remains timely as Rosenblatt asserts the importance of the efferent and aesthetic stances in literary experiences. She challenges teachers to learn more about the distinctions of these stances and to help their students understand and apply them.

After the Rosenblatt speech, four sections follow a framework based on Hickman's 1979 research. The chapters are arranged under sections about early, middle, and late childhood. The fourth section contains chapters about research completed throughout childhood. Within these sections, the researchers focus on the social aspects of children's responses and the teachers' vital roles in promoting varieties of responses.

In the early childhood section, teachers are seen promoting dramatic play, oral language development, written expression, and enjoyment of reading real literature. The children in this section are in preschool, kindergarten, or first-grade classrooms.

In the middle childhood section, teachers are seen helping their students begin to explore a variety of literary aspects: the use of literature for second language development, the efferent stance within the context of reading aloud nonfiction, the distinction between aesthetic and efferent stances within the context of independently reading fiction, and creating a positive environment for children's responses to poetry. The children in this section are in second- through fifth-grade classrooms.

In the late childhood section, teachers are seen facilitating their students' understanding of and experiences with the complexities of literary responses, such as using written journals to deepen students' responses to fiction, encouraging aesthetic discussions about novels, researching responses to books about students' own cultures, and exploring diverse responses to nonfiction. The children in this section are in fifth through eighth grade.

Part IV presents five research investigations into children's responses to literature throughout childhood. These researchers moved across many ages and grades to look at such aspects as literary theme development, drama as a response mode, the impact of picture book illustrations, literary text sets, and evaluation. The children in this section range throughout childhood, from preschool to eighth-grade classrooms.

JOURNEYING TO THE FUTURE

Although investigation of children's responses to literature is a young area of research, it is an important and growing field. Over approximately fifteen years, new knowledge has emerged concerning children's responses to literature and the critical roles that teachers play in its encouragement. While this book is a tribute to Louise Rosenblatt's tremendous influence on research in the field, it is also an exploration of where we have been during the short journey into research on children's responses to literature and where we might want to head in the future.

Only one author (Ann Egan-Robertson) specifically explored children's cultural responses to literature. This area has been neglected among researchers and educators. The populations used in some of the chapters were diverse (Hungerford, Wilson Keenan, Yocom, Holland and Shaw), but the emphases of these investigations were not specifically on cultural responses. Rather, these researchers were concerned with other aspects of children's responses to literature. With the ongoing surge of interest in literature for our pluralistic society and in multicultural literature, more investigations are needed into this area of children's literature research. Moreover, while assembling this volume under the framework of Hickman's developmental characteristics of children's response, we found it easier to acquire research involving early and late childhood responses than research completed with children in middle childhood—especially children in second, third, and/or fourth grade. Future studies also should address this area.

Among the contributors to this book are several teacher-researchers (Jacque, Wilson Keenan, Yocom, Weston, Anzul, Golden and Handloff, Egan-Robertson, and Edmiston). This type of research is a recent phenomenon in the field of educational research. Teacher-researchers provide unique perspectives and voices. More teacher-researchers are needed to study and report on children's responses to literature.

Only one author (Lee Galda) tackled the question of evaluation and the role of reader responses. Future researchers might examine how reader response fits into classroom and schoolwide qualitative and quantitative means of student assessment. One aspect of assessment that needs further investigation is the impact of reader response on student comprehension.

In the final commentary, Bernice Cullinan presents her reflections on future directions researchers might travel as they journey further into research on children's responses to literature. She suggests that these research chapters are a strong beginning point. However, we have a long way to go on our journeying.

1

The Literary Transaction:
Evocation and Response

Louise M. Rosenblatt

The term *response* seems firmly established in the vocabulary of the theory, criticism, and teaching of literature. Perhaps I should feel some satisfaction at the present state of affairs since I am sometimes referred to as the earliest exponent of what is termed *reader-response* criticism or theory.[1] Yet the more the term is invoked, the more concerned I become over the diffuseness of its usage. In the days when simply to talk about the reader's response was considered practically subversive, it would undoubtedly have been premature to demand greater precision in the use of the term. Now that the importance of the reader's role is becoming more and more widely acknowledged, it seems essential to differentiate some of the aspects of the reading event that are frequently covered by the broad heading of "response."

Response implies an object. "Response to what?" is the question. There must be a story or a poem or a play to which to respond. Few theories of reading today view the literary work as ready-made in the text, waiting to imprint itself on the blank tape of the reader's mind. Yet, much talk about response seems to imply something like that, at least so far as assuming the text to be all-important in determining whether the result will be, say, an abstract factual

The text of this chapter was presented originally as a speech to the first Children's Literature Conference, held by the School of Education at The Ohio State University in 1982. It is reprinted here from *Theory into Practice*, *21*(4), Autumn 1982, published by the College of Education, The Ohio State University, Columbus, Ohio.

statement or a poem. Unfortunately, important though the text is, a story or a poem does not come into being simply because the text contains a narrative or the lines indicate rhythm and rhyme. Nor is it a matter simply of the reader's ability to give lexical meaning to the words. In order to deal with my assigned topic, it becomes necessary, therefore, to sketch some elements of my view of the reading process, to suggest some aspects of what happens when reader meets text.[2] (Note that although I refer mainly to reading, I shall be defining processes that apply generally to encounters with either spoken or written symbols.) This will require consideration of the nature of language, especially as manifested in early childhood. Only then shall I venture to develop some implications concerning children, literature, and response.

THE READING PROCESS AND THE READER'S STANCE

Reading is a transaction, a two-way process, involving a reader and a text at a particular time under particular circumstances. I use John Dewey's term, transaction, to emphasize the contribution of both reader and text. The words in their particular pattern stir up elements of memory, activate areas of consciousness. The reader, bringing past experience of language and of the world to the task, sets up tentative notions of a subject, of some framework into which to fit the ideas as the words unfurl. If the subsequent words do not fit into the framework, it may have to be revised, thus opening up new and further possibilities for the text that follows. This implies a constant series of selections from the multiple possibilities offered by the text and their synthesis into an organized meaning.

But the most important choice of all must be made early in the reading event—the overarching choice of what I term the reader's stance, the "mental set," so to speak. The reader may be seeking information, as in a textbook; may want directions for action, as in a driver's manual; or may be seeking some logical conclusion, as in a political article. Such reading will narrow attention to building up the meanings, the ideas, the directions to be retained. Attention focuses on accumulating what is to be carried away at the end of the reading. Hence I term this stance *efferent,* from the Latin word meaning "to carry away."

If, on the other hand, the reader seeks a story, a poem, a play, attention will shift inward, will center on what is being created *during* the actual reading. A much broader range of elements will be allowed to rise into consciousness, not simply the abstract concepts that the words point to, but also what those objects or referents stir up of personal feelings, ideas, and attitudes. The very sound and rhythm of the words will be attended to. Out of these ideas and feelings, a new experience, the story or poem, is shaped and lived through. I call this kind of reading *aesthetic*, from the Greek word meaning "to sense" or "to perceive." Whether the product of the reading will be a poem, a literary work of art, depends, then, not simply on the text but also on the stance of the reader.

I am reminded of the first grader whose teacher told the class to learn the following verses:

> *In fourteen hundred and ninety-two*
> *Columbus crossed the ocean blue.*

When called on the next day, the youngster recited:

> *In fourteen hundred and ninety-three*
> *Columbus crossed the bright blue sea.*

Questioned as to why she had changed it, she simply said she liked it better that way.

I submit that this represents a problem in stance. The teacher had wanted her to read efferently, in order to retain the date "1492." The pupil had read aesthetically, paying attention to the qualitative effect, to her own responses, not only to the image of the ship crossing the sea, but also to the sound of the words in her ear, and in this instance the discomfort evidently occasioned by the reversal of the normal adjective-noun order.

Freeing ourselves from the notion that the text dictates the stance seems especially difficult, precisely because the experienced reader carries out many of the processes automatically or subconsciously. We may select a text because it suits our already chosen, efferent or aesthetic, purposes. Or we note clues or cues in the text—the author announces the intention to explain or convince, for example, and we adopt the appropriate efferent stance. Or we note broad margins and uneven lines, and automatically fall into the stance that will enable us to create and experience a poem.

Any text, however, can be read either way. We may approach novels as sociological documents, efferently seeking to accumulate evidence concerning, say, the treatment of children in the nineteenth century. The "pop" poet may select a "job wanted" advertisement, arrange its phrases in separate lines, and thus signal us to read it aesthetically, to experience its human meaning, as a poem. Sometimes, of course, readers adopt an inappropriate attitude— for example, reading a political article aesthetically when they should be efferently paying attention to facts. And many people, alas, read the texts of stories and poems efferently.

Recognizing that the reader's stance inevitably affects what emerges from the reading does not deny the importance of the text in the transaction. Some texts offer greater rewards than do others. A Shakespeare text, say, offers more potentialities for an aesthetic reading than one by Longfellow. We teachers know, however, that one cannot predict which text will give rise to the better evocation—the better lived-through poem—without knowing the other part of the transaction, the reader.

Sometimes the text gives us confusing clues. I'm reminded of a letter a colleague received. "Dear Professor Baldwin," it began, "You will forgive my long silence when you learn about the tragedy that has befallen me. In June, my spouse departed from the conjugal domicile with a gentleman of the vicinity." The first sentence announces that we should adopt an aesthetic stance. The second would be appropriate in a legal brief, since the vocabulary seems adapted to an impersonal, efferent stance.

Any reading event falls somewhere on the continuum between the aesthetic and the efferent poles; between, for example, a lyric poem and a chemical formula. I speak of a *predominantly* efferent stance, because according to the text and the reader's purpose, some attention to qualitative elements of consciousness may enter. Similarly, aesthetic reading involves or includes referential or cognitive elements. Hence, the importance of the reader's *selective* attention in the reading process.

We respond, then, to what we are calling forth in the transaction with the text. In extreme cases it may be that the transaction is all-of-a-piece, so to speak. The efferent reader of the directions for first aid in an accident may be so completely absorbed in the abstract concepts of the actions advised that nothing else will enter consciousness. Or an aesthetic reader may be so completely absorbed in living through a lyric poem or may so completely identify with a character in a story that nothing else enters consciousness. But in most reading there is not only the stream of choices and syntheses that construct meaning; there is also a stream of accompanying reactions to the very meaning being constructed. For example, in reading a newspaper or a legal document, the "meaning" will be constructed, and there will be an accompanying feeling of acceptance or doubt about the evidence cited or the logical argument.

In aesthetic reading, we respond to the very story or poem that we are evoking during the transaction with the text. In order to shape the work, we draw on our reservoir of past experience with people and the world, our past inner linkage of words and things, our past encounters with spoken or written texts. We listen to the sound of the words in the inner ear; we lend our sensations, our emotions, our sense of being alive, to the new experience which, we feel, corresponds to the text. We participate in the story, we identify with the characters, we share their conflicts and their feelings.

At the same time there is a stream of responses being generated. There may be a sense of pleasure in our own creative activity, an awareness of pleasant or awkward sound and movement in the words, a feeling of approval or disapproval of the characters and their behavior. We may be aware of a contrast between the assumptions or expectations about life that we brought to the reading and the attitudes, moral codes, social situations we are living through in the world created in transaction with the text.

Any later reflection on our reading will therefore encompass all of these elements. Our response will have its beginnings in the reactions that were concurrent with the evocation, with the lived-through experience. Thus an organized report on, or articulation of, our response to a work involves mainly efferent activity as we look back on the reading event—an abstracting and categorizing of elements of the aesthetic experience, and an ordering and development of our concurrent reactions.

I have tried briefly to suggest some major aspects of my view of the reading process—reading as basically a transaction between the reader and the text; the importance of the reader's selective attention to what is aroused in consciousness through intercourse with the words of the text; the need to adopt a predominant stance to guide the process of selection and synthesis; the construction of efferent meaning or the participation in aesthetic evocation; the current of reactions to the very ideas and experiences being evoked. To develop the capacity for such activities is the aim of "the teaching of reading and literature." We shall find support and clarification in going on to consider children's early entrance into language and into literature. It will then perhaps be possible to arrive at some implications for desirable emphasis in the child's early transactions with texts.

ENTRANCE INTO LANGUAGE

The transactional view of the human being in a two-way, reciprocal relationship with the environment is increasingly reflected in current psychology, as it frees itself from the constrictions of behaviorism.[3] Language, too, is less and less being considered as "context-free."[4] Children's sensorimotor exploration of the physical environment and their interplay with the human and social environment are increasingly seen as sources and conditions of language behavior. During the prelinguistic period, the child is "learning to mean," learning the functions of language through developing a personal sound-system for communicating with others before assimilating the linguistic code of the social environment.[5]

Recent research on children's early language supports William James's dynamic picture of the connection among language, the objects and relations to which it refers, and the internal states associated with them—sensations, images, percepts and concepts, feelings of quality, feelings of tendency. James says, "The stream of consciousness matches [the words] by an inward coloring of its own. . . . We ought to say a feeling of *and*, a feeling of *if*, a feeling of *but*, and a feeling of *by*, quite as readily as we say a feeling of *blue* or a feeling of *cold*."[6]

Werner and Kaplan, in their study of symbol formation, show us the child at first internalizing such "a primordial matrix" of sensations and postural and imaginal elements. The child's early vocables "are evoked by total happenings and are expressive not only of reference to an event external to the child," but also of "the child's attitudes, states, reactions, etc."[7] Evidence of this early sense of words as part of total happenings is the fact that some children at five years of age may still believe that the name is an inherent part of the referent. *Cat* at first is as much an attribute of the creature as its fur or pointed ears. Thus, in language as in experience in general, the child is faced with the need for a process of differentiation of perception.[8] The child's movement toward conventional linguistic forms entails a sorting out of these various elements.

Werner and Kaplan describe the sorting-out process as an "inner-dynamic or form-building" or "schematizing" activity. Acquisition of language is a "twin process," they show us, because the child must learn to link the same internal, organismic state both to the sense of an external referent or object, on the one hand, and to a symbolic or linguistic vehicle, on the other. What links a word, cat, to its referent, the animal, is their connection with the same internal state.

Bates similarly sees the emergence of symbols as "the selection process, the choice of one aspect of a complex array to serve as the top of the iceberg, a light-weight mental token" that can stand for the whole "mental file drawer" of associations and can be used for higher-order cognitive operations.[9] In other words, the child learns to abstract from the total context in order to arrive at a generalized concept of "cat."

This process of decontextualization is, of course, essential to the development of the ability to think, to apply the symbol to new contexts and situations. The "mental token" is the public meaning of the word. Understandably, parents and schools welcome and foster this phase. But much less attention has been paid to the broad base of "the iceberg" of meaning.[10] "The sense of a word," Vygotsky reminds us, "is the sum of all the psychological events aroused in our consciousness by the word. It is a dynamic, fluid, complex whole. . . . The dictionary meaning of a word is no more than a stone in the edifice of sense."[11] Along with the cognitive abstraction from past experiences which is the public meaning of the word, there are the private kinesthetic and affective elements that comprise the complex, fluid matrix in which language is anchored.

THE LITERARY TRANSACTION

The connection can now be made with the view of the reading process that I have sketched. The role of selective attention in the two kinds of reading becomes apparent. In predominantly efferent reading, the child must learn to focus on extracting the public meaning of the text. Attention must be given mainly to the "token" top-of-the-inner-iceberg, to organizing the abstract concepts the verbal symbols point to. These can yield the information, the directions, the logical conclusions that will be the residue of the reading act.

In aesthetic reading, the child must learn to draw on more of the experiential matrix. Instead of looking outward mainly to the public referents, the reader must include the personal, the qualitative, kinesthetic, sensuous inner resonances of the words. Hence attention is turned toward what is immediately lived-through in transaction with the text, toward what is being shaped as the story or the poem.

Both efferent reading and aesthetic reading should be taught. If I concentrate on aesthetic reading, it is not only because our interest here today is in children and literature, but also because it is the kind of reading most neglected in our schools.

Contrary to the general tendency to think of the efferent, the "literal," as primary, the child's earliest language behavior seems closest to a primarily aesthetic approach to experience. The poet, Dylan Thomas, told a friend, "When I experience anything, I experience it as a thing and as a word at the same time, both amazing."[12] Such a bond between language and the inner experiential matrix continues to be stressed in recent studies of children's early language. Words are primarily aspects of sensed, felt, lived-through experiences:

> Beginning about the last quarter of the first year and continuing through the second, increased differentiations of self and other, the sharpening of self-awareness and the self-concept, and the ability to form and store memories enable the infant to begin the development of affective-cognitive structures, the linking or bonding of particular affects or patterns of affects with images and symbols, including words and ideas. . . .
>
> Since there is essentially an infinite variety of emotion-symbol interactions, affective-cognitive structures are far and away the predominant motivational features in consciousness soon after the acquisition of language.[13]

Dorothy White, in her classic diary of her child's introduction to books before age five, documents the transactional character of language. She notes how, at age two, experience feeds into language, and how language helps the child to handle further experience.

> The experience makes the book richer and the book enriches the personal experience even at this level. I am astonished at the early age this backward and forward flow between books and life takes place. With adults or older children one cannot observe it so easily, but here at this age when all a child's experiences are known and the books read are shared, when the voluble gabble which is her speech reveals all the associations, the interaction is seen very clearly. Now and again Carol mystifies me with a reference to life next door, or with some transposed pronunciation which defeats me, but on the whole I know her frame of reference.[14]

White also illustrates the private facet of the child's acquisition of the public language. Having observed the actual experiences that fed into the child's words, the mother realizes that she understands the child's particular meanings and emphasis on words that even the father cannot grasp. Of course, it is such private overtones that we all draw on in our aesthetic reading.

Parents and teachers have generally recognized signs of the young child's affinity for the aesthetic stance. Joseph Conrad tells us that the aim of the novelist is "to make you hear, to make you feel—it is, before all, to make you see."[15] Children enthralled by hearing or reading a story or a poem often give various nonverbal signs of such immediacy of experience. They delightedly sway to the sound and rhythm of words; their facial expressions reveal sensitivity to tone; their postural responses and gestures imitate the actions being described. That they are often limited by lack of knowledge, by immature cognitive strategies, in no way contradicts the fact that they are living through aesthetic experiences, their attention focused on what, in their transaction with the words, they can see and hear and feel.

A most eloquent verbal sign that the story or poem is being aesthetically experienced is the child's "Read it again." White's account of her daughter's "voluble gabble" as stories are read testifies that a relaxed, receptive atmosphere, with no questions or requirements, is conducive to children's verbal expressions of that second stream of reactions to the work that is the source of "responses." White's book shows a child, even before age five, offering various kinds of verbal signs of aesthetic listening—questions, comments, comparisons with life experiences and with other stories, rejection because the story puzzles or frightens, or because it offers no links with the child's past experiences.

When an adolescent girl calls the story of a wallflower at her first dance "the greatest tragedy I have ever read" we must recognize that this is a sign of the intensity of the lived-through transaction with the text, and not a judgment on the relative potentialities of this book and, say, *King Lear*. This transactional process is especially demonstrated in early reading and listening to stories. White tells of reading to her three-year-old the story of a small boy who wakes one morning to find himself the sole inhabitant of his town. White remarks:

> All this to an older child might well represent a delirium of joy and liberty, but to Carol, whose pleasure is the presence of people, not their absence, it was stark tragedy. "He's all by himself," she said, overcome and deeply mournful. Paul's isolation obviously wounded and shocked her, but I had the feeling that in creating this dismay, the book provided her with the most tremendous emotional experience she has known in all her reading. However, here's the rub, this emotional experience was of a kind totally different from anything the author had planned to provide, for planned he had.[16]

The author, she points out, may plan a particular book, but "one cannot plan what children will take from it."

Understanding the transactional nature of reading would correct the tendency of adults to look only at the text and the author's presumed intention, and to ignore as irrelevant what the child actually does make of it. As in the instance just cited, it may be that the particular experience or preoccupations the child brings to the spoken or printed text permit some one part to come most intensely alive. Let us not brush this aside in our eagerness to do justice to the total text or to put that part into its proper perspective in the story. It is more important that we reinforce the child's discovery that texts can make possible such intense personal experience. Other stories, continued reading, the maturation of cognitive powers, will contribute to the habit of attending to the entire text or organizing the sequence of episodes into a whole. We have the responsibility first of all to develop the habit and the capacity for aesthetic reading. Responsibility to the total text and the question of "the author's intention" comes later—with all the indeterminacy of meaning that implies.[17]

The notion that first the child must "understand" the text cognitively, efferently, before it can be responded to aesthetically is a rationalization that must be rejected. Aesthetic reading, we have seen, is not efferent reading with a layer of affective associations added on later. (I call this the "jam on bread" theory of literature.) Rather, we have seen that the aesthetic stance, in shaping what is understood, produces a meaning in which cognitive and affective, referential and emotive, denotational and connotational, are intermingled. The child may listen to the sound, hear the tone of the narrative "voice," evoke characters and actions, feel the quality of the event, without being able to analyze or name it. Hence the importance of finding ways to insure that an aesthetic experience has happened, that a story or a poem has been lived-through, before we hurry the young listener or reader into something called "response." This is often largely an efferent undertaking to paraphrase, summarize, or categorize. Evocation should precede response.

MAINTAINING AESTHETIC CAPACITY

Why, if the capacities for aesthetic experience are so amply provided at the outset of the child's linguistic development, do we encounter in our schools and in our adult society such a limited recourse to the pleasures of literature? We cannot take the easy route of blaming television for this, since it was a problem already lamented at least fifty years ago.

One tendency is to assume a natural developmental loss of aesthetic capacity, or at the least, interest, as the child grows older. We often still share Wordsworth's romantic view that "Shades of the prison-house begin to close/Upon the growing boy."[18] Some believe that in the early school years children become mainly concerned with the "real" and reject "the worlds of the imaginative and the fantastic." This idea, and confusion of the aesthetic stance with the fictive, with the imaginative or fantasy, may have contributed to the neglect of literature in the middle years.

The child's problem of delimiting the objects and the nature of the real world may at a certain stage foster a preoccupation with clarifying the boundary between reality and fantasy. But distrust of fantasy should not be equated with rejection of aesthetic experience. Literary works representing "real" events and "real" people can be read with all the sensuous, kinesthetic, imaginative richness that are applied to fantasy. Imagination is needed also in cognitive processes, in the process of remembering, in thinking of the past, in thinking of alternative solutions to a problem. Again, we need to see that the reader's stance transcends the distinction between the real and the fictive.

The obvious question, in all such developmental generalization, is—to what extent are the changes observed due to innate factors and to what extent are they the result of environmental influences? Fortunately, an ethnographic emphasis is beginning to be valued in contemporary research on the teaching of English, and I should wish only to broaden its purview.[19] Hence the question: to what extent does the emphasis in our culture on the primarily practical, technical, empirical, and quantitative contribute to the reported loss of aesthetic receptivity as the child grows older? Why do we find teachers at every level, from the early years through high school and college, seeming always to be having to start from scratch in teaching poetry?

The fact of the great diversity of the cultures evolved by human beings is in itself testimony to the power of the environment into which the child is born. Anthropologists are making us aware of how subtle signals from adults and older children are assimilated by the infant. "In depth" studies of child-rearing and particular customs or rituals document the complexity of the individual's assimilation to his culture.[20] All who are concerned about education and children have a responsibility to interpret this process to our society, and to be actively critical of the negative aspects of our culture. Just as the medical profession is helping us relate our physical health to general environmental and cultural conditions, so we as professionals need to emphasize the importance of the child's general social, economic, and intellectual environment both outside and in the school.

A nurturing environment that values the whole range of human achievements, the opportunity for stimulating experiences, cultivation of habits of observation, opportunities for satisfying natural curiosity about the world, a sense of creative freedom—all of these lay the foundation for linguistic development. Reading, we know, is not an encapsulated skill that can be added on like a splint to an arm. If I have dwelt so long on the organismic basis of all language, it is because reading draws on the whole person's past transactions with the environment. Reading, especially aesthetic reading, extends the scope of that environment and feeds the growth of the individual, who can then bring a richer self to further transactions with life and literature. We must at least indicate awareness of broader underlying societal or cultural needs before we go on to talk about the teaching of reading, and especially the teaching of literature, the kind of reading our economy-minded school boards often consider elitist and dispensable.

In my sketch of the child's acquisition of the environing language system, I presented as a natural and desirable development the selective process by which the child detaches a sense of the public meaning of a verbal symbol from its personal organismic matrix. But in our society the emphasis, at home and at school, is almost entirely on that decontextualizing, abstracting process. Parents quite rightly welcome the child's abstracting-out of words so that they can be applied to other instances of the same category and be used in new situations. Of course, the child needs to participate in the public, referential linguistic system. Of course, the child needs to distinguish between what the society considers "real" and what fantasy. Of course, the rational, empirical, scientific, logical components of our culture should be transmitted.

Nevertheless, are these aptitudes not being fostered—or at least favored—at the expense of other potentialities of the human being and of our culture? The quality of education in general is being diluted by neglect of, sacrifice of, the rich organismic, personal, experiential source of both efferent and aesthetic thinking. Is there not evidence of the importance of the affective, the imaginative, the fantasizing activities even for the development of cognitive abilities and creativity in all modes of human endeavor?

Throughout the entire educational process, the child in our society seems to be receiving the same signal: adopt the efferent stance. What can be quantified—the most public of efferent modes—becomes often the guide to what is taught, tested, or researched. In the teaching of reading, and even of literature, failure to recognize the importance of the two stances seems to me to be at the root of much of the plight of literature today.

One of the most troubling instances of the confusion of stances is the use of stories to teach efferent reading skills. Is it not a deception to induce the child's interest through a narrative and then, in the effort to make sure it has been (literally, efferently) "understood," to raise questions that imply that only an efferent reading was necessary? Even more disconcerting is the neglect of the aesthetic stance when the declared aim is "the teaching of literature," when stories and poems are presented, not as exercises for reading skills, but presumably for their value as literature, for their capacity to present images of life, to entertain, to deal with human situations and problems, to open up vistas of different personalities and different milieus. Here, too, the concern in most classes still seems to be first of all with the kinds of response that can be met by efferent reading. Questions often ask for highly specific factual details— What did the boy do, where did he go, what did he see, what does this word mean? At the other extreme is the tendency to nudge the young reader toward a labeling, a generalization, a paraphrase, a summary that again requires an abstracting analytic approach to what has been read. Repeated questions of that sort soon teach the young reader to approach the next texts with an efferent stance. Studies of students' responses to literature have revealed the extent to which in a seemingly open situation the young reader will respond in ways already learned from the school environment.[21] The results of the 1979–1980 National Assessment of Reading and Literature demonstrate that the traditional teacher-dominated teaching of literature, with its emphasis on approved or conventional interpretations, does not produce many readers capable of handling their initial responses or relating them to the text.

Questions calling for traditional analyses of character or theme, for example, reveal such shallowness of response.

Educators and psychologists investigating children's aesthetic activities and development reflect a similar tendency to focus on the efferent—a legacy, perhaps, from the hegemony of traditional behaviorist experimental research methodology. Investigations of children's use of metaphor seem often actually to be testing children's cognitive metalinguistic abilities. Studies of the "grammar" of story tend also to eliminate the personal aesthetic event and to center on the cognitive ability to abstract out its narrative structure. Stories or poems can thus become as much a tool for studying the child's advance through the Piagetian stages of cognitive or analytic thinking as would a series of history texts or science texts.

IMPLICATIONS FOR TEACHING

What, then, are the implications for teaching? The view of language and the reading process I have sketched demonstrates the importance of the early years for the development of adult readers able to share in the pleasures and benefits of literature. The theoretical positions I have sketched apply, I believe, throughout the entire educational span, from the beginning reader to the adult critic. At every stage, of course, knowledge of students and books is essential to the sound application of any theoretical guidelines. At best, I can only suggest criteria for differentiating between potentially counterproductive or fruitful practices. I shall undoubtedly only be offering theoretical support for what many sensitive teachers are already doing.

A reading stance is basically an expression of purpose. Children will read efferently in order to arrive at some desired result, some answer to a question, some explanation of a puzzling situation, some directions as to procedures to be followed in an interesting activity.

Aesthetic reading, by its very nature, has an intrinsic purpose, the desire to have a pleasurable, interesting experience for its own sake. (The older the students, the more likely we are to forget this.) We should be careful not to confuse the student by suggesting other, extrinsic purposes, no matter how admirable. That will turn attention away from participating in what is being evoked.

Paradoxically, when the transactions are lived through for their own sake, they will probably have as byproducts the educational, informative, social, and moral values for which literature is often praised. Even enhancement of skills may result. By the same token, literary works often fail to emerge at all if the texts are offered as the means for the demonstration of reading skills.

Exercises and readings that do not satisfy such meaningful purposes for the child, but are considered defensible means of developing skills, should be offered separately, honestly, as exercises. If needed, they should be recognized as ancillary and supplementary to the real business of reading for meaning, whether efferent or aesthetic.[22]

I speak of both the teaching of efferent reading and the teaching of aesthetic reading because the distinctions in purpose and process should be made clear from the outset. (Of course, I do not mean to imply theoretical explanation of them to the child.) If reading is presented as a meaningful, purposive activity, and if texts are presented in meaningful situations, the two kinds of stance should naturally emerge. Texts should be presented that clearly satisfy one or another purpose. Given the linguistic development of the child, probably there should be greater emphasis in the earlier stages on aesthetic listening and reading.

This view of the two stances opens up the necessity for a new and more rounded concept of comprehension in both efferent and aesthetic reading. I shall venture here only the suggestion that this will involve attention to the transactional, two-way, process and to affective as well as cognitive components of meaning. Recent interest of some psychologists in the role of context in comprehension indicates movement in this direction.[23]

In the teaching of literature, then, our primary responsibility is to encourage, not get in the way of, the aesthetic stance. As the child carries on the process of decontextualization that serves the logical, analytic, cognitive abilities whose development Piaget traced so influentially, we need also to keep alive the habit of paying selective attention to the inner states, the kinesthetic tensions, the feelings, the colorings of the stream of consciousness, that accompany all cognition, and that particularly make possible the evocation of literary works of art from texts.

Much of what we need to do can fortunately be viewed as a reinforcement of the child's own earliest linguistic processes, richly embedded in a cognitive-affective matrix. Transactions with texts that offer some linkage with the child's own experiences and concerns can give rise aesthetically to new experiences. These in turn open new linguistic windows into the world. Recall that when I refer to a reading event, it can be either hearing the text read or having the printed text. Both types of literary experience should continue into the elementary years.

A receptive, nonpressured atmosphere will free the child to adopt the aesthetic stance with pleasant anticipation, without worry about future demands. There will be freedom, too, for various kinds of spontaneous nonverbal and verbal expression during the reading. These can be considered intermingled signs of participation in, and reactions to, the evoked story or poem.

After the reading, our initial function is to deepen the experience. (We know one cannot predict developments in a teaching situation, but we can think in terms of priority of emphasis.) We should help the young reader to return to, relive, savor, the experience. For continuing the focus on what has been seen, heard, felt, teachers have successfully provided the opportunity for various forms of nonverbal expression or response: drawing, painting, playacting, dance. These may sometimes become ends in themselves, perhaps valuable for a child's development, but only very generally relevant to the reading purposes. Such activities can, however, offer an aesthetic means of giving form to a sense of what has been lived through in the literary transaction. This can give evidence of what has caught the young reader's attention, what has stirred pleasant or unpleasant reactions. This can lead back to the text.

Requests for verbal responses create the greatest hazards. Adults may, often unconsciously, reveal a testing motive. Perhaps there will be a suggestion of what the approved or "correct" response should be. Sometimes there is a tacit steering toward an efferent or analytic stance, toward the kinds of subjects the adult thinks interesting or important. The reader is often hurried away from the aesthetic experience and turned to efferent analysis by questions such as those appended to stories in various basal readers and anthologies and by teachers' questions or tests "checking whether the student has read the text." Questions that call for the traditional analyses of character, setting, and plot are often premature or routine, contributing to shallow, efferent readings.

Some object that the formalists and poststructuralists are right in identifying literature with its system of conventions, its technical traits. My reply is that, by focusing on these components of the text, they fail to do justice to the total aesthetic experience. Metaphor, narrative structure, linguistic conventions, verbal techniques are, of course, important elements of "literary" texts, and they contribute much to the quality of the aesthetic transaction. But they are vacuous concepts without recognition of the importance of stance. Poetic metaphors or narrative suspense, for example, become operative, come into existence, only if the reader pays attention to the inner states that these verbal patterns arouse. After this repeatedly happens, we can communicate to our students the appropriate terminology—when they need it! "Form" is something felt on the pulses, first of all.

How, then, can we deal with the young reader's responses without inhibiting the aesthetic experience? Two answers to this quite real dilemma suggest themselves. First, a truly receptive attitude on the part of teacher and peers—and this requires strong efforts at creating such trust—can be sufficient inducement to children to give spontaneous verbal expression to what has been lived through. Once nonverbal or verbal comments have given some glimpse into the nature of what the young readers have made of the text, the teacher can provide positive reinforcement by leading to further reflection on what in the experienced story or poem had triggered the reactions. Comments by other children and the teacher, of course, also contribute to this imaginative recall of the experience.

Second, if for some reason the teacher finds it appropriate to initiate discussion, remarks (or questions, if necessary!) can guide the reader's attention back toward the reading event. Questions can be sufficiently open to enable the young readers to select concrete details or parts of the text that had struck them most forcibly. The point is to foster expressions of response that keep the experiential, qualitative elements in mind. Did anything especially interest? annoy? puzzle? frighten? please? seem familiar? seem weird? The particular text and the teacher's knowledge of the readers involved will suggest such open-ended questions. The habit of the aesthetic stance, of attention to concrete detail, will be strengthened for further reading. Cognitive abilities, to organize, to interpret, or to explain, will be rooted in the ability to handle responses. (And enhanced "reading skills" will probably be a byproduct!)

The young reader will be stimulated to make the connections among initial responses, the evoked work, and the text. He may then be motivated to return to the actual words of the text, to deepen the experience. As students grow older, sharing of responses becomes the basis for valuable interchange. Discovering that others have had different responses, have noticed what was overlooked, have made alternative interpretations, leads to self-awareness and self-criticism.[24]

At the opening of these remarks, I mentioned the need to clarify my own version of reader-response theory, but felt no urge to survey the gamut of competing theories. It seems important, however, to recall that the transactional theory avoids concentration solely on the reader's contribution or on feeling for its own sake, but centers on the reciprocal interplay of reader and text.[25] For years I have extolled the potentialities of literature for aiding us to understand ourselves and others, for widening our horizons to include temperaments and cultures different from our own, for helping us to clarify our conflicts in values, for illuminating our world. I have believed, and have become increasingly convinced, that these benefits spring only from emotional and intellectual participation in evoking the work of art, through reflection on our own aesthetic experience. Precisely because every aesthetic reading of a text is a unique creation, woven out of the inner life and thought of the reader, the literary work of art can be a rich source of insight and truth. But it has become apparent that even when literature is presented to young readers, the efferent emphasis of our society and schools tends to negate the potential interest and benefits of the reading. Literature is "an endangered species." By establishing the habit of aesthetic evocation and personal response during the elementary years, teachers of children's literature can make a prime contribution to the health of our culture.

NOTES

1. Tompkins, Jane P. (Ed.) *Reader-response criticism.* Baltimore: Johns Hopkins University Press, 1980, p. xxvi; Suleiman, Susan R. and Crosman, Inge (Eds.) *The reader in the text.* Princeton: Princeton University Press, 1980, p. 45.

2. Rosenblatt, Louise M. *The reader, the text, the poem.* Carbondale, Ill.: Southern Illinois University Press, 1978 presents the fullest statement of the transactional theory. The present article cannot deal with such matters as "correctness" of interpretation, the author's intention, the openness and constraints of the text, or the role of the critic.

3. This is conveniently documented by articles by 11 leading psychologists (Jerome Bruner, Richard Lazarus, Ulric Neisser, David McClelland, et al.) on "the state of the science" in *Psychology Today*, May 1982, pp. 41–59. See especially the article by Ulric Neisser.

4. Keller-Cohen, Deborah. Context in child language, *Annual Review of Anthropology*, 1978, 7, pp. 433–482.

5. Halliday, M. A. K. *Learning to mean.* New York: Elsevier, 1975.

6. James, William. *The principles of psychology.* New York: Dover Publications, pp. 245–246.

7. Werner, Heinz, & Kaplan, Bernard. *Symbol formation.* New York: Wiley, 1963, p. 18.

8. Gibson, E. J. *How perception really develops.* In David Laberge & S. Jay Samuels (Eds.), *Basic processes in reading.* Hillsdale, N.J.: Lawrence Erlbaum, 1975, p. 171; Rommetveit, Ragnar. *Words, meanings, and messages.* New York: Academic Press, 1968, pp. 147, 167; Werner & Kaplan, *Symbol formation,* pp. 23–24 and *passim.*

9. Bates, Elizabeth. *The emergence of symbols.* New York: Academic Press, 1979, pp. 65–66.

10. See Dewey, John. *How we think.* Lexington, Mass.: D. C. Heath, 1933, Ch. X; Dewey, John. Qualitative thought, *Philosophy and civilization.* New York: Minton, Balch, 1931, pp. 93–116.

11. Vygotsky, L. S. *Thought and language,* (Eugenia Hanfmann & Gertrude Vakar, Ed. and trans.) Cambridge, Mass.: MIT Press, 1962, p. 8.

12. Tedlock, Ernest (Ed.) *Dylan Thomas.* New York: Mercury, 1963, p. 54.

13. Izard, Carroll E. On the ontogenesis of emotions and emotion-cognition relationships in infancy. In Michael Lewis and Leonard Rosenblum (Eds.), *The development of affect.* New York: Plenum Press, 1978, p. 404.

14. White, Dorothy. *Books before five.* New York: Oxford University Press, 1954, p. 13.

15. Conrad, Joseph. Preface. *The nigger of the narcissus.* New York: Double-day, Page, 1922, p. x.
16. White, p. 79.
17. The problems of validity in interpretation and the author's intention are treated in Rosenblatt, *The reader, the text, the poem,* Chapters 5 and 6.
18. Wordsworth, William. Ode, intimations of immortality. *Poetical works.* London: Oxford University Press, 1959, p. 46.
19. See *Research in the teaching of English, 15*(4), December 1981, pp. 293–309, 343–354, and *passim.*
20. Bateson, Gregory, & Mead, Margaret. *Balinese character.* New York: New York Academy of Sciences, 1942; Geertz, Clifford. *The interpretation of cultures.* New York: Basic Books, 1973.
21. Purves, Alan. *Literature education in ten countries.* Stockholm: Almqvist and Wiksell, 1973.
22. Cf. Huey, Edmund Burke. *The psychology and pedagogy of reading.* Cambridge, Mass.: MIT Press, 1968 (original edition, 1908), pp. 345, 380.
23. See Harste, Jerome C., & Carey, Robert F. Comprehension as setting. In *New perspectives on comprehension,* Monograph in Language and Reading Studies, Indiana University, No. 3, October 1979.

    In a volume and an article that reflect the psychologists' usual preoccupation with efferent reading. I find this concession: "It may be in the rapid interplay of feelings . . . that the source of the creation of ideas, later to receive their analytic flesh and bones, may be found. If so, how sad it would be if it were discovered that the real problem of many readers is that their instruction so automatizes them that they do not develop a feeling for what they read or use the feelings available to them in the development of new understandings from reading." Spiro, Rand J. Constructive processes in prose comprehension and recall. In Rand J. Spiro, Bertram Bruce, and William Brewer (Eds.), *Theoretical issues in reading comprehension.* Hillside, N.J.: L Erlbaum, 1980, p. 274.
24. Rosenblatt, L. *Literature as exploration,* 1976 (distributed by the National Council of Teachers of English) develops further the implications for teaching.
25. The recent publication of *On learning to read,* by Bruno Bettelheim and Karen Zelan, with its subtitle, *The child's fascination with meaning,* and its emphasis on response, leads me to disclaim any actual resemblance to my views. These authors reiterate what many of us, from Dewey on, have been saying about the importance of meaning and the child's own feelings, and about the narrow, dull approach of much teaching of beginning reading. But the book's concentration on a doctrinal psychoanalytic interpretation of response, disregard of the process of making meaning out of printed symbols, and treatment of the text as a repository of ready-made meanings or didactic human stereotypes, add up to an inadequate view of the relationship between reader and text.

Part I

Literary Responses in Early Childhood

2

Star Wars and the World Beyond

Rachael A. Hungerford

Josh rushed to the teacher, sobbing and holding out his arm, which had a red welt across it. Nora knelt down to examine his arm and asked him what had happened. "We were playing Star Wars and Jack hit me during the fight." The other four Star Wars players rushed up to defend themselves. "You have to hit the enemies in a battle," protested Jack, "it's part of the game." "Yes," agreed Kerrie. "We have to beat Darth Vader and Josh was Darth Vader." This was the third time that week that Nora had had to stop the aggressive play that arose around the Star Wars stories. She took the group aside and talked to them about their play behavior. For a while they remembered—no hitting, no shoving.

The Star Wars friends group had sat in the book corner looking through one of the Star Wars books for almost half an hour. As soon as the block area was free, they raced over and began to build a space ship with the biggest blocks. When the ship was built, they began assigning character roles and the play erupted into a fierce argument. They shouted at and shoved each other until the teacher came to stop the play. Deprived of the physical aspects of their fantasy play, the children returned to the book corner to go through the Star Wars books again and continue their game verbally.

Few dispute and many defend the importance of both play and literature in the lives and development of young children. Both L. S. Vygotsky (1962) and Jerome Bruner (1983) view children as active creators in their own learning processes and contend that social interaction in the form of play is as important as biological processes in learning. Child psychologist D. W. Winnicott (1971) felt that "on the basis of playing is built the whole of man's experiential existence" (p. 102).

Other researchers have given attention to specific learning possibilities inherent in children's interactions with and response to literature. Marilyn Cochran-Smith (1984) stated that the early experiences children have with books and stories not only deeply enrich their experience outside of books and play an important part in language and concept development but also greatly stimulate and broaden their imaginative behavior. Denny Taylor and Catherine Dorsey-Gaines (1988) described ways in which children use print to master their surroundings and build new social and environmental relationships.

However, it is in the area of response to literature that more concrete connections can be made between literature and play and the opportunities each offers for the creation of meaning. I. A. Richards (1929) saw the worth of any literary piece to be individual, decided by personal inner nature and the nature of the world at large. Louise Rosenblatt (1976) expanded on this idea when she began to look specifically at the interaction between the reader and the text and the contribution made by both to the process of meaning making. Rosenblatt's (1978) idea is that the process of response is contained in the interaction between what the reader brings to the text and what the text provides for the reader. Such possibilities were the focus of response research studies done with young children (Hickman, 1979; Kiefer, 1982). The connections among the literature, response, and fantasy play of preschool children became the focus of my own research study (Hungerford, 1990). What happens in the lives and development of young children through fantasy play responses resulting from prolonged exposure to and interaction with a particular literature?

CONTEXT

There were several reasons why I chose to do this study in the day care center of a large northeastern university. The classes were small, with twelve children to three teachers plus several occasional student and parent aides (see Figure 2–1). The physical setting included a large comfortable area designated specifically for book sharing that housed a very extensive and varied picture book collection. The daily schedule of time and activities was open and flexible and always included and encouraged book sharing and responses of various kinds (see Figure 2–2). The children came from varied cultural backgrounds and most had had a fairly consistent exposure to literature. The basic philosophy of the teachers and the govern-

Children	Gender	Age	Adults	Position
Mikki	F	4½	Nora	Head teacher
Josh	M	4	Martha	Assistant teacher
Will	M	5	Edmund	Assistant teacher
Jack	M	4	Laura	Student aid
Alan	M	3½	Jonathan	Extended day
Adam	M	5		
Eli	M	4		
Peter	M	4		
DiAnn	F	4		
Jordon	F	4		
Kerrie	F	5		
Joie	F	4		
Jude	F	4		

FIGURE 2–1   *Setting participants*

ing parent board was similar to mine. Finally, this setting was ideal for using ethnographic research techniques and allowed me to be a participant observer.

My entrance into the setting was made quite easily. A number of adults (parent and aides) regularly came in and out of this classroom to perform various duties, such as helping with lessons, cooking and doing laundry, and conferencing with teachers. All of them made time to talk to the children, read a story occasionally, and asked about on-going lessons and projects. I slipped into the routine quickly and the children accepted me as just another adult like the others. I did not conduct lessons, supervise, or discipline, but I was always available to read stories or play games when I was there.

There were thirteen children in this classroom, six girls and seven boys, who ranged in age from 3½ to 5 years old (see Figure 2–1). They came from somewhat varied ethnic backgrounds. Mikki was new to the class that year. She came from Israel and did not speak English when she joined the group in September. Jordon was Afro-American; Eli was the child of a biracial marriage. Peter had come from West Africa with his mother and was also new to the class. Jack, too, was new in the class that year. He and his family had come from a small community in Alaska. The rest of the group were white. Will, Josh, Alan, Kerrie, Joie, and Jude had been in the same day care class since they were infants. All of the children except Peter and DiAnn had been involved with literature both in the day care setting and at home from very early childhood. They were familiar with book handling techniques, had relatively long attention spans when interacting with books, and all enjoyed books in different ways.

Time	Activity
7:45–8:00 A.M.	Teachers arrive
8:15 A.M.	Children begin to arrive
8:00–9:40 A.M.	Free play time (breakfast is served during this time)
9:40–10:00 A.M.	Circle time
10:00–11:00 A.M.	Activity time (choice)
11:00–11:50 A.M.	Outdoor time (weather permitting)
12:00 A.M.–1:00 P.M.	Lunch time/story time
1:00–2:15 P.M.	Nap time
2:15–3:00 P.M.	Snack and free play time
3:00–4:15 P.M.	Outdoor play (weather permitting) or indoor free play time
4:15–5:30 P.M.	Activity and "extend a hand" (clean up) time

FIGURE 2–2   *Daily schedule of the regular and extended day programs*

The teachers saw themselves as facilitators of a developmental process rather than transmittors or imposers of knowledge. They practiced their deeply held respect for, and belief in, the children's abilities to be active, self-directed explorers of learning. The teachers expected and encouraged interaction with peers and adults as the means to negotiate meaning, and sharing and responding to literature played a major role in creating such meaning. Within this open, flexible, and supportive environment the teachers operated in accordance with Rosenblatt's theory (1978), which suggests that response to literature is a transactional process. On the one hand, the response is individual because it is tempered by the reader's personal experiences and ideas; on the other hand, it is social because through interaction with peers and teachers meaning is negotiated and created, greatly affecting response. These teachers used book sharing and encouraged diverse responses to help children examine and extend meaning in their lives. They supported and encouraged the children to use that meaning to discover new worlds of possibilities.

Interaction with and response to literature was an everyday, ongoing activity in this setting. Children read and looked at books alone, with one or two friends, in small and large groups, with adults both in groups and individually, in informal unstructured times, and in formal structured story times. Teachers and children shared many genres of literature over time. Much of the response resulting from this sharing involved fantasy play of one kind or another. I have chosen to discuss one particular segment of book sharing because, over time, it covered all of the preceding kinds of interactions and contributed a great deal to the explorations and expansion of meaning.

STAR WARS: CHILDREN'S RESPONSES AND BEHAVIORS

Science fiction seemed a rather advanced and sophisticated genre to attract such avid attention from 3½- to 5-year-olds in their day care setting. However, some of the most intensive and extensive interactions among these preschoolers, their books, and their play involved the various Star Wars books and the children's responses to them.

Kerrie, Jack, Adam, and Joie had been intensely interested in Star Wars books and fantasy play since the beginning of the school year. As the year went on, they drew Josh, Will, and occasionally Jude into the Star Wars world of books and play. While the other six children in the setting expressed some interest in the books and the fantasy play, they were seldom invited by this core group to share the books or to participate in the play.

Kerrie was a leader and it became clear that the interest in the Star Wars books and play had originated with her, beginning with the Star Wars videos and then expanding to the books. Kerrie and her 7-year-old brother owned three of the videos and all of the story books. They often watched the videos and played Star Wars at home. At various times, Kerrie had invited one or another of the group (Joie, Adam, Jack, Will, or Josh) to her house to watch the tapes. Consequently, this group had created a shared base of knowledge from which to talk and to play. Kerrie brought in one or more of the Star Wars books at least three out of every five days. She talked about having the whole class come to her birthday party, where they would watch all three of the Star Wars videos.

The teachers shared with me the history of the book interactions and the fantasy play that had resulted in the day care class in response to these books. As the interest in Star Wars books and play grew during the year, the core group coalesced and began to ostracize other children from the play. The play frequently became aggressive, with eruptions of pushing, shoving, hitting, and shoot-'em-dead behaviors. The teachers were very concerned. Obviously, the children were using these books and play to work out and find their way through strong needs and feelings, and because this behavior came so strongly from the children themselves, the teachers were hesitant to arbitrarily put an end to it. Instead, they saw this situation as an opportunity to help the children find different, better ways of dealing with these emotions and needs. After much discussion among themselves and with the parent advisory board, the teachers took a number of effective steps to provide opportunities for the children to learn more appropriate expressions of their feelings through the Star Wars play and book interactions.

STAR WARS: TEACHERS' RESPONSES AND BEHAVIORS

The changes the teachers helped to effect in the book interactions and the fantasy play were neither arbitrarily nor forcefully imposed. These changes involved the structure, content, and action of the fantasy play that arose in response to the literary interactions with the Star Wars books.

The Structure of the Play

First, the teachers reworked the daily schedule in order to redirect some of the Star Wars play. Originally the daily schedule was set up to be free play and breakfast, circle time, free play and story time, outdoor time, lunch and story and nap time, free play, and then extended day activities for the children who were there the longest. The amended schedule had one major change. The longest free play time, which occurred after circle time, became a choice play time. Every day the teachers set up five or six different activities, and at the end of circle time the children could choose the activity in which they wanted to be involved. A maximum of four children could be in any one activity. The rather long time span and the number of choices allowed for movement when the children's interests changed. Some days, though not every day, one of the possible choices was Star Wars play. This adjustment to the schedule accomplished several things. It provided the teachers with a measure of control over who could choose to play Star Wars, and it afforded children outside the core group an opportunity to play.

The teachers then began discussions with individuals, the core group, and the whole class in circle time about the kinds of aggressive behavior going on around Star Wars. They encouraged the children to express how they felt about it. The adults in the setting also continued to be willing readers of the Star Wars books to any of the children who requested it. Most of Kerrie's Star Wars books contained long texts and were illustrated with photographs taken directly from the videos. Usually the children requested that only their favorite segments of these books be read. Within these shared readings the adults encouraged discussion about other aspects of the story beyond the war and fighting issues. The teachers brought the texts closer to the children's lives by discussing with them how they might feel if people or creatures like the Star Wars characters showed up in their back yards or neighborhoods, asking why the children hated certain characters, and determining what made these characters bad. Here the children had the opportunity to connect story to real life, explore what might happen, and talk about how they might deal with it. The children were also encouraged to think about, define, and qualify what they meant when they spoke about things being beautiful, fake, bad, real, or pretend. Through their verbal responses to exploring these stories, both their linguistic and conceptual abilities grew.

Nora, the head teacher, began writing down the names of characters, scrambling them up, and having the children take turns at different roles. This gave the children the chance to explore the ideas and behaviors of characters other than their particular favorites. When protests arose at not getting a favored role, Nora set the rule that players could have five minutes of a favorite role and five minutes of the scrambled choice role, an arrangement that satisfied them.

A power structure that revolved around both the Star Wars story sharing and the fantasy play responses had developed within the classroom. Gradually during the year, the core group had formed a very strong relationship based almost entirely on Star Wars. This group tended to separate themselves from the rest; they wanted to play Star Wars only with each other and in only certain roles. The interactions went back and forth between the fantasy play and the book sharing. At times it began with the group sitting in the book corner looking at and talking about one or two of the Star Wars books. Then they would put the books aside and take the interaction into the big block or housekeeping area to pretend play Star Wars. The interaction might also go the other way and begin with the pretend play, which usually got too rough and ended in book sharing. This group quickly found that they could continue the fantasy play using the texts and illustrations and acting out parts with their voices and hands. It was easier for them to share their favorite character in the book sharing context than in the physical fantasy play. For example, story sharing could more easily contain two Princess Leias or two Han Solos, while acting out could not. Story sharing through the books also involved other children from outside the more exclusive core Star Wars group. Group members seldom invited others to come and look at the books; however, they didn't object to others sitting with them, looking on, and commenting.

Power, residing in ownership of Star Wars artifacts and knowledge, was an invested phenomenon within the Star Wars core group as well. Kerrie owned the books and the video tapes, so in the beginning she knew the most from having heard the stories and watching the videos at home. At the day care, if the group was playing Star Wars without Kerrie, they assumed their favorite roles with some occasional arguing. If Kerrie was part of the group, however, she assumed the role of director, assigning roles and controlling the play. For many months the group was content to allow her this power.

Later, however, when most of the group had viewed the videos at Kerrie's house, shared the books at day care, and built their own solid knowledge base, they were no longer content to do what Kerrie said. Several complained to Nora that Kerrie was being bossy and telling them who they had to be. Nora suggested that those complaining talk to Kerrie about their discontent. In addition, Nora asked them how they would like to have this problem handled. She called the whole group together, including Kerrie, in the the book corner and began by saying that some children were unhappy that Kerrie was the only one who got to assign roles. Kerrie said that the books were hers and she knew the most about them. The others defended their knowledge and their desire to have a turn at running the play. Kerrie was not especially happy with this turn of events, but she didn't want to alienate her playmates. Nora helped them set up a chart of names and times that governed who was to have a turn to assign roles. This slowed the play for several days, but never stopped it.

Ultimately, Kerrie handled this by trying to persuade her friends to look at the Star Wars books with her instead of playing out the Star Wars games. This strategy left her with a measure of her former power because she still owned the books and could say who sat next to her and helped turn the pages.

Jude was only an occasional member of the Star Wars group. She had no particular favorite character but was willing to take on a variety of roles. It appeared that often she joined the group only for the sake of playing and not for what they were playing. However, Jude was also the only other member of the class to own a Star Wars book *(The Ewoks)*. Whenever she brought the book to day care, the other group members, except Kerrie, were ready and willing to accord her the authority and group control they usually gave to Kerrie and her books. Ownership of the book was an acknowledged source of knowledge and power. Kerrie preferred to hold that power on her own and share the book as she chose. Often she refused to let an adult read it to the group. Jude, on the other hand, though aware that this control could be hers, wasn't especially interested in wielding it. She often sought an adult to read the story to the group and seemed much more concerned with getting on with the story than with personal control of who was listening.

Jack concentrated most of his energy and attention on combat fantasy play. He had quickly picked up on this aspect of the Star Wars books and expanded the battle scenes impressively. This specialty gave him a measure of authority as well as the others' respect for his imaginative extensions of the war. Joie and Kerrie tended to squabble over who was going to be Princess Leia, but Kerrie was usually willing to let the role go because she recognized that she retained more control through ownership of the books.

The children involved in this sequence of events were exploring and learning a great deal about themselves and the issues of power. They all understood that ownership offered power—ownership of knowledge as well as of objects. They respected and listened to Kerrie until they were comfortable with and confident in their own interpretations of the Star Wars stories, roles, and fantasy play possibilities. Nora built on this confidence by having them discuss their dissatisfaction with Kerrie and by helping them sort out a workable solution. Nora was, in effect, telling them that they had a legitimate problem and that they were capable of working it out themselves. She was there to help but not to impose. She provided the opportunity for the children to make the connections between the problem and their own abilities to solve it all within the context of their own interactions with the book and the resulting fantasy play response.

The Content of the Play

The teachers provided for the expansion of ideas in the content of the play as well. In the further classroom, which housed the extended day program, Jonathan (a teacher) had helped the children create a space travel environment based directly on the Star Wars books and play. With the children's help, he provided props in the form of headphones, a microphone, a control panel, helmets, and egg carton oxygen tanks. The children used all of these to initiate and explore ways of surviving in space. He also helped the children make a large painted cardboard sun, several planets, and many tinfoil stars, which they hung from the ceiling. A continuum of interaction around this setup continued for many weeks. Jonathan and the children planned a pretend space trip to Mars. Every other day or so they spent time discussing how the trip was going, how far they had traveled, what they might expect to see, and when they might return. Parents became very interested and asked many questions concerning the trip. In conjunction with this aspect of the Star Wars interests, Jonathan displayed and read a number of nonfiction picture books on various aspects of space. Jonathan was very adept at redirecting the Star Wars interest and play. He continued to be willing to read the Star Wars books when requested, but his questions and comments directed their thinking toward the equipment in space ships, the kinds of space occupations the characters had, and the things the characters had to do in

order to survive in space. He helped the children to broaden their
interests and ideas beyond the war and fighting aspects of the story
and to consider different points of view and possibilities.

The space props and factual information about space expanded
not only their personal information base but also provided opportunities for a different kind of fantasy play. The props encouraged
thinking about and exploring special equipment, surviving in
space, traveling in space, and discovering man-made and natural
aspects of space. Fantasy play that grew out of these props and the
nonfiction book interactions seldom resulted in fighting or shooting behaviors. The children extended this knowledge and response
to include other things. It was their idea to pretend that the tricycles
were small moveable space ships and to build tall, elaborate rockets
in the big block area.

The Action of the Play

The interactions with Star Wars books and fantasy play produced
strong indications of how these children were exploring many ideas
about themselves, their world, and their own abilities to accomplish
what they needed to in order to create meaning for themselves. This
exploration was, perhaps, most apparent with the action of the story.
Typical of their ages, these children engaged in various forms of
rough and tumble play as they tested the limits of their own bodies,
the tolerance of the society, and the setting around them. Such play
had a ready outlet in Star Wars stories, whether in books or play. The
children expressed themselves through imitation and exploration of
the characters and their actions. In this sense, the play arose out of
story or, at least, story provided the medium for play expression.
Understanding the strength and importance of these needs and of
having a means to express them, the adults in this setting did not
deny the interest or banish it from the classroom. In creative and
positive ways, the adults helped these children to put the aggressive
behavior back into story from whence it came.

Edmund (another teacher) spent many days helping the children
create a large Star Wars book of their own. He provided big sheets
of newsprint, crayons, time, encouragement, and interest. The children provided the ideas. Any child who wanted to was welcome to
draw a picture of the Star Wars character he or she liked, hated, or
most wanted to be. Edmund labeled the drawings, which were
mostly done in a group setting accompanied by much talk about the
characters being depicted (see Figures 2–3, 2–4, 2–5).

Next Edmund met with the children individually and in small
groups and they dictated to him what they wanted to say about the
characters. He wrote it down and read it back to them. They could
express any of their ideas about the characters and the actions no

Figure 2–3   *An Ewok*

matter how violent or aggressive. Edmund bound the book pages together with yarn and put it on an accessible shelf to be shared with other classmates and with parents.

Out of this dictated book project came the idea, from the children, to dramatize a Star Wars story for the neighboring class and for parents. The children had done other dramatizations and knew that the first thing they needed was a script. Edmund began the group writing project by providing one line from a Star Wars story. The result was a four-page dictated script that eventually was dramatized for parents. Edmund and Nora emphasized that the dramatization had to demonstrate behavior that was acceptable in the classroom, so the children had to find alternative ways to handle situations that involved fighting or shooting.

Within these story and script discussions and writing, the teachers were acknowledging with the children the existence of the violence. How could it be denied? The children had seen these videos as well as other violent ones. Such violence, at least in a visual and oral context, was a part of their lives. Rather than denying and trying to banish violence, the teachers helped the children

FIGURE 2–4   *Darth Vader*

explore other ways to handle it. In writing about the Star Wars characters and their actions, the children had the opportunity to express their own feelings of aggression. In their dictated stories they could fight and shoot as much as they needed or wanted to—safely. Ideas expressed in words about story characters were not going to hit back and hurt physically. Edmund, talking with them as he took their story dictations, was not judgmental and did not reprimand them for having bad ideas. Through writing they could explore violence and the possibilities of their own competence in handling it. Thus story powerfully offered both containment and exploration of frightening ideas while encouraging the personal ability to understand and assure survival.

Writing the script and dramatizing it offered further opportunity for construction and exploration of meaning. Here was a different kind of story, one that would lead to real action of their own chosing and direction. With the help of the adults, the children came up with different ways to handle violent, aggressive behavior:

FIGURE 2–5   *C3PO*

nets, cages, and imprisonment in caves instead of guns, laser beams, and swords leading to death and destruction. Monsters in a cave could be imagined by the audience and didn't have to appear. Such enemies could be contained instead of destroyed. The children were also furthering their understanding of drama through a specialized kind of play within play that could accommodate fighting behavior in a pretend fashion with pretend weapons. Expressing hostile behavior in text and drama was safer; no one got hurt, no one got scolded or sent to their cubby. Their awareness of pain and violence and their need to find ways to deal with it were acknowledged. The children used their abilities to find more positive ways to deal with violence. Through creating their story they accomplished what they needed.

The idea of finding more positive and less hurtful ways to deal with hostility was evident in the physical fantasy play that came out of these story creations. After the stories and play script were written and dramatized, the everyday Star Wars pretend play changed. The children continued to exhibit fighting behavior, but they began to deal with fighting in different ways. Kerrie, especially, found some satisfaction in punishing the bad Star Wars characters in the books by smacking the illustrations with her hand or pounding them with her fist. Will, Josh, Kerrie, Jack, Adam, and Joie all acted out bits and pieces of the story with their voices and their hands as they looked through the books. They were successfully fighting an invisible enemy instead of each other.

Will was especially timid about taking on any role that involved fighting and that might have led to actual hitting or shoving. He avoided those roles by always being an Ewok or Chewbacca. The day that Jude brought in her Star Wars book, Jack and Adam finally convinced Will to be Han Solo, a major warrior. Will, however, did not immediately join the play. He stood to one side watching and refusing Jack's attempts to get him to fight. Finally, Will figured out a way to get into the play and not have to fight or get hurt. He threw himself on the floor at the feet of the fighters and declared that he had been stunned by a laser gun. This action had an immediate effect on the play. After all, Han was an important character and was needed for the battle. All play immediately concentrated on reviving Han. Adam, as Luke Skywalker, finally succeeded by rubbing Han's back. Now the idea of being stunned and then revived had captured their interest. Here was a new aspect of the play to be explored and developed. A kiss on the cheek, a hug, or a back rub were all nurturing and positive ways to handle the results of a heavy fight. Will had found a way to be a warrior and not lose face because he didn't want or like to fight; in addition, he had centered attention on a more gentle but just as interesting play idea.

CONCLUSIONS

Interactions with Star Wars books and the resultant fantasy play provided long-term, multifaceted opportunities for the creation and exploration of meaning. The book interactions and the play presented integrated opportunities for the children to investigate many aspects of their living. The children examined both new and familiar roles and abilities, expanded their general factual knowledge, broadened their interests in space, explored behavior and emotions, and discussed concepts of reality, fantasy, good and evil, beauty, and death. They also learned the value of story as a place to express what was often unacceptable in action. Their play allowed them to discover different, more acceptable ways of handling their fears and aggressions. Social power was investigated and strongly reflected by the children involved in Star Wars books and activities. Teachers took advantage of the opportunities presented in the children's responses to influence the structure, content, and action of the play. Ultimately this involvement led to negotiation of appropriate activities and extensions of meaning making for the children.

Young children interacting with literature are not only acquiring literacy competence or just enjoying literature. They are directly and actively creating purposeful social and individual meaning for their lives. The importance of play in the growth and development of young children has long been acknowledged. When such play occurs in conjunction with literature, it offers extraordinary opportunities for exploration and learning. Star Wars play and response grew out of the immediate needs and interests of these preschoolers. It was important and useful that they had long flexible blocks of time, open space, and constructive but not intrusive supervision as the environment in which to respond to the stories and play at Star Wars. More open and flexible time and space arrangements would be useful in elementary classroom settings as well.

Adults contributed a great deal to the growth and learning of the preschoolers at this day care center. Adults need to relinquish rigid control of the group and their personal expectations. They must provide enough supervision and structure to prevent injury but not so much as to critically inhibit individual and social learning. Teachers need to resist imposing their own interpretations of life, as well as of literature, too strongly on the children. They can be strong literacy models by making literature available and being willing to read, discuss, and take dictation. Helping children find their own ways of dealing with strong emotions, aggression, nurture, and cooperation takes more insight and understanding than imposing a dictated curriculum. Children of all ages deserve respect for themselves and for their particular ways of being in the world. They present us with vast and unique opportunities to explore the source of meaning creation. They know what they are doing.

PROFESSIONAL RESOURCES

Benton, Michael (1978). Children's responses to stories. Paper given at the fourth symposium of the International Research Society for Children's Literature. Exeter, Eng.: Exeter University.

Bergen, Doris (Ed.) (1988). *Play as a medium for learning and development: A handbook of theory and practice*. Portsmouth, NH: Heinemann Educational Books.

Bissex, Glenda L. (1980). *Gnys at wrk*. Cambridge, MA: Harvard University Press.

Bruner, Jerome (1983). *Child's talk*. New York: W. W. Norton.

Cochran-Smith, Marilyn (1984). *The making of a reader*. Norwood, NJ: Ablex.

Galda, Lee, & Pelligrini, Anthony (Eds.) (1985). *Play, language and stories: The development of children's literate behavior*. Norwood, NJ: Ablex.

Hickman, Janet (1979). *Responses to literature in the school environment: Grades K–6.* Unpublished doctoral dissertation, The Ohio State University.

Hungerford, Rachael (1990). *Creating meaning: An ethnographic study of preschoolers, literary response and play.* Unpublished doctoral dissertation, University of Massachusetts.

Kiefer, Barbara (1982). *The response of primary children to picture books.* Unpublished doctoral dissertation, The Ohio State University.

Richards, I. A. (1929). *Practical criticism.* New York: Harcourt Brace.

Rosenblatt, Louise (1976). *Literature as exploration.* New York: Noble & Noble.

Rosenblatt, Louise (1978). *The reader, the text, the poem: The transactional theory of the literary work.* Carbondale: Southern Illinois University Press.

Singer, Jerome (1973). *The child's world of make believe.* New York: Academic Press.

Taylor, Denny, & Dorsey-Gaines, Catherine (1988). *Growing up literate.* Portsmouth, NH: Heinemann Educational Books.

Vygotsky, L. S. (1962). *Thought and language.* Cambridge, MA.: The MIT Press.

Winnicott, D. W. (1971). *Playing and reality.* London: Tavistock Publications.

CHILDREN'S LITERATURE

Books for young explorers. (1972). (4 vol. set). Washington, DC: National Geographic Society.

Razzi, James (1979). *Star Wars Darth Vader's activity book.* New York: Random House.

Star Wars, the ewoks. (1978). New York: Random House.

Star Wars, the maverick moon. (1979). New York: Random House.

Vinge, Joan D. (1983). *Star Wars, return of the Jedi.* New York: Scholastic.

3

The Judge Comes
to Kindergarten

Deborah G. Jacque

ALANA: How can the little one get out of jail if they threw away the key?
SETH: I know how! They can take it out of the trash.
BOBBY: How can they reach it if they are in chains?

My kindergarteners were learners who followed their own individual processes of discovery no matter what they were learning. As the above dialogue shows, problem solving among themselves was a process in which they felt comfortable and used much imagination. When I read another primary teacher's article (Beaver, 1982) about young children and their responses to literature read aloud more than once, I began to understand that my kindergarteners, too, structured their learning experiences around books read aloud by practicing some things over and over until they gained ownership of them. When Joetta Beaver completed repetitive readings of *Say It!* (Zolotow, 1980), she discovered that every time her primary grade students heard the story read again, their range and depth of responses increased and deepened. She felt that this was because they had more opportunity to fill in gaps about the story's meaning and to make more connections among their developing meanings.

I became very excited about the prospect of exploring and enlarging another teacher-researcher's work in the area of young children's responses to stories read in repetition. As a kindergarten teacher in a small rural school with a predominantly white population, I wanted to know what kinds of learning and responses were going on among students during my repeated readings of a story. I realized that my kindergarteners' internalized representations of stories were dependent on their developmental level (Applebee, 1977). I also knew that my kindergarteners, like all young children, actively participated in the creation of meanings by bringing their own life and literary experiences to each book that I read aloud to them (Cochran-Smith, 1984). Furthermore, the limits of my children's language experiences were the limits of their various worlds, and their everyday experiences were directly linked to their understandings of what went on around them (Meek, Warlow, & Barton, 1978). With all of this in mind, I set about undertaking a teacher-researcher investigation of my own kindergarten students' responses to literature in a book read in repetition.

THE JUDGE COMES TO KINDERGARTEN

This study of my kindergarten involved repeated readings of the picture book *The Judge* (Zemach, 1969). This book was about a judge and how he sentenced people to go to jail. Each prisoner told the judge about the "horrible thing coming this way." Throughout the book, the five different prisoners used repetitive, rhyming language that expanded as each approached the judge—such as, "Its eyes are scary, Its tail is hairy, Its paws have claws, It snaps its jaws, I tell you judge we all better pray!" The final four wordless pages portrayed the fifth prisoner being carted off by two guards, the appearance of the horrible thing's face at the judge's door, the horrible thing eating the judge, and the five released prisoners walking off together.

Over a two-week period, I read *The Judge* five times to my fourteen kindergarten students. Each read-aloud session was about twenty minutes long. I read aloud in our meeting area, where my students usually felt relaxed because they could sit however they wanted. They were encouraged to speak up and comment on anything as stories were read aloud. I also allowed questions and comments before and after the story was read to them. After each session, I left the book on my desk where it was easily accessible to my students to use whenever they wished.

I chose to videotape only the first and last sessions and to audiotape the middle three sessions. I wanted to focus on the expected changes between the first and fifth readings for body language and all five sessions for oral responses. I viewed the videotapes many times and listened to both the videotapes and audiotapes for the exact quotes used in this chapter. Using qualitative research methods, I searched for patterns across the five read-aloud sessions.

First Reading

The first afternoon, as I read the story *The Judge,* my students sat very quietly. They seemed to put their full concentration into processing the story. Seth guessed that "the creature is supposed to be coming." Cotie repeated the word "pray." Roy pointed out that "tale and jail" were rhyming words. Bobby's inquiry, "What's a scoundrel?", evoked numerous guesses, such as "a robber," "a bad person," "a killer," and "pirates that steal gold." I did not verify or negate their guesses, but, rather, I allowed them to keep their own thoughts. When the word "nincompoop" was read, the whole class laughed. Roy realized that the same repetitive phrases were being told to the judge by all the people being sent to jail: "Please let me go, Judge, I didn't know, Judge. That what I did was against the law. I just said what I saw. A horrible thing is coming this way, creeping closer day by day."

As the four wordless pages were shared, many of the children sat wide-eyed as they studied the illustrations that showed the horrible thing in the window behind the judge, the horrible thing at the door, the horrible thing consuming the judge, and the five prisoners released from jail. "There it is—right in the window!" exclaimed Bobby as he saw the horrible thing's head appear behind the sitting judge. "Oh, what a creature!" sighed Cotie as he saw the whole horrible thing eating the judge.

Second Reading

During a morning story time two days later, *The Judge* was again shared. Most of my students were excited about hearing the story again. One child said, "We already heard this!" However, immediately several children chimed in and shouted, "It's good! We want to hear it again!" Many of the children moved in closer during this read-aloud sesson.

As I read about the prisoners, Roy correctly recalled that there were five prisoners in this book. Cotie knew when the phrase "We all better pray" was going to be said by each of the five prisoners. Bobby joined Cotie in repeating "We all better pray" throughout the rest of the book. A discussion again occurred about the word scoundrel. Molly asked, "What's a scoundrel?" Cotie answered Molly by insisting the it was a "killer." Molly turned to me for verification and I went to the dictionary, which defined a scoundrel as a mean worthless person and a villain. However, Cotie insisted that the meaning should be killer and the rest of the class agreed.

Molly was excited about the appearance of the elegantly dressed female, prisoner number four, and called out, "I like this part!". Several children repeated the phrase "day by day." Seth repeated my reading of each prisoner's number (e.g., "This is prisoner number four"), and he wondered what the prisoners had done. Bobby joined Cotie in repeating "We all better pray" throughout the rest of the book. Toby repeated the phrase "creeping closer day by day." As I read the phrase "nincompoop, ninnyhammer, dimwit, dunce," the whole class laughed.

Third Reading

Three days later I shared *The Judge* again during the afternoon. Roy continued to notice the rhymes in the text and pointed out that the judge's responses were in rhyme. For example, when the judge said, "There must be something wrong with his brains. Put him in chains.", Roy pointed out that "brains and chains" were rhyming words. When prisoner number three, a young boy, was again identified as a "scoundrel," many voices called out the word "killer." However, Tina offered her opinion that the judge might be the scoundrel and said "maybe he's somebody bad."

Molly and Tina expressed their delight with the upcoming appearance of the elegantly dressed lady and the judge's use of the word "nincompoop." Several children began to chime in on many repetitive phrases: "We all better pray," "day by day," and "creeping closer day by day." Roy, Seth, and Cotie repeated "the eyes are scary." The word "prisoners" was repeated by three quarters of the class. Bobby asked the same question that Seth had asked in the last reading, "What did the prisoners do?" When the "nincompoop, ninnyhammer, dimwit, dunce" phrase was read, everyone laughed.

During the wordless pages, upon seeing the "horrible thing" at the judge's door, Cristal said, "Uh-oh! There it is!" Keith shouted to the judge, "Run, run, judge!" Then Cotie shouted, "No, eat him up!" And Cristal answered, "Yeah!"

Afterward several children wanted to take *The Judge* to their rest time. We decided to make out a list for turn-taking during the next week. I kept a xeroxed class list displayed on the wall near the book, and my students checked off their names as they used the book over the ensuing days. The next morning while out at recess, my children created a chasing game that involved the word "nincompoop."

Fourth Reading

Three days later we again had the chance to read *The Judge* during the morning. This session took place exactly one week after the initial reading. My students seemed to have an overall sense of the story, its sequence, and repetitions. As each prisoner arrived before the judge, over two thirds of my students predicted events before they happened. Bobby did not want everyone to laugh when "nincompoop, ninnyhammer, dimwit, dunce" was read aloud. Rather, he wanted everyone to wait and laugh afterward so that he could hear the words read clearly.

Over three quarters of my students repeated almost word-for-word the phrases: "We all better pray," "day by day," and "Creeping closer day by day." The word killer was loudly stated by Cotie as the word scoundrel appeared in the story, and several children repeated Cotie's use of the word killer for scoundrel. Cotie and other children also used body language to emphasize their meaning of the word killer by making facial and arm movements that dramatized killing motions.

Many children verbally growled, using detailed facial expressions, when I repeatedly read, "It growls, it groans." Alana was quite concerned for prisoner number three, who was a young boy. The judge told the guard, "Lock him up and throw away the key. He can't fool me." She wondered, "How can the little one get out of jail if they threw away the key?" Seth replied, "I know how! They can take it out of the trash." Bobby then wondered, "How can they reach it if they are in chains?"

As I shared the four wordless pages, the children moved even closer to me and the book. As they scanned the page where the horrible thing was eating the judge, Keith added something new to their observations and excitedly shouted, "That's either flame or some of his blood!" Others gathered even closer, and Keith proudly pointed to the red flame or blood coming out of the horrible thing's mouth or nostril.

Fifth Reading

Two weeks after the initial reading and four days after the previous reading, we gathered together for the final read-aloud session of *The Judge*. I felt as though I was not needed as the reader. My students read along with me, making predictions, repeating language, and acting out many parts of the story. While showing the illustrations and using a soft voice, I encouraged my students to take over the reading themselves, and they did so with great enthusiasm and ownership of the text.

The phrase "We all better pray" intensified every time each prisoner appeared before the judge. When "creeping closer day by day" was read, Cotie and Cristal acted this part out together. They used their hands and facial expressions to move closer and closer to each other. Bobby became very angry and repeated his request for silence during the reading of "nincompoop, ninnyhammer, dimwit, dunce. He said, "I hate people who were talking." We decided to try it again his way. Everyone listened to me read "nincompoop, ninnyhammer, dimwit, dunce" and then burst out laughing. However, Roy complained, "That's bad! I couldn't laugh having to wait."

When the first wordless page was about to show the horrible thing behind the judge, Roy leaned back and hid behind another child. When the second wordless page appeared showing the horrible thing in the door facing the judge, Roy moved out from behind his friend and looked carefully at this illustration.

After the story was finished, Molly and Tina wanted me to turn back so that they could look at the wordless pages again. They were examined in great detail by the whole class. Everyone was talking to each other about what was happening in the illustrations and pointing our specific details, such as the "flame or blood" coming from the horrible thing's nostrils or mouth. However, the consensus among my students seemed to be that this was blood from eating the judge. At this point I was not involved with their discussions, as they were talking to each other and confirming their meanings of the story. They were huddled very close to the book, touching and pointing to items of interest to each other. I left *The Judge* on my desk for children to borrow, and they frequently did over the next two weeks.

THE KINDERGARTENERS OWN THE JUDGE

The review of first and last videotaped sessions demonstrated the clear ownership that my students had developed throughout the five repeated readings of *The Judge*. During the first reading, almost all of my students sat almost motionless, concentrating and processing this new book being read aloud to them. During the last reading, my students were physically moving their bodies to enact parts of the story (e.g., the two girls creeping closer and closer together as I read) or in anticipation of upcoming parts (e.g., Roy hiding behind a friend just as the horrible thing hid behind the judge in a window). Predictions and repetitions were made continually. Many comments were made about various parts of the story, especially the wordless pages.

My students had concentrated on parts rather than on the whole story, as Hickman (1981) found out in her study of young children's responses. My children were fascinated with certain words— nincompoop, scoundrel—and using pictures to construct the story line. Their abilities to analyze the story were best seen in their detailed scanning of the illustrations for meanings and story. I was excited to see that the children had built a shared social context together, processing, developing, and practicing this story over and over, just as Beaver (1982) had discovered in her repetitive readings of *Say It!* to her primary students.

Predictions and Repetitions

The number of predictions and repetitions went from one or two voices during the second reading to the ability of all my students to read the entire story with me the fifth and final time. The illustrations more than the text provided clues for my children's abilities at prediction, as the illustrations signaled their recall of certain words, phrases, and rhymes. My young students relied upon illustrations to provide meaning to the story and details of its meaning. Their insistence that they be given time to explore the final four wordless page after each reading demonstrated the extreme importance they held for visual information.

However, when it came to the text repetition, the cumulative nature of this story lent itself very well to my children's language abilities. When each prisoner arrived, more details accumulated upon those all ready shared about the horrible thing. Thus, each prisoner had to repeat the previous descriptions and add his or her new insights. This provided an excellent frame within which my young children could enjoy repetition and prediction. Once they realized the repetitive pattern and accumulation of new information about the horrible thing, they could join in with my reading. The frame of this text is much like the traditional poem, "This is the House That Jack Built." This kind of text structure allowed my students to participate in reading with me.

With the patterns of repetition and prediction working so strongly in text and illustrations, my student were able to build increasing ownership based upon the sharing of their individual interpretations of text and pictures. By sharing their unique verbal responses, the entire class came to appreciate and understand more of the story as a whole. The key element in this ownership-building was the students' repeated exposures to the text and illustrations and my willingness to give them time for discussion with me and, especially, with each other.

Vocabulary

Cotie was fascinated with the usage of the word scoundrel. The first discussion of its definition happened during the first reading. Then, during the next reading, even after I had read the dictionary definition of scoundrel, Cotie changed the meaning to fit within her own developmental understanding of it. The rest of the class agreed with her. In the third session, Cotie made sure that it became killer instead of scoundrel because she insisted that another child use killer rather than scoundrel. By the fourth reading, Cotie dramatically stated this word substitution, and several children repeated it. During the final session, all of the children were using the word killer for scoundrel. It seemed that the whole class had changed the author's language to fit into language that was within their own level of development. This observation concurs with Applebee's (1977) view that children's internalized representations of stories depend on where they are developmentally.

However, the "nincompoop, ninnyhammer, dimwit, dunce" phrase was not changed. Rather, this phrase became part of my students' vocabulary. During all the readings, they laughed at this phrase. By the third reading, they had acquired ownership of this phrase strongly enough to take it into another social context. As I watched my kindergarteners create a tag game involving the word nincompoop, I was reminded of Cochran-Smith's (1984) study of preschoolers and her identification of young children's abilities to carry "text-to-life." That is, young children often take something from a story they have heard and add it to their own lives, especially in play. And Hickman (1981) found that children in early childhood comprise the only group to use dramatic play as a response to literature. Here, my students took a part of the story they most enjoyed and added to their play at recess.

Inquiries

Throughout all the readings, the number of questions asked by my kindergarteners increased. During the first and second reading, children wanted clarification of what a "scoundrel" was in the story. And when the dictionary did not satisfy their need for its meaning, they arrived at their own consensus on what they would have it mean. Individual children asked more and more specific questions, such as: "Why do they have to throw away the key?" and "What did the prisoners do?" This use of heuristic language (Halliday, 1975) allowed my students to wonder, explore, and gain information about illustrations, text events, and vocabulary that they did not understand. I was thrilled that they often turned to each other for help in understanding and did not rely on me as the font of knowledge. This was the style of inquiry and discovery I encouraged among my students. I felt that this orientation facilitated problem solving and encouraged them to search for meaning among the illustrations and text.

Body Movements

The increase of body movements demonstrated my students' growing understanding of the story. Hickman (1981) found young children to be the only group that uses body movement to convey their meanings of the story. During the first reading, my students sat quietly as they heard the story and saw the illustrations. During the middle three readings, as my students discussed meanings (e.g., scoundrel), explored wordless pages in detail, and gained owner-ship of the text, they began to use certain body language in connection with words, phrases, and illustrations. The best example was when the phrase "nincompoop, ninnyhammer, dimwit, dunce" was read. This passage brought my students closer to the book and brought bursts of laughter. By the final reading, the students used body language in many different ways to convey meaning. For example, Cotie and Cristal acted out "closer day by day" together, children acted out the meaning of scoundrel with killing hand motions, and Roy physically hid his body from the horrible thing as it appeared behind the judge. These children were actively using their bodies to create their unique and shared meanings of this text (Cochran-Smith, 1984).

Illustrations

The illustrations in this book helped support the repetitive, predictable nature of the text. My kindergarteners used the illustrations as clues to what text matched them. They relied on the illustrations to help them construct their unique and shared meanings of the story. They often crowded closer to the book to examine the illustrations in great detail. They all had favorite illustrations and wouldn't hesitate to call out their favorites as they appeared in the book.

The four wordless pages produced the most inquiries, comments, and dramatic body movements. Each time these pages were shown, my students found more and more to talk about in the illustrations. They scanned them closely during each reading and needed to talk out loud about what they saw, understood, or questioned in these illustrations. During the final reading, this wordless section was looked at twice by the whole class. This overall reaction to these wordless pages demonstrated to me the importance of illustrations and how much visual learning can take place when picture books are read to young children.

IMPLICATIONS

The growth of understanding developed through the repeated reading of one story was astounding. I feel that any story should be read aloud more than once to young children because they are given the opportunities to separate, organize, and internalize information. Parents, educators, and anyone reading to young children should be aware of the special and individualized processing that goes on during repeated story readings. Children should be allowed to comment and ask questions throughout the story because this is their natural way of sorting and processing information. The story reader can ask simple why and what questions so that young children can comfortably answer questions at their own level of development.

Time is always a consideration to an educator. The time given to several readings of one story could prove to be a very important part of young children's development of language structure, story structure, sense of organization, and word meanings. This important part of learning is often overlooked—the "text-to-life" connection (Cochran-Smith, 1984).

I also came to see the importance of my students' aesthetic responses, especially those involving body language, as a means of constructing their unique and shared responses. Rosenblatt (1982) suggested that teachers should be careful to avoid overanalyzing stories through discussions. Rather, she suggested that "questions can be sufficiently open to enable the young readers to select concrete details or parts of the text that had struck them most forcibly" (p. 276). I took this suggestion a step further and allowed my young students opportunities to discuss the book with me and among themselves during the reading more than after the story had been read. The immediacy of the current illustration and text provided my kindergarteners with concrete contexts for discussion, argument, comment, inquiry, and use of body language. Teachers of young children in preschool and primary grades should be cognizant of the need to permit students time for verbal responses during the story and not just after the book is finished.

I realized how much my repeated readings of this book helped my students to gain ownership of it when, one month later, one of my students came to me for *The Judge.* This child said, "Do you still have the judge book? I want to read it." I explained that I had returned it to the library. However, hand-in-hand we left the classroom and headed down the hall to the library in search of *The Judge.*

PROFESSIONAL RESOURCES

Applebee, A. (1977). A sense of story. *Theory into Practice, 16*(5), 342–347.

Beaver, Joetta (1982). Say it! Over and over. *Language Arts, 59*(2), 143–148.

Cochran-Smith, Marilyn (1984). *The making of a reader.* Norwood, NJ: Ablex.

Halliday, M. A. K. (1975). *Learning how to mean: Explorations in the development of language.* London: Edward Arnold.

Hickman, Janet (1981). A new perspective on response to literature: Research in an elementary school setting. *Research in the Teaching of English, 15* (December), 343–354.

Meek, Margaret, Warlow, Aidan, & Barton, Griselda (1978). *The cool web: The pattern of children's reading behavior.* London: Atheneum.

Rosenblatt, Louise (1982). The literary transaction: Evocation and response. *Theory into Practice, 21,* 268–277.

CHILDREN'S LITERATURE

Zemach, Harve (1969). *The judge.* Illustrated by Margot Zemach. New York: Farrar, Straus & Giroux.

Zolotow, Charlotte (1980). *Say it!* Illustrated by James Stevenson. New York: Greenwillow Books.

4

Reading Aloud
in a Primary Classroom:
Reaching and Teaching
Young Readers

Janice V. Kristo

Over the last twenty years, changes in the way we think about reading and reading instruction have signaled a radical shift from a basal reading program using a detailed teacher's manual to a program based on the use of children's books. Professionals in the field have studied and written extensively about using literature and the reading program (Hansen, 1987; Harste, Short, & Burke, 1988; Huck, Hepler, & Hickman, 1987; Newman, 1985; Routman, 1988; Short & Pierce, 1990). What needs to be studied further are the ways children experience books and teachers' role in this process.

This chapter describes highlights of a two-year observational study of first-grade teacher Mary Giard from Bangor, Maine, and ways her students learn about books and reading from each other. All children in this classroom are read to everyday and use only literature as the content of their reading program. Mary's sophisticated way of talking about books with children fascinated me. Had I not known this was a first grade, I would have thought it to be a much higher grade level or a class of very gifted first graders. However, neither was the case. I knew at that point that I wanted to study Mary's interactions with her students over books as well as the ways children experience literature in this classroom.

As many teachers nationwide move toward using more literature in the classroom, it becomes increasingly important to document the ways individual teachers work with literature in the classroom. Implications for both the teacher and students are explored here within the context of Mary's read-aloud sessions.

An analysis of the data from observations, videotaping, and samples of recorded teacher interaction with children over books led to an understanding of the ways children experience literature and offers insights into the role of the teacher. Mary became my teacher. She taught me that "spirited" readers thrive in a community built around opportunities for all readers (including the teacher) to interact with each other over books they read, those they listen to, and those they write for themselves. These spirited readers are also in an environment in which listening to high-quality children's literature is one of the most important features of the school day. Students interact throughout the story and are given time to respond to the text in memorable ways.

After two years of data collection and analysis, it became apparent that story time (as read-aloud time is called in this classroom) serves as the centerpiece of the curriculum from which all else flows and that the teacher's role in preparing and orchestrating story time is crucial. The power of reading aloud to children is widely documented in the literature (Butler, 1980; Clark, 1976; Cohen, 1968; Durkin, 1966; Mason, Peterman, & Kerr, 1989). This chapter further elucidates how critical the teacher's role is in orchestrating powerful read-aloud sessions. The curriculum is set in motion by using a carefully chosen book for story time, much like one who finds the perfect stone and throws it into a pond with just the right flick of the wrist: a ripple effect is the result. There is a ripple effect throughout the curriculum, as the title Mary chooses is linked to a theme under study. The book may illustrate a particular writing technique that appears in the children's writing, or it may help to illustrate a point made earlier in the day during the reading mini-lesson, and so on. Story time also sets the ground work for the study of all kinds of literature. The kinds of interaction between the teacher and students are explored through the ways Mary invites a variety of responses to literature and the nature of those responses. Over time students learn to become literature critics and how to articulate their own growth as readers.

SHAPING THE CONTOUR AND TEXTURE OF STORY TIME

Because Mary is an avid reader and browser of bookstores and libraries, she knows, quite literally, what's out there and what titles will be good child and curriculum matches. Mary sees opportunities in books she wants to share during story time. She seeks ways to make the curriculum in her classroom seamless by extending some of the elements of reading "instruction" time (occurring earlier in the morning) into the noon-hour story time. Other important aspects that contribute to establishing the reading terrain in the classroom are qualities Mary believes help to achieve a democratic and community atmosphere in the classroom but are also vitally linked to literacy learning. Figure 4–1 lists components of Mary's program and purposes for story time.

Mary herself is an explorer of the literary terrain. Interspersed through story time are questions and "noticings" about the text or illustrations she genuinely wonders about. For instance, as Mary invites discussion about Langstaff's and Keat's (1971) versions of *Over in the Meadow*, she asks, "Could I add something I noticed that was similar between the two texts? I noticed that the pattern of the story was alike. Remember when I read the two texts, some of you were snapping your fingers and moving to the language of the story? Did anyone notice that?" She invites students to see how observant they can be; she listens carefully to what they want to talk about, what they notice about the artwork, what patterns they hear in the text, and what, generally, interests them about the text. There is a continual flow of interaction between Mary and the students during the reading of the text. She doesn't encourage them to hold back until the story is finished; they are expected to be active while she is reading aloud. Mary takes part in this active, ongoing thinking aloud about text as another one of the listeners. Children appear to monitor this interchange and will request that Mary go on with the reading if the discussion seems to be going on too long.

I've chosen to use the terminology of the cartographer—for example, contour and texture—because such terms aptly describe contextual features of the classroom. Contour and texture connote shape and appearance in an environment; the classroom contour and texture are shaped by the climate or tone established by Mary's demonstrations of what it means to be a reader and by her valuing learner responsibility, personal decision making, and individual response. Another critical component of the contour and texture is Mary's degree of personal preparation in order to engage her young readers with literature. Figure 4–2 summarizes important considerations for the classroom environment and teacher preparation (adapted from Allen, Giard, & Kristo, 1991).

Story Time Rituals

Most, if not all, of Mary's group interactions take place as a community gathering on the floor. Mary's welcoming of children into the story group is like the inviting of the tribe into the special tent for the rituals of storying to begin. This is similar, in intent, to Howard's (1989) description of her gathering times with young students in a private school in Vermont:

> Obviously, we "gather" quite a bit, and I do see these gathering times as important punctuation points in the day, allowing us time

The principal begins day with a poem

Writing time:
  Author's chair
  Writing folders—status of class
  Minilesson
  Individual and group conferences
  Share circles

Reading time:
  Minilesson using predictable literature
  What do you notice?
  What did you discover about print?
  Helping children discover reading strategies
  Tapping cueing systems:
    graphophonemic
    semantic
    syntactic
    pragmatic
  Groups and self-selection—status of the class
  Buddy reading; debriefing

Story time:
  She shares the best

Theme study

Math

Purposes of Story Time:
  Creates a community of enthusiastic literature lovers
  Exposes students to a wide variety of literature
  Helps students make informed book choices for independent
    reading
  Creates an atmosphere for students to develop discussion skills
  Develops listening and thinking skills
  Allows an opportunity to demonstrate a respect for a variety of
    responses to literature
  Develops a cohesive program for students by using books as the
    basis for all activities
  Demonstrates good oral reading skills and enthusiasm for print
  Gives students an opportunity to practice literary strategies such as:
    Making predictions
    Discussing story development
    Characterization
    Point of view
    Setting
    Theme
    Techniques used by the author or illustrator
    Parts of a book (dedication, end pages, copyright, etc.)
    Comparing and contrasting themes, authors, illustrators, etc.
    Response to literature through discussion, writing, artwork,
      dramatics, etc.

FIGURE 4–1   *Components of Mary's first-grade reading program*

Classroom environment:
1. Do I have a chart or paper available for noting repetitive lines, student comments, and/or extension activities?
2. Do I have a special place for read-aloud books so students can easily find them?
3. Do I have a mechanism that lets students know it is time for read aloud (predictable schedule, light, music, etc.)? To what extent do I demonstrate that this is an important time of the day?
4. Have I established guidelines for read-aloud time? What should students be doing during this time?

Teacher preparation:
1. Have I read the text myself? Do I know the text well enough to share it enthusiastically with the group?
2. Do I feel this is a good story or poem, or am I only reading it on someone's recommendation?
3. Have I looked at background information about the author, illustrator, or writing that might add to students' understanding and appreciation of the book?
4. How will I introduce the text?
5. How will I establish an appropriate mood for the story or poem?
6. How can I help students make connections between this text, author, or illustrator and others studied?
7. Have I considered ways for students to extend their appreciation of the book?
8. If this story or poem is part of a unit, how will I help students see the text as part of a larger picture?
9. If I plan to use the text as a vehicle for discussing reading strategies, do I have a clear picture of how it could be used for this purpose without sacrificing the enjoyment of the read-aloud session?

FIGURE 4–2   *Story-time checklist*

to draw breath, step back, and refocus on the next activity. These group times give time for talk and reflection, time for me and my students to evaluate the last piece of work, or to relax before the next one. (p. 229)

Although Mary may read aloud during other selected times of the day, she always sets aside from thirty minutes to an hour each day after lunch. The children automatically gather around her on the floor as they see Mary sitting with either a tempting new book or the continuation of a favorite chapter book. It is fascinating to watch Mary settle even the most restless listener by using some aspect of the story as a verbal clue that the story is about to begin. For example, when reading *The Lion, the Witch, and the Wardrobe* (Lewis, 1961), she might suggest that children close their eyes to imagine what they might see if they were to enter the wardrobe.

Cazden (1988) writes about the importance of students being able to see one another for real discussion to occur. Mary has easily accomplished this with the group "gathering" arrangement. Mary believes that a special kind of bonding occurs with this kind of arrangement; it signals that something very special is about to happen—in this case, story time.

A calmness pervades the classroom as Mary begins a book. During story time she and the children are both engrossed with the book and in the book. Story time is an invitation for the classroom community to enter the magical kingdom of literature. It provides the community with a consciousness of literature by providing a common core of interactional experiences with literature. Borrowing from Smith (1988), this is the kind of literacy club that provides membership for all and excludes none. Martin (1989) states that "We have to read if we are to learn to read." It is clear from my observations that we need to add that children also need to listen to literature in order to learn how to read. Children in this class are actively engaged with the text as Mary reads aloud. Mary is committed to bringing the finest literature to children; she knows the books she chooses to share aloud. Her dramatic readings, her consistent eye contact with the children, and her invitations to engage in literary talk relays the powerful message that there is something very special to discover between the covers of a book.

Literary Unfoldings

Story time is a kind of literary unfolding for children. It provides children with a wide literary buffet; they begin to develop a taste for particular authors and kinds of literature. Mary might begin the year with selections by Ezra Jack Keats. By sharing many works by one author or illustrator, children begin to understand what Mary means by "making connections" between and among texts. She wants to informally assess whether children note similarities in Keats's artwork by their discussions and art responses and to what extent they are able to describe the setting, characters, and so on in Keats's books. The literary buffet expands as Mary shares everything from realistic fiction and fantasy books to nonfiction selections to accompany a unit on the ocean. Mary's personal favorite, C. S. Lewis's *The Lion, the Witch, and the Wardrobe* is shared. Many teachers would not consider using this advanced fantasy with such a young group. However, observing her classes over the last several years has convinced me that Mary's enthusiasm for the book, her very dramatic performance—facial expressions, body language, and eye contact—and her openness for children to interact throughout the reading make a more advanced text challenging but within the reach of young listeners' comprehension. The children's understanding of this text is also seen in rich and varied ways through their art work, journal entries, and drama responses. Literary unfoldings through the vehicle of story time stimulate children to want to learn to read in this classroom, and Mary shows that it's worth it. Martin (1989) suggests that

> If children who have failed to learn to read are to be motivated, a great deal of the motivation must come from a growing realization that books are worth reading. You cannot tell them that. Until a child experiences a book which really moves him in some way, catching him up in its action, he cannot know what the world of books has to offer. (p. 54)

Mary sets the reading tone in this classroom by demonstrating that she is a reader, that she enjoys being one, and that she is still growing as a reader. She shows genuine excitement and enthusiasm about being a reader and shares her own puzzlement over what she reads. For example, at one point Mary talked about her own passion for fantasy and her need to expand and sample from other genres, such as biography. Chambers (1985) discusses the notion of flat-earth reading. He suggests that we need to become more intergalactic in our reading by sampling from a wider array of genres.

I witnessed continual demonstrations of Mary literally cascading children with books in a multitude of ways throughout the day, sometimes in very obvious ways and at other times in more quiet, less direct ways. For instance, Mary might add several versions of fairy tales to a display table in anticipation that a child or two will discover them during the day. At other times Mary might enthusiastically talk about discovering a new book by a favorite author or illustrator at a local bookstore or library and engage children in conversation about what they know about the writer or artist.

Literary Noticings

Particular aspects of the text such as book design, endpapers, dedication page, style of illustration, print format, as well as responses to literary characteristics are explored in a depth similar to Hilliker's (1986) intense exploration of themes with her kindergartners. Mary continually asks children what they think and what they notice about text. Done often enough, children, too, want to share their own book discoveries. They seem to want to "try on her mind," a notion discussed by Crews (1986).

These "noticing" episodes are similar to FYI—For Your Information—a procedure credited to Edelsky (1987) as described by Staab (1990). In discussing teacher mediation in the whole language classroom, Staab describes the FYI as a bit of relevant information presented very briefly. For instance, after Mary shared

John Langstaff's *Over in the Meadow* (1957), a student initiated a discussion about the differences in illustration as compared with the version by Ezra Jack Keats (1971), shared earlier in the week. Mary used this as a springboard to invite students to make other comparisons by noting differences between the endpapers, dedication, and language pattern in both books. The use of the FYI strategy made sense as children appeared primed to examine similarities and differences between and among texts. Learning about text may appear to occur in an incidental way; however, Mary seems to hold a kind of literary map in her head about the noticings she has made about the text under study. She typically initiates discussion by probing the concept of likenesses and differences between and among texts by simply posing the question, "What do you notice about these texts?" Obviously, this question is open-ended, and Mary, often, is treated to an unexpected comment that leads to some aspect of the text she may not have noticed. This kind of relaxed, often open-ended, book talk allows these young listeners to try on their own literary maps for size.

STORY TIME AS THE FORUM FOR BOOK TALK

Talking about books is of primary importance in this classroom. Children are active participants throughout each story time; Mary encourages a response from every child. She invites them to become story detectives, to problem solve, to notice every aspect they can find about text, and to feel free to talk about it. From their study of this classroom, Allen, Giard, and Kristo (1991) state that: Their responses are not limited to listening in a literal way, but go beyond listening both in inferential and evaluative ways, as indicated by twelve different responses (see Figure 4–3) varying from nonword reactions to critical analysis of text. These responses can be grouped into the four categories.

Nonword responses. Active listeners often indicated their participation throughout story time by responding in ways that did not interrupt the flow of the story. Eyes can be closed, hands can be clenched, and bodies can be contorted in a variety of ways that relate directly to the events or descriptions of the story. These responses, so personal they seem almost involuntary, attest to the active meaning making occurring during a story.

Literal word responses. Responses of this type fell into two broad categories: mimicking of unique words or sounds, and questions or statements about the meaning of specific words. Some words or phrases seemed to entice students because of the combination of sounds. "Trit-trot, trit-trot" and "whoopy once, whoopy twice" were

1. Giving nonword responses
2. Comparing to other works of literature
3. Making statements about the language
4. Commenting on physical characteristics of the book
5. Offering alternative versions of the story
6. Sharing opinions about the characters and their motivations
7. Mimicking unique and/or appealing words or sounds
8. Stating pleasure or displeasure with the events or ending
9. Asking important questions
10. Relating the story to their personal experiences
11. Making judgments about the book's merit
12. Extending the book

FIGURE 4–3   *Student reponses during story time*

often repeated by students, not only during the story but while they were participating in a variety of activities. Other words seemed to capture the students' attention because the meaning wasn't clear. "What does bold mean? That's a funny word." Questions such as this were answered by students within the group. This activity afforded Mary an opportunity to informally evaluate the word knowledge of her students.

Evaluative responses. Just as adults choose and respond to books in a variety of ways and for a variety of reasons, students used the story time arena to offer a variety of opinions about the physical characteristics of the book:

"Why isn't there a dedication?"
"I don't like these illustrations."
"I didn't picture him looking like that."

A story hour that includes these kinds of responses offers the whole group an opportunity to look at the book from a variety of perspectives. Additionally, Mary is then able to foster critical evaluation of text by the students.

Students responding at this level move well beyond the physical characteristics of the book as they attempt to understand the characters and their motivations as well as the author's intentions. For example, during the oral reading of the Narnia series, a common point of discussion centered not only around the witch's words and actions but also her intentions.

"I don't understand why the witch did that."
"I wonder why the author made her look like that?"

When students are interacting with story at this level, a natural course seems to be toward examination of their own thoughts and values. As students begin to move the story into their own lives and relate it to their own experiences, the stage is set for understanding the universality of literature.

Extension responses. As a community of readers—individually, with friends, and as a group—these students developed an extensive background of literature. Students self-selected books for sustained silent reading, jointly selected books for reading with a friend, and voted as a group for the story time read-aloud book. During the course of the year, students not only studied specific authors and illustrators, they also experienced selections from all genres of literature. This practice enabled students to draw from a wide variety of literary models to compare and extend any given piece of literature. Responses ranged from social commentaries to alternative versions of text.

"This woman isn't like the women we've seen in other fairy tales."
"I think C. S. Lewis should have written this one first. I think I'll write a different ending so it could be."

Students who extend a piece of literature in this manner do not see reading as separate from either the rest of the curriculum or their lives.

In the following episode, Mary elicits book extension activities for Susan Jeffer's *Snow White* (1980). However, before she does so, she asks students to comment about Jeffer's artwork as a lead into discussing response activities.

MARY: What do you think of Susan Jeffer's artwork? Donna?
DONNA: Pretty.
MARY: What was pretty about it?
DONNA: She uses lots of flowers that are pretty.
MARY: Anything else about her artwork? Bonnie?
BONNIE: She shows purple and pink flowers that are matched nicely together. Some paintings are black and white and some paintings are colorful pictures.
MARY: Yes. Some are colorful and some tend to have a pattern. How do you suppose Susan Jeffers did this artwork? How do you suppose she made all of these beautiful fine lines?
BEN: A sharp pencil.
MARY: A sharp pencil? That sounds like a possibility. Will?
WILL: Maybe a sharp color crayon.
MARY: Why do you think it wouldn't have been a regular crayon?
WILL: Because it would be hard to get it in neatly.

MARY: Yes, it would be hard to get those fine details, wouldn't it? What else do you suppose she could have used besides a pencil or a colored pencil?

WILL: A black crayon.

MARY: Maybe a black crayon—

ALICIA: Paint.

MARY: She might have used paint, although it would have been quite difficult with that fine, fine artwork. Will?

WILL: Pen?

MARY: That's what I was wondering. It looks as though she might have used some india ink, maybe, here with a pen.

MARY: If you were going to do something to extend this book—what kind of things could you think of that would be appropriate? Donna.

DONNA: We could draw flowers like she did.

ALICIA: We could make puppets.

BONNIE: We could make a book about her.

WILL: We could draw a picture we like best from the book.

Empowering Listeners to Use Literary Language

Story time, bursting at the seams with lively book talk, spilled out into all the curriculum. For example, the effects of an in-depth study of fairy tales at the beginning of the year led into discussions of the role of women in fairy tales and of how this genre differs from stories that really could have happened and seeped into writing time as some children chose the fairy tale genre for their stories and added an illuminated look to the first letter of their own version of *Snow White* or an original fairy tale.

The fairy tale theme crept into the reading minilesson as children practiced their reading skills using the big book version of the Ahlberg's (1978) *Each Peach Pear Plum*. The math lesson in the afternoon provided children with addition and subtraction practice using Jack's magic beans. Story time provided the forum for authentic book language—personal interpretations and transactions from all members of this reading community. Mary read from Trina Schart Hyman's (1982) version of *Rapunzel:*

> When Rapunzel was twelve years old, the witch took her deep into the forest to a place where a tall tower stood, surrounded by thorns. High at the very top was a small room with just one window. The witch shut Rapunzel inside, and then sealed up the door and took down the stairs."

Mary stopped there and invited interaction:

MARY: Why do you suppose the witch did this? She got what she wanted. Why is she locking this 12-year-old child up in a tower? Nathan?

NATHAN: She doesn't want her to get out or maybe because the witch doesn't want anybody to rescue her.

MARY: Ok, Dawn. What do you think?

DAWN: It's because she only wanted a kid that was pretty for a while but because she is so pretty she gets real mean. She really doesn't like beauty.

MARY: OK. Those are two super ideas. What do you think, Tammy?

TAMMY: I have two ideas. Maybe she wants to kill her or maybe she thinks that she's prettier and the witch can't stand the beautiness of her.

MARY: Yes, it's like what other story we've read this week?

ALLISON: Snow White.

MARY: Sort of like Snow White. Allison?

ALLISON: Maybe she doesn't like her so she's locking her up. Maybe she just wants to see what happens when she gets a little older.

MARY: Could be. What do you think, Jim?

JIM: I think a snake's in there and she wants the snakes to eat her.

MARY: You think she wants the snakes to eat Rapunzel? What do you think, Randy?

RANDY: Maybe she doesn't like that she's so pretty and she thought she'd grow up like her.

This genuine, uncontrived book talk makes for empowered listeners, readers, and literary critics. Mary triggers in her first graders what we want to see happen with more mature readers—engagement in lengthy and "meaty" conversations about literature and genuine puzzlement about what was read.

Mary introduced another kind of book talk by engaging children in a conversation about how they select books for their independent reading. This kind of conversation helps young readers bring their own thoughts about reading to a more conscious level. All the children gathered in a circle on the floor while Mary transcribed their responses:

MARY: How do you choose what you're going to be reading? Readers make choices for different reasons; it's really interesting for us to hear how we all do that. Nathan, how do you make a selection?

NATHAN: I just choose a book, and I look through it. Then I make my decision if it's good or not. If it isn't, I just put it back, and I get another book and I keep going until I find one I like.

SANDY: I just go through the book and look at the pictures.

MARY: So, you rely on the pictures quite a bit? Somebody else, what do you do to make a choice? Jim?

JIM: I look at the cover first then I read the title and a page to see if it sounds interesting and if it doesn't sound interesting then I put it back and pick up another book.

MARY: OK. Will, what do you do?

WILL: If I find a bad book, I don't care. I just write about it anyways. I don't care.

MARY: Why would you want to spend time on a book that you don't care about? Tell me more about that.

WILL: Because I don't want to spend my whole reading time looking for a book.

MARY: OK. So, you want to spend your time being productive even if it's something you're not particularly fond of? That's interesting.

MARY: Could I share with you something that I do to choose books? I like to pick the same kinds of books to read over and over. I have favorite types I like, but I find that as I get older I haven't been fair to myself because there really are a lot of good books that I just haven't even explored before. I find when I try something new and different, I really end up liking it. I used to like mostly books about make believe kinds of things—fantasy. Will and I were talking about fiction books the other day. I told him that I used to read primarily fantasy and sometimes mysteries. I don't usually like books that are about real things—like, biographies. But if I do try other kinds I find that I really get interested in them. So, I have a lot of different kinds of books in our room for different reading tastes. How many of you just have a favorite type of book that you would like to read all the time? What's your favorite kind of book, Jim?

JIM: Science books.

ALLISON: I like everything.

MARY: You like every kind! How about you, Randy?

RANDY: I like the Berenstein Bear books.

MARY: It sounds like most people have a particular favorite. How do you begin to learn about other books so that you can make some new choices?

ALLISON: I take the book out from the library, I look at the back of it or look at the title to see if it sounds interesting. If it sort of sounds interesting, I take it out and I start reading it. If it doesn't, then I put it back and I find another one and I do the same thing.

MARY: OK. Do any of you ever take advantage of the opportunity to find out about other books from your friends? Do any of you ever get recommendations from another friend that says, "Gee, this was a great book! You might want to look at it."? Has anybody ever had that experience in here yet? Just a couple of you?

MARY: My other question to you would be, how many of you have decided to read a book because you've heard me read it or talk about it?

SANDY: I have!

What do you notice about me as a reader?

What do you notice about each other as readers?

What reading strategies work best for you?

What do you need to do to become a better reader?

What might be the advantage of keeping a list of the books you have read? How would it help the class?

How does reading aloud help you as a reader?

Why is retelling a story important?

When you are finished with this book, what are you going to do next?

What are your reading goals?

Do you believe that the more you read, the better you become?

Why do we read everyday?

If you are reading aloud with a buddy, how does it help that person? How can your buddy help you? How can you become a better buddy reader?

Take a look at this poem (or story). What discoveries can you make about the text?

FIGURE 4–4   *Types of questions that empower readers*

Mary's talk about books with first graders is very sophisticated; in fact, it is similar in tone to what I would have with college students. The classroom community becomes a forum for every child, as well as the adult reader, to practice using language to engage in talk about books and the reading process.

Mary's book talk is characterized by her conversational, relaxed, and adult tone; no childish, condescending language or tone from this first-grade teacher! Mary's invitations and acceptance of responses from every student, her patience in allowing time for students to formulate responses, and her use of highly sophisticated language about the reading process (i.e., text, strategies, genres of literature, response to literature, types of questions, etc.) seem to encourage students to want to participate at this more advanced level of book talk—a level beyond what one would typically expect from first graders.

Figure 4–4 offers offers a sampling of additional questions that seem to allow students to be more powerful and empowered readers. They are, in fact, allowed to take the driver's seat as readers.

The nature of these questions helps students to think of themselves as more powerful readers and shows that they have a responsibility in becoming readers. Mary's strategy of inviting a response from each student confirms that all students are readers. Everyone in this group, including Mary, demonstrated membership in the literacy club (Smith, 1988).

This kind of language-rich environment finds support from the work of researchers such as Halliday (1973), Vygotsky (1978), and Newman (1985) and suggests that learning language is an active and social process in which the teacher plays an active role. In Mary's room, children learn how to talk the language of books in order to grow and thrive as readers.

MASSAGING AND COMBING TEXT

Mary's comments about the book selection process for story time suggest that she continually brainstorms books, possible responses, and connections to these books in her mind. She looks for ways to lead children to a rich and in-depth study of books and to make connections among and between texts. Mary massages and combs each text for response possibilities, curricular connections, and what children might learn about reading strategies. Massaging and combing text describes Mary's process of exploring the literary terrain of a text—that is, discovering the surface and deep structures. Examples of surface structure include: rhyming words, punctuation marks, use of capital letters, arrangement of print, particular consonant and vowel sounds, and so on. Aspects of deep structure include possibilities for response (i.e., art, drama, writing, music, etc.) and questions that help to extend and enrich the comprehension of the text.

This process is part of the in-depth preparation Mary does when the text lends itself to this kind of exploration. It provides Mary with a mind set for looking carefully at what texts offer for children to discover. In determining why a particular text was chosen for story time, Mary looks for the following:

Ways the title, topic, and/or author might connect with previous story time books, a book a student is reading, or a genre or theme previously or currently studied.
Concepts, words, and ideas that beg for invitations to interact.
Ways to investigate the craft of the writer.
Response opportunities.

This massaging and combing of text gives Mary a sense of direction, questioning possibilities, and ways to engage children in book talk. All of this prework with a text gives Mary a good beginning understanding of the text, but it is her students who set the pace of story time. In the next stage of the process, Mary duplicates the text, usually one with predictable language, and asks students to make discoveries. What do they notice about the text? How good are they at being detectives? This leads to a rich discussion of the literary terrain and is one strategy for helping young readers practice critical thinking and problem solving about text.

CONCLUSIONS

Martin (1989) discusses the value of teachers and students sharing books together in terms of drawing readers to the real point of reading rather than concentrating on surface features of text. This sharing is also an important opportunity to consider aspects of the reading process and the work itself. In this classroom, the study of one book or a set of books within a genre leads to the next as Mary helps children see connections between and among the books they read. She gives book talk invitations such as "See what you notice today about the artwork in this book by Trina Schart Hyman. How does it compare with other books illustrated by her?" "What would you say about Trina Schart Hyman and her style of art?" "How does this version of *Little Red Riding Hood* (1983) compare with the others we've read?" "What did you notice about Ezra Jack Keat's version of *Over in the Meadow* (1971) and that by John Langstaff?" Culler (1980) states, "It is clear that the study of one poem or novel facilitates the study of the next: one gains not only points of comparison but a sense of how to read" (p. 109). Mary typically asks divergent questions and welcomes and expects a diversity and a plethora of responses. Cairney (1988) recommends the following: "Read literature to your students which can be analyzed, criticized, assessed, interpreted, compared, and linked with their own knowledge and experiences." Atwell (1984) echoes this recommendation and further suggests that "we link books with our own knowledge and experiences and generally get inside written language" (p. 241).

Children learn about books and the language of literature from Mary and each other. It is clear that in this classroom where good books abound, where children read many self-selected texts, and where students have extensive experiences with books during story time, they develop an understanding of how reading works and of the joy of good literature. Mary continually challenges children to apply this knowledge through book talk. Books hold a place of honor and prestige in this classroom. They have become the glue that binds the classroom community into a network of readers. As one child so aptly described his literacy experiences in this classroom, "Reading is the funnest thing that ever happened to me!"

PROFESSIONAL RESOURCES

Allen, J., Giard, M., & Kristo, J. (1991). Read aloud: Prime time instruction. *New England Reading Association Journal, 27,* 2–13.

Atwell, N. (1984). Writing and reading literature from the inside out. *Language Arts, 61,* 240–252.

Butler, D. (1980). *Cushla and her books.* Boston: The Horn Book.

Cairney, T. (1988). Literature in the classroom: The making of literate learners. In A. Hanzl (Ed.), *Literature: A focus for language learning* (pp. 14–24). Melbourne: Australian Reading Association.

Cazden, C. B. (1988). *Classroom discourse: The language of teaching and learning.* Portsmouth, NH: Heinemann Educational Books.

Chambers, A. (1985). *Booktalk.* New York: Harper and Row.

Clark, M. (1976). *Young fluent readers.* London: Heinemann Educational Books.

Cohen, D. (1968). The effect of literature on vocabulary and reading achievement. *Elementary English, 45,* 209–213, 217.

Crews, F. (1986). Theory for whose sake? *The Quarterly of the National Writing Project and the Center for the Study of Writing, 8,* 4–9.

Culler, J. (1980). Literary competence. In J. P. Tompkins (Ed.), *Reader-response criticism: From formalism to post-structuralism* (pp. 101–117). Baltimore, MD: The Johns Hopkins University Press.

Durkin, D. (1966). *Children who read early.* New York: Columbia Teachers College Press.

Edelsky, C. (1987). *Talk and context: A truly intimate relationship.* Unpublished manuscript.

Halliday, M. A. K. (1973). *Explorations in the functions of language.* London: Edward Arnold.

Hansen, J. (1987). *When writers read.* Portsmouth, NH: Heinemann Educational Books.

Harste, J. C., Short, K. G., & Burke, C. (1988). *Creating classrooms for authors: The reading-writing connection.* Portsmouth, NH: Heinemann Educational Books.

Hilliker, J. (1986). Labelling to beginning narrative. In T. Newkirk & N. Atwell (Eds.), *Understanding writing: Ways of observing, learning and teaching* (2nd ed.) (pp. 13–22). Chelmsford, MA: The Northeast Regional Exchange.

Howard, E. (1989). On teaching, knowledge, and "middle ground." *Harvard Educational Review, 59,* 226–239.

Huck, C., Hepler, S., & Hickman, J. (1987). *Children's literature in the elementary school* (4th ed.). New York: Holt, Rinehart and Winston.

Martin, T. (1989). *The strugglers.* Milton Keynes, Eng.: Open University Press.

Mason, J. M., Peterman, C. L., & Kerr, B. (1989). Reading to kindergarten children. In D. S. Strickland & L. M. Morrow (Eds.), *Emerging literacy: Young children learn to read and write* (pp. 52–62). Newark, DE: International Reading Association.

Newman, J. M. (Ed.). (1985). *Whole language: Theory in use.* Portsmouth, NH: Heinemann Educational Books.

Routman, R. (1988). *Transitions: From literature to literacy.* Portsmouth, NH: Heinemann Educational Books.

Short, K. G., & Pierce, K. M. (Eds.). (1990). *Talking about books: Creating literate communities.* Portsmouth, NH: Heinemann Educational Books.

Smith, F. (1988). *Joining the literacy club: Further essays into education.* Portsmouth, NH: Heinemann Educational Books.

Staab, C. F. (1990). Teacher mediation in one whole literacy classroom. *The Reading Teacher, 43*, 548–552.

Vygotsky, L. (1978). *Mind in society.* Cambridge, MA: Harvard University Press.

CHILDREN'S LITERATURE

Ahlberg, J., & Ahlberg, A. (1978). *Each peach pear plum.* New York: Viking.

Grimm Brothers (1983). *Little red riding hood.* Illustrated by T. S. Hyman. New York: Holiday.

Grimm Brothers (1982). *Rapunzel,* retold by B. Rogasky, illustrated by T. S. Hyman. New York: Holiday.

Jeffers, S. (1980). *Snow White.* Retold by F. Littledale. Illustrated by S. Jeffers. New York: Scholastic.

Keats, E. J. (1971). *Over in the meadow.* New York: Four Winds.

Langstaff, J. (1957). *Over in the meadow.* Illustrated by F. Rojankovsky. New York: Harcourt.

Lewis, C. S. (1961). *The lion, the witch, and the wardrobe.* New York: MacMillan.

5

The Jolly Postman Comes to Call: Primary Writers' Response to Literature

Jo-Anne Wilson Keenan

Once upon a bicycle,
So they say,
A Jolly Postman came one day
From over the hills
And far away . . .
With a letter for . . .

So begins Janet and Allen Ahlberg's book *The Jolly Postman or Other People's Letters* (1986). When he rode into my classroom, carrying his sack of mail for favorite folk and fairy tale characters, he provided a means for the children to write letters in response to familiar stories.

These letters became part of our classroom postal system, which was set up initially so that members of our classroom community could write to each other, but after reading aloud a variety of folk and fairy tales and *The Jolly Postman,* we added the names of the characters to our class mailboxes. The system consisted of two wooden boxes with dividers that were labeled with the children's names, a small basket of notepaper, and a few markers.

We soon had mailboxes for Cinderella, the three bears, and the wicked witch from Hansel and Gretel. Later, we also wrote to characters from other favorite picture story books. The mailboxes were available to all of the children in the classroom, and they could write letters whenever they wished. Occasionally I would schedule a brief period of time in which all of the students in the class were requested to write a letter of response to a story character.

My idea for this mode of response is connected to Louise Rosenblatt's belief that

> In aesthetic reading, we respond to the very story or poem that we are evoking during the transaction with the text. In order to shape the work, we draw on our reservoir of past experience with people and the world, our inner linkage of words and things, our past encounters with children's spoken or written texts. (Rosenblatt, 1982, p. 270)

As the "aesthetic reader" of the "text" that is my classroom, I drew upon my reservoir of encounters with children's spoken and written texts. In earlier research (Wilson, 1988), I found that seemingly reluctant urban writers were able to retell and write down familiar texts when emphasis was placed on content rather than constraints or conventions of writing. The responses to literature described in this chapter extend that research.

I was also trying to find a way to enhance the experience of literature for my students. As Rosenblatt states, "After the reading, our initial function is to deepen the experience. . . . We should help the young reader to return to, relive, savor the experience." (Rosenblatt, 1982, p. 275)

I felt that the letters were an activity that could

> offer an aesthetic means of giving form to a sense of what has been lived through in the literary transaction. This can give evidence of what has caught the young reader's attention, what has stirred pleasant or unpleasant reactions. This can lead them back to the text. (Rosenblatt, 1982, p. 276)

I also believe that the letters to the story characters offer the affective, imaginative, fantasizing activities that Rosenblatt suggests:

> Of course, the child needs to distinguish between what the society considers "real" and what fantasy. Of course, the rational, empirical, scientific, logical components of our culture should be transmitted.
>
> Nevertheless, are these aptitudes not being fostered—or at least favored—at the expense of other potentialities of the human being and our culture? The quality of education in general is being diluted by neglect of, sacrifice of, the rich organismic, personal, experiential source of both efferent and aesthetic thinking.

> Is there not evidence of the importance of the affective, the imaginative, the fantasizing activities even for the development of cognitive abilities and creativity in a variety of modes of human endeavors? (Rosenblatt, 1982, p. 274)

The concept of evoking these responses in writing further connects to Hickman and Hepler's statement that

> Talk is the most obvious but not the only way, that children explore meaning in literature. . . . The community of readers furnishes an eager audience as well as a pool of resource ideas for response activities that go beyond talk—using story as the core of a drama for instance, or as a basis for writing, or for interpretation with paints or collage. (Hickman & Hepler, 1982, p. 21–24)

The idea of the literary letter is specifically suggested by Johnson and Louis in *Literacy Through Literature* (1988).

THE READERS AND WRITERS

The readers and writers whose letters are presented here were members of a primary whole-language classroom in a northeastern city with a population of 160,000 people. There were twenty-six students in the classroom. The children were Hispanic, white, and African-American. Half of the children were bilingual speakers of both English and Spanish. Many of the children were bussed to school to achieve racial balance. The curriculum of the classroom was child-centered and designed to provide the students with a multitude of opportunities for reading and writing. Half of the students had been members of the classroom for both first and second grade. Most of the letters presented here were written when the children were in first grade. For the purposes of this chapter, I focus upon the writing of four boys and two girls.

Each day, the children participated in a class meeting that helped build the classroom into a community. The idea for the class meeting comes from the book *Positive Discipline* (Nelson, 1987). During the meeting, the class sat in a circle and passed around a favorite object. Whoever was holding the object had the floor and could compliment or thank someone else in the class for a kindness. Next, we discussed items from an agenda that was posted prior to the meeting. Children could sign up on the agenda to discuss an issue with the rest of the class, and other children could offer suggestions for dealing with the issue. If time allowed, we'd pass the object around again and invite children to tell a story or share a page from a favorite book, news, writings, or small treasures brought from home.

When the children responded in writing to the stories in *The Jolly Postman* (Alhberg & Alhberg, 1986), the characters came alive for them. Letters directed to the characters addressed incidents in the stories themselves. Others suggested extensions of the stories, and many reflected the kind of talk that was taking place in the class meeting each morning. Just as students complimented and gave advice to each other, they also complimented and advised story characters.

The reading in the classroom comprised shared, guided, independent, and read-aloud time, as described in *Reading in Junior Classes* (Mooney, 1985). At the time that many of the pieces in this chapter were written, the children were emergent readers and their own readings of the traditional tales were close approximations of the texts. This means that they often engaged in reading-like behavior by following and retelling the story in the book, although they were not saying the exact words that were on the page. Some children relied on their prior knowledge of stories, familiar refrains, or picture cues to guide them through a text.

The children were learning to write through a process approach, as described by Donald Graves (1983). In my earlier years of teaching, I might have hesitated and thought that these students were not ready to engage in written responses to literature. I might have held them back until their spellings were closer to conventional form or until they could read with greater accuracy. But, instead, I allowed the children to set aside "conceived or real constraints" (Harste, Woodward, & Burke, 1984) and I attempted to create a "receptive, nonpressured atmosphere" similar to the one Rosenblatt (1982) encourages to help children adopt the aesthetic stance in reading. As a result, the children created nonconventional writing that signifies its genre to our adult literate community (Harste, Woodward, & Burke, 1984). The pieces of writing presented here are recognizable as letters because they generally contain the recipient's name and are signed by the writer. I did not direct the children to follow a specific format, although I did write letters myself that served as models for the children. The intentions of the pieces are clear, and the writers addressed a specific audience. The letters are mainly first drafts, and capitalization, punctuation, and spellings are not conventional. The letters were a valuable means of learning because they provided the emergent readers and writers with an opportunity to engage with a familiar piece of literature on their own terms in a way that reflected their knowledge of written language. The students were gaining access to the literacy process through involvement in the process (Harste, Woodward, & Burke, 1984).

The children chose to write to the characters for their own purposes, and thus they created authentic texts within the context of the practices of the classroom. I became the audience and often wrote back in the persona of the characters to ask a question and extend the opportunity for another writing event. This type of response was a variation on a dialogue journal in the form of letters rather than journal entries. For several months, the children never questioned the identity of the respondent, they were simply delighted when they received a letter from a story character.

In the beginning I initiated the making of a mailbox for a character, but as time went on, the children began to take ownership of this as well. One day Corey wrote to me and complained that he was not getting enough mail. I wrote back to him and asked him if he would like to become the jolly postman. His next letter stated that he would love the job. I brought him a mail carrier's hat and affixed a label reading "The Jolly Postman." His main duty was to distribute letters that had not been collected from mailboxes, but he saw another dimension to his job and began adding labels to the mailbox for other characters to whom he wished to send mail. He brought in a copy of *The Brave Little Tailor* for me to read to the class and took it upon himself to add a mailbox for the tailor. Upon the death of Jim Henson, he added a mailbox for Whembly Fraggle, one of Henson's characters from another book that Corey had brought in from home. As Rosenblatt states, "Children's sensori-motor exploration of the physical environment and their interplay with human and social environments are increasingly seen as sources and conditions of language behavior" (1982, p. 270). The story characters' mailboxes were providing a safe place for the children to carry out this exploration and interplay.

LETTERS

This chapter presents the children's letters and comments on the use of the letter as an extension of an aesthetic response to literature. I present the children's messages in both original form and in conventional spelling. I then explain the message and the knowledge of written language that is reflected in that piece of writing. The names of the children in the pieces are pseudonyms.

Frequently, initial messages comprised a few words that the children could write in conventional spellings, such as "I love you." Although these letters were simple, the messages were the first signs that the children were developing the habit and capacity for aesthetic reading (Rosenblatt, 1982). They were often accompanied by drawings. In addition to exploring the writing of their first messages, the children were also building a vocabulary of lines and forms (Gardner, 1980) and combining them into fixed patterns for the familiar objects in their world and in the stories. The drawing and writing were developing simultaneously. This development concurs with Harste, Woodward, & Burke's idea that although art is often thought to develop before writing, the relationship is reciprocal and becomes mutually supportive to written language literacy in the broadest sense (Harste, Woodward, & Burke, 1984). The children also included their names and the names of the story characters in these early letters. The use of names in these pieces coincides with Dyson's (1984) idea that names are reference points in learning about print. In addition, the children used labels on the mailboxes as a means of discovering the spelling of a character's name. Other messages were written in the emergent stages of spelling, in which children represent words with one or two letters. Later pieces were longer and allowed the children to express in more detail what had been lived through in the literary transaction. They also reflected the children's acquisition of additional knowledge of the workings of written language, including the development of the principles of directionality, return sweep, spacing between words (Clay, 1975), and spelling.

Hector

Hector wrote a series of letters to Cinderella. Hector showed that he was familiar with the characters, setting, and motifs of this familiar tale, but his response was not limited to these. Although Hector was at an emergent stage in his drawing and writing, he was effectively using written language to create an aesthetic response to a piece of literature. His message reads "I Love you Love Hector." He drew the pumpkin coach, complete with horse and coachman (see Figure 5–1). Hector recreated the scene from the fairy tale by weaving circles, lines, mandalas, and triangles into a picture.

These types of scenes are described by Gardner (1980) as typical drawings of young children. Hector also inserted a heart into the middle of the letter o in the word you, perhaps as a means of expressing his feelings more deeply than the letter would by itself. He moved freely between writing and art and created this new symbol by decorating a standard form. This process is called a border skirmish (Harste, Woodward, & Burke, 1984) and is based upon the flexibility principle described by Clay (1975).

Hector made one revision in the piece, marking over the letter u in the word Love to correct the spelling to L-o-v-e. He maintained this spelling the second time he wrote the word. Hector delighted in writing to Cinderella.

Maria

Like Hector, Maria also wrote a letter to a story character. She wrote to Arthur, the main aardvark in Marc Brown's Arthur series.

FIGURE 5–1   *Hector's piece*
The message reads: "I Love you Love [Hector]."

Like Hector, Maria wrote a message that she could spell conventionally. She also drew a picture of Arthur in a manner similar to the way in which Hector drew Cinderella's carriage. Maria added another piece to her text. She drew a picture of a flower and wrote the words "red rose" next to it (see Figure 5–2). The flower added a new dimension to Maria's text because it originated from another popular text in the classroom, *The Red Rose* (Wright Group, 1983). In this story, the main character gives his wife a red rose. The red rose became a popular motif in the children's drawings. Maria's response of presenting a red rose to the character Arthur came from an idea she had found in another text. Maria was linking her past encounter with a written text with a present one (Rosenblatt, 1982).

Raoul

Raoul was another writer who frequently corresponded with a story character. His favorite was the wicked witch. Raoul's first message to the witch stated, "The Wicked Witch, I wish that (wish that you) were alive" (see Figure 5–3).

When the witch received this letter, she wrote back to him:

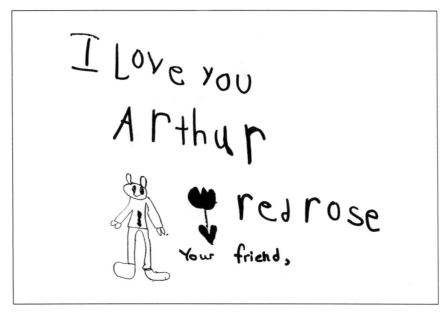

FIGURE 5–2   *Maria's piece*
The message reads: "I Love you Arthur. red rose. Your friend, [Maria]."

Dear Raoul,
   I am alive! [Then, adding a bit of humor, she queried:] Are you fat? Please write back soon.

Love,
The Wicked Witch

Raoul quickly responded, "No, I am not fat, okay?" (see Figure 5–4).

Raoul's frequent absences from school sometimes interfered with his social interactions in the classroom. One day when I noticed that Raoul was becoming comfortable with the other children and making friends, I capitalized on the witch's loneliness and isolation and left a letter in his box asking him how he had made so many friends. The letter read:

Dear Raoul,
   I hear that you have made many friends lately. Will you tell me the secret to making friends? I am lonesome. Thank you.

Love,
The Wicked Witch.

Raoul wrote back promptly, "You need to be friendly so you can get some friends and you have a lot of friends. Love" (see Figure 5–5).

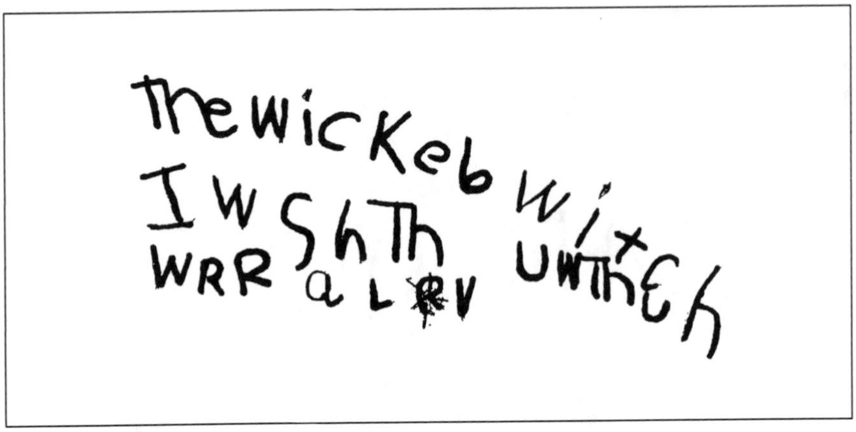

FIGURE 5–3   *Raoul's first piece*

VO‡MNF TOCA

FIGURE 5–4   *Raoul's second piece*

Raoul's letters transcended the boundaries of fantasy and became a conversation between himself and the witch. The letters also became a place where humor could be shared and compliments, advice, and self-awareness could be extended. This sharing had been a goal of our class meetings, but the literary exchange became a more personal forum for addressing these issues. Through the letters, Raoul was also able to consider the possibility that this story character could come alive for him and show another side of herself. He could consider that her attitudes toward others might come from loneliness and a feeling of isolation. He could also think through the ways in which he was working out similar issues in order to help and assure her that she did have friends. This experience "has as its by products the educational, informative,

U neD TO
B FrD iE
SoU cavn
gt sm
FrnDS
and U
HU a It
av FrnOS. LOVE

FIGURE 5–5   *Raoul's third piece*

social, and moral values for which literature is often praised"
(Rosenblatt, 1982).

Raoul's knowledge of written language was also being enhanced
in the process. Raoul was finding models for written language in
the label on the mailbox and in the letters that were being written
back to him. In the first two letters most of his spellings were stage
II (Graves, 1983) or stage III, where he was employing mainly
initial final and some medial consonants. For example, he spelled
fat as f-t, and wish as w-s-h. He was also using letter name spellings
for the word you, which he spelled with the single letter U. He
showed evidence of return sweep in his first letter, where he
returned to the left margin to begin the second and third lines of
his text. He also showed awareness of audience in both pieces, in his
salutation addressing the witch and in his exclamation, "okay?" at
the end of the second letter.

In his third letter, Raoul was employing vocabulary from his
reading—to, can, and, LOVE. He improved the spacing between
the words in his piece and employed plural form and end-stop
punctuation. The content of this piece was also longer and more
detailed than the others.

FIGURE 5-6   *Sharee's first piece*
The message reads: "I like your crown and your dress."

Sharee

Sharee used the postal system often and generally chose to write to Cinderella. Her letters, even responses to my exchanges with her, usually consisted of pictures of Cinderella in her finery accompanied by a written compliment (see Figure 5-6). These responses reflected the type of compliments that were being given in the daily class meetings. Sharee was able to add these written messages because, unlike Hector or Maria, she took the risk of attempting functional spelling from the beginning of the year.

In one of Sharee's letters, she superimposed her picture on the written text. The piece has a three-dimensional effect, as balloons, hearts, birds, smiling butterflies, and insects float past Cinderella. Although the double text makes this piece somewhat difficult to discern, it shows the mutually supportive relationship between

Figure 5–7 *Sharee's second piece*

drawing and writing. The letter also seems to indicate the degree of Sharee's familiarity with the character and the details of the tale and the amount of detail she invested in this response. In the letter, Sharee tells her "I like your dress, Cinderella. It is pretty because of the way it is decorated." (see Figure 5–7). Sharee was the first child to tell me that she had figured out that I was the one writing back in the persona of the story characters.

In her writing, Sharee used a little of the vocabulary from her reading: I, and, is, the, way. She also spelled words at stage IV (Graves, 1983), as she used initial, medial, and final consonants and vowels as placeholders.

Corey and Andrew

Two of the boys, Corey and Andrew, made personal connections with literature that extended beyond the classroom. Rosenblatt cites Dorothy White's discussion of her young daughter's response to books:

> The experience makes the book richer and the book enriches the personal experience even at this level. I am astonished at the early

age this backward and forward flow between books and life takes place. With adults and older children one cannot observe it so easily, but here at this age when all the child's experiences are known and the books are read and shared . . . the interaction is seen very clearly. (Rosenblatt, 1982, p. 272)

I found the interaction between literature and personal experience recorded clearly in the letters of Corey and Andrew. Corey, who was our jolly postman, made connections between his experiences at home and the books in the classroom. In the following response, Corey began by telling the main character in the story *Madeline* (Bemelmans, 1958) that he had two of her stories on tape as cartoons. Then he went on to retell the story that he knew from the classroom. Almost incidentally, he revealed his knowledge of the story as he mentioned characters, setting, events, details and feelings of the characters (see Figure 5–8). Corey addressed Madeline as "you" throughout the text of the letter, which shows that he definitely considered the story character to be his audience. His story also conveyed a sense of fun. In writing his letter to Madeline, Corey returned to, relived, and savored the experience of the story (Rosenblatt, 1982).

He labeled his letter as draft number one, which indicates that he was concentrating on content and would go back to work on conventions later. Corey had many conventional spellings in his piece; however, his other spellings were mainly stage IV spellings (Graves, 1983). Corey also used plural form and employed vocabulary from his reading. He left spaces between the words in his piece and was beginning to use punctuation.

Andrew came into first grade as a fluent reader who took pride in reading to others. He also involved himself in his response to a story character. He wrote to Mike Mulligan (Burton, 1939) and invited him to come to his house to dig a hole for him so that he could make a swimming pool for his family. Andrew gave Mike his exact address so that Mike would be sure to find the house. Andrew also drew a detailed picture on the back of the letter showing Mike digging the hole (see Figure 5–9). Andrew's letter is mainly an invitation, and it shows that he understood the story well enough that he didn't need to retell it. Mike would be the perfect solution to Andrew's desire to provide a pool for his family and he is imagining the thrill of having Mike come to his house.

Andrew's story indicates that, like Corey's, this letter was a first draft. Andrew had mainly conventional spellings in his letter and was attempting the use of commas and end-stop punctuation. He also employed the alternate form of addition signs in place of the word and.

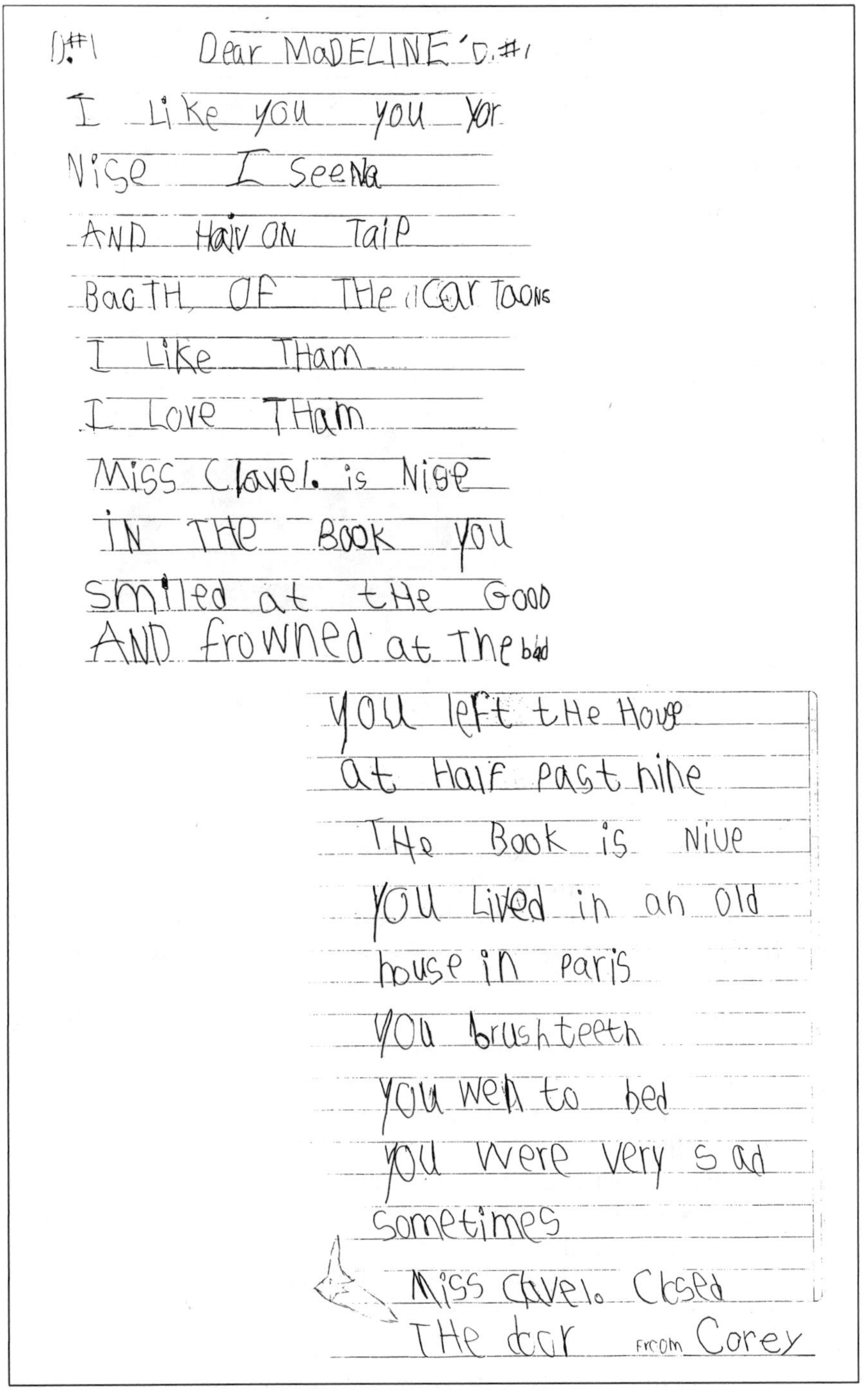
D#1 Dear MaDELINE 'D.#1
I LiKe you you yor
Nise I SeeNa
AND Haiv ON TaiP
BaGTH OF THe Car TOONS
I Like Tham
I Love THam
Miss Clavel is Nise
IN THE BOOK you
smiled at tHe GOOD
AND frowned at The bad
you left tHe House
at Half past nine
THe Book is Nive
you Lived in an old
house in paris
you brushteeth
you wen to bed
you were very sad
sometimes
Miss Clavel Closed
THe door From Corey

FIGURE 5–8 *Corey's piece*
The message reads: "Dear Madeline, I like you. You are nice. I seen and have on tape both of the cartoons. I like them. I love them. Miss Clavel is nice. In the book you smiled at the good and frowned at the bad. You left the house at half past nine. The book is nice. You lived in an old house in Paris. You brush teeth. You went to bed. You were very sad sometimes. Miss Clavel closed the door. From, [Corey]."

FIGURE 5–9   *Andrew's piece*

CONCLUSIONS

I found that the visits from the jolly postman were an enjoyable means of inviting responses to literature in my classroom. The letters helped me discover what had caught the children's attention and what stirred their reactions. The letters provided an opportunity for the children to respond to literature while engaging themselves in literacy. The letters offered an aesthetic means of giving form to a sense of what has been lived through in the literary transaction and deepened the experience of literature for my students as they returned to, relived, and savored the experience (Rosenblatt, 1982).

In concurrence with my previous work (Wilson, 1988), I found that greater knowledge of written language was revealed when children took risks and felt comfortable expressing themselves in functional spelling. I also found that a more detailed response to literature was shared when children take the risk and produce texts in functional spelling. Furthermore, responses were richly enhanced when children drew upon home-based experiences.

Hector and Maria, for example, wrote their brief responses using a few familar words they could spell in conventional spellings. Because they did not take the risk of writing words in functional spelling, they limited the amount of detail they shared in those responses. They also limited the amount of information that the reader has about their response. Raoul, Sharee, and Corey, on the other hand, utilized functional spelling and were able to provide a more detailed sense of what had been lived through and drawn from their literary interactions. Their use of functional spelling provided the flexibility to create a text that extended beyond the constraints of the words they could spell conventionally. Their letters do not necessarily indicate that their responses were realized more deeply than Hector's or Maria's, but the detail gives the reader more information about their responses. Andrew, who was able to spell a wide range of words in conventional spelling, was also able to employ this flexibility in his letter and thus revealed the richness of his response that was connected to a home-based experience.

Initial letter writing served as the springboard for additional responses, including more letters and writing in other genres. The letters also offered opportunity for further responses in other modes. They led to spoken conversations with the children and reading aloud from books, like those the children brought in from home. Children also created their own illustrations and designed bulletin board displays as artistic responses to literature. Puppet shows were held in the classroom, and Corey's role as postman became extended dramatic play.

Any teacher can bring the jolly postman into the classroom and provide students, even those in the earliest stages of written language development, with means for aesthetic response to literature. All you need is one or two divided wooden boxes; they do not have to be elaborate—one of mine is a CD storage box, the other is an old pie box I found at a flea market. The number will depend upon the number of your students and how many characters you wish to include, as you need a slot for each. You also will need some gummed labels and some notepaper. Include a mailbox for yourself so you can write letters that provide a model for the students.

The children will become engaged in literacy as they respond to and reconstruct texts and discuss characters, events, and settings. The letters will also indicate the next steps for instruction in the conventions of written language, but teachers should exercise caution and make prudent choices about the degree of convention they expect in first drafts. Too much emphasis on convention and constraint will reduce the risks that writers are willing to take and will limit the detail of the responses.

In working with these writers, I noticed how much they delighted in writing to the story characters. They looked upon them as old familiar friends. I specifically noted that the boys in this integrated urban setting responded to the literature as readily as the girls. Further research could focus upon the nature of young urban boys' written responses to familiar literature. Research could also focus upon the nature of the extended conversations in the texts of letters stemming from response to a character.

PROFESSIONAL RESOURCES

Clay, M. (1975). *What did I write?* London: Heinemann.

Dyson, A. (1984). Emerging alphabetic literacy in school contexts: Toward defining the gap between school curriculum and child mind. *Written Communication, 1* (1), 5–55.

Gardner, H. (1980). *Artful scribbles: The significance of children's drawing.* New York: Basic Books.

Graves, D. (1983). *Writing: Teachers and children at work.* Portsmouth, NH: Heinemann Educational Books.

Harste, J., Woodward, V., & Burke, C. (1984). *Language stories & literacy lessons.* Portsmouth, NH: Heinemann Educational Books.

Hickman, J. & Hepler, S. (1982). The book was Ok, I love you. *Theory into Practice, 21* (4).

Johnson, T. D., & Louis, D. R. (1988). *Literacy through literature.* Portsmouth, NH: Heinemann Educational Books.

Mooney, Margaret (Ed.). (1985). *Reading in junior classes.* Wellington, New Zealand: Department of Education.

Nelson, J. (1987). *Positive discipline.* New York: Ballantine Books.

Rosenblatt, L. M. (1982). The literary transaction: Evocation and response. *Theory into Practice, 21* (4), 268–277.

Wilson, J. (1988). *Multiple contexts: Tapping the writing abilities of innercity writers.* Doctoral Dissertation, University of Massachusetts.

CHILDREN'S LITERATURE

Ahlberg, J., & Ahlberg, A. (1986). *The jolly postman or other people's letters.* Boston: Little, Brown.

Bemelmans, Ludwig (1958). *Madeline.* New York: Viking.

Brown, Marc (1980). *Arthur's valentine.* Boston: Little, Brown.

Burton, Virginia L. (1939). *Mike Mulligan and his steam shovel.* Boston: Houghton Mifflin.

Cinderella—Letter included in (1986), *The jolly postman or other people's letters.* Boston: Little, Brown.

Cowley, Joy (1983). *The red rose.* Auckland, New Zealand: Shortland Publications.

Hansel and Gretel—Letter included in (1986), *The jolly postman or other people's letters.* Boston: Little, Brown.

Line, Kathleen (Ed.). (1963). *The brave little tailor* in *Fifty favorite fairy tales.* Chosen from *The color fairy book* by Andrew Long. New York: The Nonesuch Press Limited.

Part II

Literary Responses in Middle Childhood

6

What's a Bustle?

Judy A. Yocom

ANTHONY: What's a bustle?
TERESA: It's like a piece of material that makes the dress blow up.
MAGGIE: You put it in back to make it go out and back.
COLIN: It goes like this. [demonstrates]

As in many primary school classrooms, these children are sitting on a rug in a corner of their classroom. Their attention is given to the classroom teacher, who is reading a story aloud. The responses just quoted occurred while the classroom teacher was reading aloud from the book, *The Glorious Flight Across the Channel with Louis Bleriot* (Provensen, 1983).

A child sitting on the rug listening to the classroom teacher read a story responds to that story with verbal and nonverbal behaviors. Anthony needed to know about a bustle, and Teresa provided a description. During this read-aloud event, the children were actively engaged in the story and were encouraged to participate and share their responses.

The observation and evaluation of children's responses is an essential component of the read-aloud activity. The classroom teacher is generally seen as the person responsible for the nurture and development of children's literary experiences. Often the task of bringing children and books together has been viewed as the domain of the librarian, but teachers, as well as librarians, carry the responsibility for bringing children and books together.

Research studies investigating the significance of reading aloud to elementary school children often have focused on a particular aspect of children's increased learning potential, such as increased vocabulary knowledge (Cohen, 1968; Porter, 1969). However, this narrow focus of measurement leads to a limited interpretation of the effects of reading aloud and ignores the richness of the children's responses. Alternatively, research that focuses attention on both the verbal and nonverbal responses of children "on and off the rug" moves beyond measuring a final outcome, a product, to describing the nature of the read-aloud event—the process. This chapter presents such process-focused research, done by a teacher-researcher, which collects and evaluates the children's responses.

As teacher-researchers, classroom teachers have the advantage of being a part of the social context of the elementary classroom environment. They can systematically and continually observe and record their students' responses to children's literature read aloud daily throughout the school year. They have access to all of the children's work, which may, in less obvious ways, reflect their responses to stories read aloud. Teachers also can observe and record the children's responses throughout the school day without having to limit observation to a predetermined period of time each day or to targeted days each week, as would be the case with an outside observer.

DeLapp (1980) writes:

> If classroom and teaching research is to make contributions to our understanding of the processes of education, the results, in the final analysis, must be meaningful to classroom teachers. It is their actions and understandings at the classroom level that determine to an important degree the processes of education in our schools. (p. 5)

THE DYNAMICS OF THE READ-ALOUD EVENT

The read-aloud activity can be seen as a sociocultural literary event. The literature on the topic of reading aloud to children suggests that during this story-time activity children learn about the text or story and also form concepts about language and experiences that may be new or different from those previously experienced (Martinez & Roser, 1985).

The act of reading is also understood to be a transaction involving the reader and the text (Rosenblatt, 1978). In the case of young children, a willing adult acts as an intermediary and reads aloud the text to the child. For many years, Rosenblatt has spoken of the importance of acknowledging the social setting of the act of reading. She writes:

> Any encounter between readers, teachers, and texts in a classroom has as its setting the society, the community, the ethos of the school, the total curriculum, the cumulative social concepts embodied in the works presented to the pupil over the years, and the earlier experiences with literature at home and in school. The dynamics of the particular classroom, in turn, provide a context for the individual students' evocations and responses. (Rosenblatt, 1985, p. 50)

The study on which this chapter is based (Yocom, 1987) was implemented to explore the nature of the responses of second-grade students in an international school to children's literature read aloud by the classroom teacher. The school was located in a suburb of Paris, France. The enrollment of the school represents approximately fifty countries. This investigation of children's responses was not limited to the classroom but included the exploration of children's responses at home to the books read aloud in the classroom. The study lasted an academic school year.

PROCEDURES

To explore the nature and extent of the children's responses to the books read aloud in the classroom, research questions were tentatively proposed that concentrated on three areas of investigation:

1. Children's responses during the read-aloud events.
2. Children's responses outside of the read-aloud events but centered in the classroom.
3. Children's responses in the home.

Forms of data collection included four sets of questionnaires sent to the parents during the school year, audiotapes of the read-aloud events, which were later transcribed, and field notes of observations that recorded the verbal and nonverbal responses of the children outside of the read-aloud events. The read-aloud events were audio-taped daily throughout the school year, parental questionnaires were sent in October, December, March, and June, and field notes were kept in a journal throughout the study.

THE SECOND-GRADE CHILDREN

All classes at second-grade level were balanced in terms of the number of children from the United States, the number of children

Name	Nationality
Kristian	Netherlands
Ali	United States
Tze Khong	Malaysia
Teresa	Spain
Caitlin	United States
Colin	United States
Greg	United States
Malia	United States
Piper	United States
Hamoudi	Lebanon
Rana	Saudi Arabia
Christoph	Switzerland
Doris	Kenya
Maggie	United States
Oko	Tanzania
Goncalo	Brazil
Paul	England
John	Venezuela
David	England
Megan	United States
Thomas	France
Yike	Belgium
Anthony	China
Alex	Norway
Alexis	France
Julie	Brazil

FIGURE 6–1   *Class list of second-grade children*

who did not speak English as their first language, the number of boys and girls, the number of children who spoke no English, and the number of countries represented. During the school year the class list changed when families moved to other job assignments or new families were transferred to Paris. Throughout the school year the class size ranged from twenty-two to twenty-four students (see Figure 6–1).

The children came from families in which one or both parents held high positions in the government of their country, were assigned to an embassy, or held positions at the upper executive level in the business community. In general terms, the parents were professionals of upper middle to high socioeconomic status. Many of the children spoke a language other than English in their homes, but the unifying factor in the classroom was the use of English as the language of instruction.

One of the basic principles of instruction in an international school is not to focus on what is different—that is, the nationalities of the children or the home language spoken—but to concentrate on what the children have in common. Each of these second-grade children brought their unique cultural heritage to the classroom. Many of them spoke haltingly and groped to express themselves in English. Some of the children came from cultures with non-Western values. Their lunchboxes did not contain peanut butter and jelly sandwiches but did hold tabouli, rice, crepes, and other nationalities' dishes. Yet, they also brought the ability to create unity amidst diversity. During the school year the class became a collective international community. This study explored the children's responses to literature in this international setting during the course of a school year.

DURING THE READ-ALOUD EVENT

From an analysis of over one-hundred transcriptions, five loosely defined categories of children's responses emerged:

1. Children's responses as literary linkage.
2. Children's responses as explanations.
3. Children's responses to characters.
4. Children's responses related to their world.
5. Children's responses to illustrations.

Children's responses were fluid, so the categories served as general markers or guidelines in understanding the responses. These categories were neither discrete nor mutually exclusive.

Literary linkage is defined as a response in which a connection is made between an aspect of the read-aloud book and some feature of another book. The children in this study, for example, linked the author of the read-aloud book with other books that author had written. Literary linkage became more pronounced throughout the school year.

During the reading of *The Story of Jumping Mouse* (Steptoe, 1984), the children voiced their interest in the habits of snakes and then related the eating habits of snakes to a song:

CHRISTOPH: Ms. Yocom, turn to that page where the snake is.
GREG: I know what snakes do, they swallow it and then it goes down to the end of them and they digest it.
JOHN: He had to swallow it because snakes don't chew.
GREG: Snakes can swallow pigs?
COLIN: Yeah, they can cause in Teresa's world book or something I saw it showed a pig. And, like, after they swallowed it whole, they don't chew it. They press their poison and . . .

TERESA: But, Ms. Yocom, how can a snake he has this little mouth, how does he swallow it in one gulp?

MS. YOCOM: He doesn't. It is part in and part out. Slowly goes into the mouth.

MAGGIE: Like the song, "I'm Being Swallowed by a Boa Constrictor." Like it say . . .

ANTHONY: Oh, yeah, I know that.

MAGGIE (sings): Gee, he swallowed my knee.

During the reading of *The Glorious Flight Across the Channel with Louis Bleriot* (Provensen, 1983), Anthony made a general observation about the way the story chronicled the building of Bleriot's many planes. His general comment triggered explanations from the other children.

ANTHONY: He stopped at Bleriot seven and we never heard Bleriot eight.

COLIN: Cause it would be a long time. It would be like that thick [demonstrates] if telling about everything.

GREG: It only told about eight planes.

MAGGIE: Some books do that. They have lots of information to tell. And if they write all of it, it will probably be really, really thick book. And that would be hard to sew together and publish. So they don't want to sew that many pages.

Children's responses to the books during the read-aloud events matured over time. Response patterns that permeated the transcriptions and became noticeable and more prevalent over the course of the school year were:

An increase in child-initiated questions.

An increase in child-initiated answers to questions voiced by other children.

An emergence and continued increase in the amount of children's opinion supported by book information.

An increase in children's elaboration of verbal responses.

An emergence of children's references to responses of other children.

A lengthening of sequences of child-to-child responses.

An emergence and continued interest in illustration and text congruency.

Children's responses grew in quantity as well as quality. Transcriptions of the read-aloud events ranged from a few pages in the autumn to seventeen pages in late spring. Thus, a long period of time was necessary for children's responses to develop and be expressed during the read-aloud event.

In the fall, isolated individual responses were voiced by the children. Months later, children's literary understanding became evident. In the spring, a unit on folk and fairy tales was introduced. During the reading of the folk tale *Salt* (Zemach, 1965), the children were concerned about the marriage of the princess. The following sequence of the children's responses was typical in terms of its length and adherence to the topic of discussion. This conversation also exemplifies responses that conform to the accepted boundaries of a book discussion. Interspersed in this discussion are the children's prior knowledge and experiences of a marriage ceremony.

JOHN: I think the father took the gold away and, um, he used that money for Ivan and the princess to get married.

COLIN: Well, it doesn't cost that much to get married.

TERESA: Yes, it does.

PIPER: Yes, it does. It cost a lot for the food and the wedding gown and all that other stuff.

COLIN: I know, but they already had that cause she was going to get married to the other brother.

CHRISTOPH: He got the rest of the money because he told everything to his father. So his father took the money and spent it on the dresses and . . .

COLIN: And they . . .

CHRISTOPH: And gave the rest of the money to Ivan.

TERESA: But that can't be, because when he arrived, um, the oldest brother already brought his papers cause he was going to marry with the princess. She already had her gown. They already reserved the food and everything. So he must have not wasted anything. And his brothers gave him back the gold and the silver.

COLIN: She probably is the first wife.

AFTER THE READ-ALOUD EVENT

Children continued to respond to the children's literature read aloud in the classroom after the read-aloud events. Children's responses to the read-aloud books were observable in many of the daily activities of the classroom: silent sustained reading, snack time, a field trip, and in casual conversations. The children's verbal responses during the school day were expressed in a quick, spontaneous, and evanescent manner.

Children's responses to the read-aloud books were also evident in their writing, artwork, and nonverbal behaviors. Although there were observable examples of a direct connection between the read-aloud books and children's writing and illustrations, the children did not appear to initiate or incorporate information from the read-aloud books directly. In the following exerpt from the transcription of a reading of *Arrow to the Sun* (McDermott, 1974), Piper shares:

> The last time you read this, it was the morning that I was writing my book. So I tried to make my sun like that. And it turned out to look like a regular sun.

Nevertheless, the children responded positively to suggestions to incorporate information from the read-aloud books in their own writing. During the reading of *Lyle Finds His Mother* (Waber, 1974), the children wondered if there was another book about Lyle. In the following sequence of responses, one way to read more about Lyle was suggested:

TERESA: Maybe there's another book there, um, found Mrs. Primm and Lyle and Lyle's mother all live together.
MS. YOCOM: That could be. You know, we could almost make a book like that ourselves, couldn't we?
PAUL: We could make a book of Lyle.

After more discussion, the children wrote stories about Lyle. Hamoudi's story (see Figure 6–2) is an example from a child whose second language is English.

The read-aloud books were displayed throughout the classroom, and the children actively sought them for silent sustained reading and other free moments during the school day. On occasion, more than one child wanted to read a particular read-aloud book at the same time. These situations were resolved by the children sharing the book in different ways. Children also mirrored behaviors that occurred as part of the read-aloud events. The journal entry dated October 29 read:

> During S.S.R. [silent sustained reading] Malia took her stuffed animal that she brings to school and placed it on the bar of the double glass door. She then set her chair facing the stuffed animal and sat down. She was reading, whispering, a book, *Bedtime for Frances*, and looking up at the stuffed animal.

IN THE HOME ENVIRONMENT

The questionnaires were designed to elicit from parents a record of the nature of children's responses in the home to the read-aloud books. The parental responses on the questionnaires and casual comments made in conversations indicated that the children con-

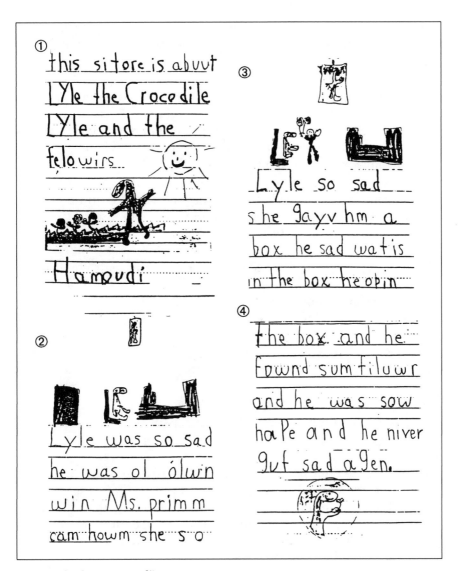

FIGURE 6-2   *Hamoudi's story*
(1) This story is about Lyle the Crocodile, Lyle and the flowers. [Hamoudi]
(2) Lyle was so sad. He was all alone when Ms. Primm came home. She saw
(3) Lyle so sad. She gave him a box. He said, "What is in the box?" He opened
(4) the box and he found some flowers, and he was so happy and he never got sad
again.

tinued to respond in the home to the books read aloud in the
classroom. These behaviors were demonstrated in various ways.

Some responses of the children were direct and obvious; other
responses were elusive and ephemeral. Even when the responses of
the children were captured and noted, it was difficult for parents
to express and adequately convey the nature of their children's

responses to another person. Caitlin's mother expressed the difficulty of recording her daughter's responses to the read-aloud books:

> I cannot be specific here, but I know that Caitlin responds at home to the stories read in class in very subtle ways, a comment here; a question there and a look of understanding and similarity about certain issues especially regarding nature and animals, decision making working out a deal, etc.

Yfke's mother noted a change in her daughter's reading behavior, as illustrated by the following quotes. In response to the first questionnaire, sent in October, she wrote:

> Yfke does not tell anything about the stories you read. When asked, she showed me a book she had herself, *The Girl Who Loved Wild Horses*. Yfke does not allow me to read a book to her but she does love you reading in the class.

However, when the second questionnaire was sent in December, she said:

> The last library session Yfke got a book which I had to read to her. She allowed me to read a book to her for the first time in two years!

Although the children might not initiate responses to the books read aloud in the classroom, if parents expressed interest in these books, children would share their responses more directly. This situation suggests that if parents express overt interest in read-aloud books, children will respond by sharing their responses with family members in more observable ways.

Parental responses on the questionnaires were overwhelmingly positive about the activity of reading aloud to their children in the classroom. The responses indicated that parents believed reading aloud to their children in the school positively influenced their children's reading habits, their interest in and motivation to read children's literature on their own, and their ability to critically evaluate the quality of the books they read. The degree of support for reading aloud to children in the classroom was especially significant. Parents believed that reading aloud in the classroom was beneficial for the growth of their children as independent readers.

In the comments section of the questionnaire, one mother spoke of her daughter's increased interest in reading and described her daughter's literary behaviors in some detail:

Maggie's interest in reading has certainly been sharpened and stimulated by your approach. She spends long periods reading to herself in a highly concentrated manner. She has also become discriminating in the quality of literature and illustrations that she reads (or is read to in class). She will discuss with me why a particular story was especially good, i.e. the illustrations were photos artistically taken; the plot was interesting; the book won the Caldecott, etc. She does love reading!

The responses of the parents on the questionnaires made it evident that the children did respond to the books read aloud in the classroom outside of the school environment.

FACTORS THAT ENCOURAGE CHILDREN'S RESPONSES

Throughout the school year, the children's developing skills in maintaining, utilizing, and focusing their attention on the read-aloud books was clearly evident. Children's responses were not limited to the read-aloud events but were evident in other activities during the school day. A classroom environment that encourages children to respond to literature on and off the rug is critical. A number of components of this environment were identified.

An Atmosphere of Acceptance

An atmosphere of acceptance of children's individual responses is important in creating a nonthreatening, nonjudgmental environment in which children feel safe and comfortable in sharing their responses with others. Initially, children appeared hesitant in expressing their responses to the read-aloud books and seemed even more hesitant if they did not agree with other children's responses. An atmosphere in which differences in opinions are viewed as appropriate and acceptable is fundamental to children sharing their responses with others.

A Community of Shared Experiences

The read-aloud events create an opportunity for children to expand their language capabilities. Children increasingly responded to the read-aloud books and to their peers over the course of the school year. The read-aloud events introduced children to books, to authors, and to an understanding of a book discussion. These events also provided the children with an increasing reservoir of knowledge of children's literature that, in turn, leads to a deeper sense of literary development. This experiential base of literacy created a situation in which all the children shared common experiences. With this commonality of literary experience, children who did not speak English as their first language seemed more confident in expressing themselves. These children were in a position to hear native speakers of English in a natural context of communication.

The commonality of literacy experience during the read-aloud events also provided the children with a forum in which to respond to the books outside of the read-aloud time. For example, the children discussed the books with their peers during snack time and shared the read-aloud books in small groups during silent sustained reading. Opportunities for these literary, language-learning experiences among the children outside of the read-aloud sessions were essential for nurturing the children's responses.

Guidance and Modeling of Responses

One important aspect of the reader's role was to guide and expand children's initial responses to the read-aloud books. This guidance was fostered by asking open-ended questions throughout the story that redirected the children's attention to an unexpected avenue. Questions that ask why seek an interpretation—for example, "Why did Jumping Mouse begin his difficult quest?" The question "Do you know any other stories that have a character like this one?" asks children to go beyond the literal level and make connections beyond the immediate text. Initially, the children's responses were meager, but once they understood and felt that their ideas were given value they were less hesitant. This process did not happen overnight; it needed many weeks of careful nurturing to develop.

In the spring, Maggie brought her paperback book, *The Frog Prince* (Grimm, 1979) from home to share with the class. During this read-aloud event, Colin shared the opinion that if he were the frog prince, he wouldn't have married the princess because she was so mean. Several children responded to the marriage of the frog and the princess. In the following sequence of responses, there was an underlying and tacitly accepted knowledge that in a literary discussion the responses must stay within certain limits. When the children voiced their explanations, they supported their opinions with information from the book. This behavior suggests that the children understood that response, although personal, is still tied to the book.

CHRISTOPH: Maybe it was right to marry her because instead he would stay forever a frog. Nobody would help him.
GREG: Yeah, but she already helped him. So he could have run off somewhere else.

CHRISTOPH: Yeah, but it's good that he, that it's good that she had the golden ball because nobody else would have golden ball. Then if the ball would fall she would just let it go.

PIPER: Also this is only a fairy tale and usually fairy tales end happily. You know, they usually get married at the end of a fairy tale.

COLIN: But it would still end happily if the prince went off and married somebody else.

PAUL: And turned back into a frog!

PIPER: But he didn't know anyone else. He didn't know any other girl except for the sisters. I think, and you didn't see them, so really there was no other choice.

ALEX: Like, if she know he was a prince. I bet she would throw him against the wall 'cause that if she knew that the frog would turn to a prince, um, I bet she would throw him against the wall to take away the spell.

Children's deepening and discerning responses to the books read aloud did not happen spontaneously. Initially a model was needed to provide a framework in which the children could define and express their own responses to the read-aloud books. For many children, these read-aloud events were their first experiences in school in which they were encouraged to express their responses to books read aloud to them.

By reading aloud to the children daily, by sharing her enthusiasm for and interest in the read-aloud events, and by sharing extra information about particular authors and books, the classroom teacher provided a positive model of a reader. These actions clearly demonstrated to the children that reading and responding to children's literature are important and valuable activities in the classroom.

Selection of Books

The selection of children's literature in read-aloud events was central to awakening children's critical and discerning eye for quality. (See Appendix A for a list of books to read aloud.) Elements of quality to target include text, illustrations, and text–illustration congruity. The selection of appropriate books depends on such criteria as knowing the children, their literary needs and interests, their depth of literary understanding, and their background in children's literature. This understanding is needed to select read-aloud books that spark the interest and enthusiasm of the children. Personal knowledge of a wide range of children's literature is invaluable.

Insightful Observation of Parents

Parents provided insightful observations of aspects of their children's literary development, and their input helped to broaden the understanding of children's responses to literature. The parents in this study were very receptive to recording areas of their children's literacy development and sharing that information with the teacher-researcher. Information provided by the parents was critical to describing the responses of the children to the read-aloud books. Without this parental input, the classroom teacher's perception of children's literacy development could have been distorted and limited.

Goncalo was a case in point. He sat quietly and listened but rarely responded verbally during the read-aloud events. His silence easily could have been construed as nonresponse. On one parental questionnaire, his mother reported that Goncalo enjoyed hearing stories read aloud and "pushed" the family so that he would not be late for school and miss part of the read-aloud events. His mother wrote:

> Goncalo was very insecure in changing schools especially coming from a first grade with 16 kids, two teachers and lots of individual attention. think your morning reading 'set up' made him very comfortable and relaxed. He commented at home about your 'good ideas' and imagination. He really took an interest in reading and felt confident as the year progressed and he could notice his own progress and improvements. He enjoys talking about the books, authors, and illustrators.

Without this type of information from the parents, it could have been assumed that Goncalo did not respond to the read-aloud books because he seldom if ever contributed verbally during the read-aloud events. Parents and classroom teachers sharing their knowledge of the children provide the context in which children's literacy development is best understood.

Value of Rereading Selected Books

The value of rereading children's literature was supported by the children's increased depth and length of responses. Children were receptive to each of the three rereadings of a single book. Native American tales such as *The Story of Jumping Mouse* (Steptoe, 1984), *Arrow to the Sun* (McDermott, 1974) and *Annie and the Old One* (Miles, 1971) worked particularly well in eliciting children's responses. Folk tales such as *The Funny Little Woman* (Mosel, 1972) and *The Fool of the World and the Flying Ship* (Ransome, 1968) also worked well. The children were especially curious about folk tales and their authorship.

During the reading of *The Frog Prince* (Grimm, 1979), Colin explained:

COLIN: It means, like, the Brothers Grimm went around the world and got some of them and she told it in a different way. But the Brothers Grimm didn't even make them up because they must got them from other people.

MS. YOCOM: That's right. The other people were telling them.

PAUL: How do they know this folk tale?

PIPER: Because of the people that were telling them.

PAUL : But how do they know?

COLIN You see, they make them up.

The rereading of books was initially met with responses such as "But we already read that book." However, the attitude conveyed in this response soon disappeared and was replaced with general enthusiasm as the children experienced interest and pleasure in exploring a read-aloud book in more perceptive ways.

Children did not accept the reiteration of information previously shared in earlier read-aloud events. Although certain books were read aloud three times, each additional reading was perceived as an opportunity to learn something new about the book. The children did not consider the rereading as merely an opportunity for review.

The Story of Jumping Mouse (Steptoe, 1984) truly touched the children's interest. The following sequence of responses illustrates that children are comfortable with stories less concrete than most published stories:

CHRISTOPH: It's better that he is an eagle because instead if he is a mouse he can't see the flowers above. So when he's an eagle he can see down, he can see the Far Off land better, cause if he is down below he only sees earth. He looks, up he sees the under flowers.

COLIN: And nothing can try and get him because he is too big. They couldn't get him. He could get the snake.

CHRISTOPH: Right. The opposite.

GREG: I wonder how like the snake . . .

ANTHONY: Like see, Christoph says he can see the Far Off better. He didn't need to go anywhere. Remember Magic Frog said it was good that your kindness has brought you to the Far Off land. He didn't need to go anywhere.

Reader–Writer Connections

In their own writings and their self-identity as authors, children made connections with authors of the read-aloud books. These connections were shared with the parents. Children began to speak of themselves as writers of books. John's mother wrote:

I am happy to see John taking the interest he does in books. He seems to like writing stories. I'm impressed with his understanding of the involvement it takes in producing a book. The last book we finished here at home John said, 'Boy does that author know how to write a good book.' He also asked if there was another book by this author and along the same theme. In the past John would just say that's a nice story and let it go. When he tells his brother about books, authors, publishing, illustrations and even how story titles come out in the reading of books, he tells this with a note of authority in his voice.

CONCLUSIONS

Children brought varying levels of experience with children's literature to the read-aloud activity. These events were an introduction to children's literature for some children, the enhancement of interest for other children, and the augmentation of knowledge and pleasure for other children. However, no matter what their level of literacy development, children spoke positively about hearing stories read aloud daily and continued to express favorable comments about the books.

The children exhibited positive behaviors as a result of reading in the classroom and in the home. Among these reading behaviors were the increased duration of periods of quiet independent reading, a deepening interest and enjoyment in reading, an increased tendency to seek the read-aloud books and other books by particular authors, and the initiation of literary discussions with peers, the classroom teacher, and parents.

The deepening of children's responses to the read-aloud books depended on an extended period of time for development. During the school year, this literary development matured as the children acquired and utilized an expanding reservoir from which to draw their literary responses. Whether the children were verbally responding or actively listening, their literary development continued to grow with each read-aloud event.

Time and opportunity were needed for children to articulate and express their responses to the read-aloud books, and children whose first language was not English needed even more time to adequately express their responses in a group situation. During the school year, the children increased their interest in other children's responses, verbally referred back to other children's responses, and learned to acknowledge the acceptability of different opinions. Children appeared to acknowledge that the book was not the only source of a better understanding of the story.

IMPLICATIONS FOR THE CLASSROOM

The findings of this study confirm the benefits of daily read-aloud activities. Based on the work presented here, the following sections offer suggestions to help classroom teachers effectively incorporate reading aloud into their daily routine.

Provision of a Daily Read-Aloud Event

Start each day with a read-aloud event. By beginning the day with literature and a format for exchanging ideas, the teacher can bring the children together and emphasize the importance of reading. Having the read-aloud event at the same time each day lets the children know that, no matter what happens, a story will be read aloud. The read-aloud event should not be contingent upon getting work done or finding the time. Story time is for all children all the time.

Knowledge of Children's Literature

With a finite number of hours in the day in which to undertake paperwork and the other demands on classroom time, it becomes essential to find effective ways to identify good literature for the children. *The Horn Book* and *The Reading Teacher* are journals that provide information on children's literature. A priority is to establish a working relationship with librarians, who know the books in their libraries and are excellent resources. *Children's Literature in the Elementary School Classroom* (Huck, Hepler, & Hickman, 1987) is another source for books and suggestions on how to introduce them to children.

Knowledge of Children's Personal and Literary Interests

Knowing books is only part of organizing a read-aloud program. By knowing the children's interests, teachers can select appropriate books to stimulate, challenge, and entertain the children during the activity of reading aloud. Some books, though commendable literature, may not spark the interest of a particular class. As the school year progresses, the children's general interests will become apparent. Introduce them to books of all genres and make a point of including poetry.

Reread Selected Children's Literature

Rereading lets the children delve more deeply into a book. It also encourages children to go beyond the surface text and become acquainted with characters, themes, and author's intent. Having a shared sense of story also may give children more security in which to voice their responses. Rereadings also convey to the children that some books are too valuable to read once and throw away.

Techniques of Reading Aloud

The read-aloud event cannot be effective unless the teacher has the active attention of the children. Create a calm atmosphere. In order to catch and hold the children's attention, the teacher's voice needs to be fluid and expressive, not loud or strident as if reading at them or reading over a layer of inattention. A teacher who finds the book interesting will generally convey that enthusiasm vocally. Eight items were assessed by the Reading Aloud to Children Scale (RACS) to contribute substantially to the quality of the read-aloud performance. According to Lamme (1986), these items are:

1. Child involvement in the story reading.
2. Amount of eye contact between reader and audience.
3. Putting expression into the quality of the reader's voice.
4. Pointing to words and pictures in the books.
5. Familiarity with the story.
6. Selection of the book.
7. Grouping the children so that all could see the pictures and hear the story.
8. Highlighting the words and language of the story.

Communication with Parents

A questionnaire that formally gathers information on children's responses in the home may be developed (see Appendix B for a sample parent questionnaire). Informal conversations with parents is another avenue for collecting information. Questionnaires can have problems, as described by one parent:

> That's the trouble with questionnaires. They never let you say what you want to. You answer the questions, but it isn't what you totally want to say.

If parents perceive that classroom teachers are interested in their children's literary responses beyond the classroom, then a mutual working relationship can develop.

Finally, an essential element in providing a rich environment for nurturing children's responses to literature in the classroom is an adequate school, classroom and/or public library. With readily available sources of books, teachers can provide their students with a strong literacy program that allows them to pleasurably discover such characters as Alice and her wonderland, Max and his monsters, Charlotte and her web, Snow White and her wicked stepmother, and Mike Mulligan and his steam shovel.

PROFESSIONAL RESOURCES

Cohen, D. (1968). The effect of literature on vocabulary and reading achievement. *Elementary English, 45,* 460–463.

DeLapp, S. (1980). *Dilemmas of teaching: A self-reflective analysis of teaching in a third–fourth grade informal classroom.* Unpublished doctoral dissertation, The Ohio State University.

Huck, C., Hepler, S., & Hickman, J. (1987). *Children's literature in the elementary school.* Troy, MO: Holt, Rinehart & Winston.

Lamme, L. (1986). Reading aloud to young children. *Language Arts, 53,* 886–888.

Martinez, M., & Roser, N. (1985). Read it again: The value of repeated readings during storytime. *The Reading Teacher, 38,* 782–786.

Porter, J. (1969). *Effect of a program of reading aloud to middle grade children in the inner city.* Unpublished doctoral dissertation, The Ohio State University.

Rosenblatt, L. (1978). *Literature as exploration.* New York: The Modern Language Association of America.

Rosenblatt, L. (1985). The transactional theory of the literary work: Implications for research, In C. Cooper (Ed.), *Researching response to literature and the teaching of literature: Points of departure.* Norwood, NJ: Ablex.

Yocom, J. (1987). *Children's responses to literature read aloud in the classroom.* Unpublished doctoral dissertation, The Ohio State University.

CHILDREN'S LITERATURE

Grimm, J., & Grimm, W. (1979). *The frog prince.* Mahwah NJ: Troll Associates.

Hoban, R. (1976). *Bedtime for Frances.* New York: Harper and Row Junior Books.

McDermott, G. (1974). *Arrow to the sun.* New York: Viking.

Miles, M. (1971). *Annie and the old one.* Boston: Little, Brown.

Mosel, A. (1972). *The funny little woman.* New York: Dutton.

Provensen, A., & Provensen, M. (1983). *The glorious flight across the channel with Louis Bleriot.* New York: Viking.

Ransome, A. (1968). *The fool of the world and the flying ship.* New York: Farrar, Straus & Giroux.

Steptoe, J. (1984). *The story of jumping mouse.* New York: Lothrop.

Waber, B. (1974). *Lyle finds his mother.* Boston: Houghton Mifflin.

Zemach, H. (1965). *Salt.* New York: Farrar, Straus & Giroux.

APPENDIX A

List of Books Read Aloud

Albert's Toothache by Barbara Williams. Illustrated by Kay Chorao. New York: Dutton, 1974.

Annie and the Old One by Miska Miles. Illustrated by Peter Parnall. Boston: Little, Brown, 1971.

Anno's Medieval World by Mitsumasa Anno. New York: Putnam, 1980.

Arrow to the Sun by Gerald McDermott. New York: Viking, 1974.

A Baby Sister for Frances by Russell Hoban. Illustrated by Lillian Hoban. New York: Harper and Row Junior Books, 1964.

A Bargain for Frances by Russell Hoban. Illustrated by Lillian Hoban. New York: Harper and Row Junior Books, 1978.

Ben's Dream by Chris Van Allsburg. Boston: Houghton Mifflin, 1982.

A Birthday for Frances by Russell Hoban. Illustrated by Lillian Hoban. New York: Harper and Row Junior Books, 1976.

Bedtime for Frances by Russell Hoban. Illustrated by Garth Williams. New York: Harper and Row Junior Books, 1976.

Best Friends for Frances by Russell Hoban. Illustrated by Lillian Hoban. New York: Harper and Row Junior Books, 1976.

The Big Snow by Berta Hader & Almer Hader. New York: Macmillan, 1981.

Blackberry Ink by Eve Merriam. Illustrated by Hans Wilhelm. New York: Morrow, 1983.

Blueberries for Sal by Robert McCloskey. New York: Penguin, 1976.

Bread and Jam for Frances by Russell Hoban. Illustrated by Lillian Hoban. New York: Harper and Row Junior Books, 1964.

The Bremen Town Musicians by Jacob Grimm & Wilhelm Grimm. Illustrated by Janina Domanska. Mahwah, NJ: Troll Associates, 1980.

Cinderella by Marcia Brown & Charles Perrault. New York: Scribner, 1954.

Cinderella by Charles Perrault. Illustrated by Susan Jeffers. New York: Dial Books Young, 1985.

Crow Boy by Taro Yashima. New York: Penguin, 1976.

Duffy and the Devil by Harve Zemach. Illustrated by Margot Zemach. New York: Farrar, Straus & Giroux, 1973.

Eats by Arnold Adoff. Illustrated by Susan Russon. New York: Lothrop, Lee and Shepard Books, 1979.

Everyone Knows What a Dragon Looks Like by Jay Williams. Illustrated by Mercer Mayer. New York: Scholastic Book Service, 1976.

The Fool of the World and the Flying Ship by Arthur Ransome. Illustrated by Uri Shulevitz. Chicago: Farrar, Straus & Giroux, 1968.

The Frog Prince by Jacob Grimm & Wilhelm Grimm. Illustrated by Robert Baxter. Mahwah, NJ: Troll Associates, 1979.

The Funny Little Woman by Arlene Mosel. Illustrated by Blair Lent. New York: Dutton, 1972.

The Garden of Abdul Gasaza by Chris Van Allsburg. Boston: Houghton Mifflin, 1979.

George and Martha: Rise and Shine by James Marshall. Boston: Houghton Mifflin, 1976.

George and Martha: Tons of Fun by James Marshall. Boston: Houghton Mifflin, 1980.

The Girl Who Loved Wild Horses by Paul Goble. New York: Bradbury Press, 1978.

The Glorious Flight Across the Channel with Louis Bleriot by Alice Provensen & Martin Provensen. New York: Viking, 1983.

Gorilla by Anthony Browne. New York: Knopf, 1985.

Hansel and Gretel by Paul Galdone. New York: McGraw-Hill, 1982.

Hansel and Gretel retold by Rika Lesser. Illustrated by Paul O. Selinksy. New York: Dodd, 1984.

Harry the Dirty Dog by Gene Zion. Illustrated by Margaret B. Graham. New York: Harper and Row, 1976.

Harvey's Hideout by Russell Hoban. Illustrated by Lillian Hoban. New York: Scholastic, 1980.

Horton Hatches the Egg by Dr. Seuss. New York: Random House, 1940.

The House on East 88th Street by Bernard Waber. Boston: Houghton Mifflin, 1975.

It Doesn't Always Have to Rhyme by Eve Merriam. New York: Antheneum, 1977.

It Could Always Be Worse by Harve Zemach. New York: Farrar, Straus & Giroux, 1976.

King Grisley Beard by Jacob Grimm & Wilhelm Grimm. Illustrated by Maurice Sendak. New York: Farrar, Straus & Giroux, 1973.

A Light in the Attic by Shel Silverstein. New York: Harper Junior Books, 1981.

The Little Engine That Could by Watty Piper. Illustrated by Richard Walz. New York: Putnam, 1984.

Little Red Cap by Jacob Grimm & Wilhelm Grimm. Translated from German by Elizabethe Crawford. Illustrated by Lizabeth Zwerger. London: Neuge-bauer Press, 1983.

Little Red Riding Hood by Jacob Grimm & Wilhelm Grimm. Retold and illus-trated by Trina Schart Hyman. New York: Holiday, 1982.

The Little Wood Duck by Brian Wildsmith. New York: Oxford University Press, 1983.

Lovable Lyle by Bernard Waber. Boston: Houghton Mifflin, 1969.

Lyle and the Birthday Party by Bernard Waber. Boston: Houghton Mifflin, 1973.

Lyle Finds His Mother by Bernard Waber. Boston: Houghton Mifflin, 1974.

Lyle, Lyle Crocodile by Bernard Waber. Boston: Houghton Mifflin, 1973.

Maggie and the Pirate by Ezra Jack Keats. New York: Scholastic Book Service, 1979.

Make Way for Ducklings by Robert McCloskey. New York: Viking, 1941.

The Man Who Loved Books by Jean Fritz. Illustrated by Trina Schart Hyman. New York: Putnam, 1981.

Mike Mulligan and His Steam Shovel by Virginia Lee Burton. Boston: Houghton Mifflin, 1977.

Millions of Cats by Wanda Gag. New York: Putnam, 1977.

Miss Nelson Is Back by Harry Allard. Illustrated by James Marshall. Boston: Houghton Mifflin, 1982.

Miss Nelson Is Missing by Harry Allard. Illustrated by James Marshall. Boston: Houghton Mifflin, 1977.

The Month Brothers: A Slavic Tale by Samuel Marshak. Translated by Thomas Whitney. Illustrated by Diane Stanley. New York: Morrow, 1973.

O Sliver Of Liver by Myra C. Livingston. Illustrated by Iris Van Rynbach. New York: Antheneum, 1979.

Once a Mouse by Marcia Brown. New York: Antheneum, 1982.

The Ox-Cart Man by Donald Hall. Illustrated by Barbara Cooney. New York: Viking, 1979.

Pelican by Brian Wildsmith. New York: Pantheon, 1983.

The Pet Show by Ezra Jack Keats. New York: Macmillan, 1972.

Peter's Chair by Ezra Jack Keats. New York: Harper and Row Junior Books, 1983.

Pinkerton Behave by Steven Kellogg. New York: Dial Books Young, 1979.

The Problem with Pulcifer by Flaoence P. Heide. New York: Harper & Row, 1982.

The Riddle of the Drum: A Tale from Tizapan, Mexico. Retold by Verna Aardema. Illustrated by Tony Chen. New York: Scholastic Book Service, 1978.

The Random House Book of Poetry for Children. Selected by Jack Prelutsky. Illustrated by Arnold Lobel. New York: Random House, 1983.

Rumpelstiltskin by Jacob Grimm & Wilhelm Grimm. Illustrated and retold by Donna Diamond. New York: Holiday, 1983.

Rumpelstiltskin by Jacob Grimm & Wilhelm Grimm. Illustrated by Paul Galdone. Boston: Houghton Mifflin, 1985.

Salt by Harve Zemach. Illustrated by Margot Zemach. New York: Farrar, Straus & Giroux, 1965.

Sam, Bangs and Moonshine by Evaline Ness. Troy, MO: Holt, Rinehart and Winston, 1966.

Shadow by Blaise Cendars. Translated and illustrated by Marcia Brown. New York: Scribner, 1982.

The Sleeping Beauty by Trina Schart Hyman. Boston: Little, Brown, 1977.

Snow White and the Seven Dwarfs. Jacob Grimm & Wilhelm Grimm. Translated by Randall Jarrell. Illustrated by Nancy E. Burkert. New York: Farrar, Straus & Giroux, 1972.

Stevie by John Steptoe. New York: Harper Junior Books, 1969.

Stone Soup by Marcia Brown. New York: Scribner, 1947.

The Story of Jumping Mouse by John Steptoe. New York: Lothrop, 1984.

The Straw Maid by Anita Lobel. New York: Greenwillow, 1983.

Strega Nona by Tomie de Paola. Englewood Cliffs, NJ: Prentice-Hall, 1975.

The Trip by Ezra Jack Keats. New York: Scholastic, 1979.

The Werewolf Family by Jack Gantos. Boston: Houghton Mifflin, 1980.

Where the Sidewalk Ends: Poems & Drawings by Shel Silverstein. New York: Harper Junior Books, 1974.

Whistle for Willie by Ezra Jack Keats. New York: Viking, 1964.

Why Mosquitoes Buzz in People's Ears: A West African Tale by Verna Aardema. Illustrated by Leo Dillon and Diane Dillon. New York: Dial Books Young, 1975.

The Wreck of the Zephr by Chris Van Allsburg. Boston: Houghton Mifflin, 1983.

APPENDIX B

Parent Questionnaire

1. Has your child talked at home about any of the books read aloud by me? If so, can you describe the event?

2. Has your child expressed an interest in any of the authors or in a particular book that was read aloud in the classroom? If so, which ones were noted?

3. Has your child requested that you read aloud to him/her any of the books read aloud in the classroom? If so, could you name the book or author?

4. Has your child read to you any of the books read aloud in the classroom? If so, could you describe the event?

5. Has your child talked about any of the illustrations or illustrators of these books with you?

6. Has your child signed out from the library any of the books or authors I have read aloud, or has he/she requested that any of these books or authors be purchased and added to his/her own book collection?

7. Has your child responded to any of the books, in other ways than noted by these questions? For example, has your child dramatized any of the plots, stories, or characters from the books?

8. Has your child commented on the quality of these books read aloud, either negatively or positively? The comments could be directed to the story or the illustrations, or both.

9. Has your child talked with you about his/her own writing of stories? If so, could you recall a specific time and describe it?

10. Has a particular author or book sparked an interest in your child's own writing?

11. Has your child talked about books or authors read aloud by me earlier in the year?

12. Have you noticed a change in your child's reading behaviors? If so, can you describe these behaviors?

13. Has your child commented on the books that have been reread this year? If so, could you describe the comments?

14. Please give other comments, if any:

7

Dances Between Stances

**Kathleen E. Holland
& Leslie A. Shaw**

> We have ignored the fact that our reading is not all-of-one-piece.
> We read for information, but we are also conscious of emotions
> about it and feel pleasure when the words we call up arouse vivid
> images and are rhythmic to the inner ear. . . . Our present pur-
> pose and past experiences, as well as the text, are factors in our
> choice of stance. (Rosenblatt, 1991, p. 445)

Children can move between two stances, efferent and aesthetic, as
they hear literature read aloud or as they read books themselves.
Within the context of one book, children can also shift in and out of
the efferent stance, where they focus on acquiring information, and
the aesthetic stance, where they focus on what they are experiencing, thinking, and feeling. However, Rosenblatt (1991) has suggested that there should exist "a 'predominate' attitude or stance,
efferent or aesthetic, on the part of the reader" (p. 445).

This movement, or dance if you like, between the two stances has
been little explored. In the context of reading aloud one children's
trade book, teachers presumably maintain a predominant stance
for their students, so as not to confuse them; however, if this is true,
no research presents a picture of how teachers signal the predominant stance to their students. Furthermore, we have not investigated the interplay between the two stances as teachers read aloud
to students.

With this vacuum of research in mind, we reviewed the videotapes
and transcripts of one teacher, Mary Lou Mack, reading aloud the

nonfiction children's trade book, *Bugs* (Parker & Wright, 1987), to second and third graders over four consecutive days. We wondered if Mrs. Mack had maintained a predominant stance—in this case an efferent, information-seeking stance. Simultaneously, we wondered how she had signaled a predominant stance without confusing her students. Lastly, we investigated to see if and how the secondary aesthetic stance had occurred.

THE CLASSROOM CONTEXT

Mrs. Mack was a reading and writing teacher whose position was funded through special state monies designated for urban desegregation of schools in Massachusetts. The teachers in her urban school, located in western Massachusetts, had decided to use these monies to support Mrs. Mack's instruction of students in need of help with their literacy development or in need of enrichment and challenge in their literacy development. Mrs. Mack's expertise among her colleagues was in the area of writing process (Calkins, 1986; Graves, 1983), in which she had received extensive training. She also had a great and endearing love of children's literature and wanted to become more knowledgeable about using it more often in her teaching.

During the 1988–1989 school year, Mrs. Mack and I participated in a year-long collaborative ethnographic research study (Holland, Bloome, & Solsken, 1991; Solsken & Holland, 1990) investigating the effects of process writing on urban multicultural students having difficulty with their literacy development. I asked Mrs. Mack to participate with me in this study because she was planning to use more children's literature, with an emphasis on daily read-aloud experiences for her students.

Mrs. Mack met every day for a one-hour writing workshop with a mix of second and third graders who were having difficulties with their literacy development. During the four days of this study, Mrs. Mack had seventeen students: eleven second graders and six third graders. There were twelve boys and five girls. This pluralistic population had eight white European, five African-American, one Korean, one Middle Eastern, and two Hispanic students. The last four students spoke English as a second language. Rather than sticking strictly to the writing workshop framework of a minilesson, writing/conferencing time, and author's circle, Mrs. Mack adapted her time to include daily read-aloud time and writing/conferencing time. Author's circle and minilessons were interjected when time and need allowed for them.

During this year-long study, Mrs. Mack and her students agreed to be videotaped while she read aloud five fiction and five nonfiction children's trade books. These trade books were preselected by

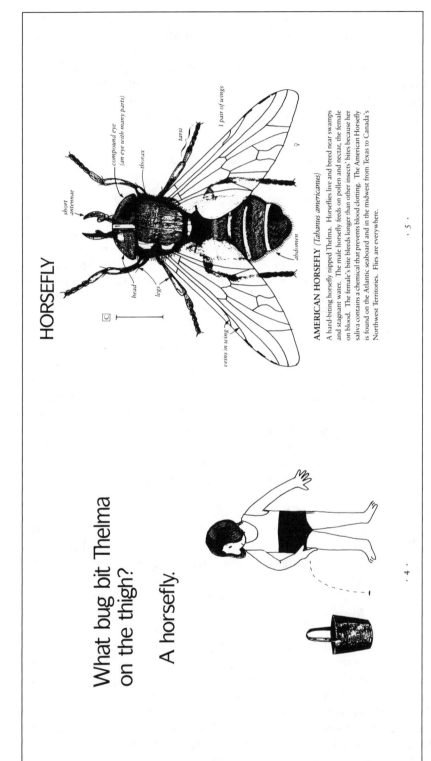

FIGURE 7–1   *Pages 4 and 5 on the American Horsefly*

me (Holland) to assist Mrs. Mack in using more children's literature and to explore how children's literature might influence children's writing genres. Mrs. Mack could suggest changes in titles at any time. This chapter investigates the longest read-aloud experience, *Bugs,* as a case study to shed light upon the phenomenon of dancing between stances.

BOOK CONTEXT

During the first week of March, 1989, Mrs. Mack read aloud *Bugs,* a forty-page information book (i.e., nonfiction) for elementary children that presented sixteen common insects through a riddle, diagram, and a one-paragraph description containing factual information (see Figure 7–1). At the back of the book are picture glossaries, an animal kingdom phylum chart, and a bibliography. After prereading this book at home, Mrs. Mack, who was told to complete the videotaped read-aloud books in her own usual way, decided to share the book over a series of consecutive days. She wanted to be sure she had enough time each day to read and talk about three to five bugs with her students.

MAINTAINING THE PREDOMINANT
EFFERENT STANCE

From the beginning of the book, Mrs. Mack began signaling the predominant efferent stance to her students by suggesting what information about insects they were to learn and by attempting to frame boundaries for the appearances of the efferent and aesthetic stances. Initially, she delineated three reading contexts for each insect in this book: (1) the rhymed riddle, (2) the labelled diagram, and (3) the paragraph description, complete with common and scientific insect names.

After she read the initial horsefly riddle and gave the correct answer herself, Mrs. Mack explained the notion of couplet and rhyme. She then read the riddle again and had the children join her in responding with the correct answer. The dialogue that resulted from this initial reading is transcribed in Figure 7–2.

The second reading context explored the labelled diagram of the horsefly. Mrs. Mack led her students through their first reading of a scientific diagram. She emphasized those aspects of insect information she deemed important for them to carry away: the line continuum that showed a horsefly's length in real life, the symbol and type of metamorphosis, and the insect body parts that her students needed to attend to and learn: head, antennae, legs, name (i.e., tarsi) and number of leg parts, thorax, wings with veins, and abdomen. Mrs. Mack did not cover all the labels or symbols on the

TEACHER: This little book starts off with on one page you're going to have a little riddle and then on the next page it's gonna to give you some real information about the subject, which is bugs.

TWO OR THREE STUDENTS: Bugs, bugs.

(Teacher reads the riddle about Thelma being bit on the thigh by a horsefly.)

TWO OR THREE STUDENTS: It rhymes.

TEACHER: It rhymes. All right, It has the same sound. Yes, it is a rhyming book in that on each page there is a couplet. When you have two lines in poetry and the last word in each line has the same vowel sound as the following line then you have what we call a rhyme. Rhyming words and it then becomes a couplet. Couplet means two. Like you know a married couple. That means two people. One. Two. Well another rhyming couplet would be—one, two, buckle my shoe.

DONNY: A couple of twins.

TEACHER: Three, four, shut the door.

SEVERAL CHILDREN WITH TEACHER: Shut the door.

TEACHER: Those are couplets. So here's a couplet. On each one of these pages we hear a couplet. (Teacher then reads the riddle again so the children can guess the answer.)

TEACHER, CHILDREN, AND TEXT: A horsefly.

TEACHER: So thigh and fly are rhyming words, all right? Now, this page [Figure 7–1] tells about the horsefly. And on this page you'll see the parts of the bug. And this line tells you exactly how long the bug is in real life. And this here, this "C" it could say "C," "S," or "I." It means if it changes completely—it, by when it's a baby til it's a full grownup—or it changes a little or not or, or, or a lot. Now a "C" means complete change—complete metamorphosis. And that means that when it was a baby it looked entirely different from what it grew up to be. And we'll have other ones that are only simple, simple changes in the way they look. And then others incomplete—not completely changed. Yes, honey?

CHERYL: What are those green things that, um, are up on the top—the green things?

TEACHER: The green things? All right, now the green thing's the head. The top part, these two little things on top, are called the short antennae. Antennae means there are two antennae. There are two things, two feelers that stick out and they, they sense what's going on around them. They can almost see with those feelers antennae.

JERRY: I know how they can bite people.

TEACHER: These things are called their legs and they're in parts. Then the legs of a bug usually have a few parts. I believe it's six. But let me see . . . 1 . . . 2 . . . 3 . . . 4 . . . 5 . . . 6 . . . 7. That leg—7 parts. This main body is called a thorax. Then this funny leg is called a tarsi. And he has wings and there are veins in the wings. The wings are very thin. And this part of him is called his abdomen. Now down there it tells the Latin name, which some scientist named the regular old horsefly probably a long time ago.

MARCUS: American?

TEACHER: He's called, he's an—[reads from the text:] "American Horsefly." Aren't we lucky? We have him all to ourselves, Marcus? [Reads from the text:] "Tabanus Americanus." That's the name of the American Horsefly!

MARCUS: Tabanus Americanus?

TEACHER: Uh-huh, that's what it says!

FIGURE 7–2   *Transcription of the initial reading of the horsefly riddle and diagram*

diagram. She did not read or discuss the label "compound eyes (an eye with many parts)" or the gender symbol (♀).

In the third reading context she focused the children's attention on two parts. First, she read the common name (i.e., American Horsefly) and the scientific Latin name (i.e., Tabanus americanus). Second, she proceeded into a full reading of the description containing factual information about the horsefly. She held vocabulary discussions about the meaning of stagnant, blood clotting, blood coagulating, and the Atlantic Ocean (i.e., "the ocean we live near").

Mrs. Mack's delineation of the three reading contexts for each insect was maintained throughout the entire book. This procedural display (Bloome, 1986) consistently involved movement from the riddle to the diagram to the paragraph description. She read the riddle and allowed guessing by students before shifting their attention to reading some of the diagram labels and symbols. She always focused upon the symbols for insect length, metamorphosis, and gender. She did not require her students to read all the labels. For example, on the flea she skipped such labels as palpl, combs, breathing spiracles, coxa, trochanter, femur, tibia, and she even dropped her previous emphasis on the leg parts (i.e., tarsi). Rather, she consistently emphasized certain body parts: head, antennae, thorax, abdomen, wings, six legs, and eyes.

On the second day, one change in her procedural display occurred during the reading of the diagrams, which continued into days three and four. Mrs. Mack began to interject the common and scientific names into the diagram reading context. Then, when finished, Mrs. Mack shifted directly into reading the paragraph description.

Bloome (1986) has defined procedural display as follows:

> As teachers and students interact, they build on each other's behavior, displaying appropriate procedures that count as getting the literacy lesson done. . . . In procedural display, teacher and student are collaborators in displaying those interactional procedures that count as the literacy lesson. (p. 73)

The first clue to how Mrs. Mack signalled predominant and secondary stances without confusing her students came in her procedural display. In *Bugs*, she took advantage of three different reading contexts—riddles, diagrams, and paragraph descriptions—and attempted to delineate a focus for her students within each.

The Illustrated Riddle

After the efferent introduction of couplets and rhyming given for the horsefly riddle, this reading context evolved into a competitive game. Mrs. Mack read the riddles without showing her students the illustrated page. Her students competed to solve the riddle. The aesthetic nature of this game between teacher and students was especially apparent in the laughter and wild guessing, which was encouraged. Cheating was even permitted, as children leaned on Mrs. Mack's lap as she turned a page to read a riddle and some tried to peek at the riddle illustration. Also, children used the book outside of the read-aloud context for writing or simply perusing, so they were prepared to answer the riddles. The loudest laughter often came from Mrs. Mack, who consistently encouraged an aesthetic stance during the riddle game. Almost the only efferent statements she made were to remind the wild guessers that the riddle needed to rhyme!

The full-page riddle illustrations provided another place where aesthetic responses occurred. Children responded with laughter to a drawing of smoke behind a centipede scurrying across the floor. Another time, children responded with repulsion to the picture of a spider that had dropped into a child's cup of cider.

Mrs. Mack set a boundary around the illustrated riddle that encouraged aesthetic responses. Since all sixteen riddles were read and answered within one minute, this aesthetic boundary was secondary to the predominant efferent stance.

The Labelled Diagram

In sharp contrast to the aesthetic boundary of the riddle, the context of the insect diagram, with its labels and symbols, was delineated by Mrs. Mack as the predominant efferent boundary. Within the confines of these diagrams, Mrs. Mack continually kept her students' attention focused upon acquiring certain information about characteristics of insects, how to read and interpret symbols, and which labels to attend to during this reading event.

Another strategy employed by Mrs. Mack to keep the predominant focus on the efferent stance was her use of scaffolding. Bruner (1983) saw scaffolding as one concept used to express the significance of communicative interactions between adults and children that are basic to the expansion of learning in children. Focusing on mother–child interaction, Bruner (1983) suggested that successful communication on one level is always a launching platform for attempts at communication on a more adult level. Mrs. Mack framed and supported the first readings of these diagrams with her students on one level by leading them through this new reading event. She emphasized that they should read and carry away the following insect information from the diagram:

1. Insects have three body parts: head, thorax, abdomen.
2. Insects have six legs.

3. Insects have antennae attached to their heads.
4. Insects may have wings.
5. Insects have eyes.

She also began teaching them how to read three diagram symbols concerning metamorphosis, size, and gender. She showed them the black scale line symbol that showed the insect's real size. She introduced the symbols—C,I,S, each within a square—abbreviating complete, incomplete, or simple metamorphosis. And, on the second day, she used the chalkboard to illustrate the scientific symbols for male and female (♂ and ♀). By the end of the first day, she had read four bug diagrams—horsefly, cicada, ant, and tick—with her students framing the five labels and all but the last symbol as the most important information to glean from the diagrams.

By the second day of bug diagrams—flea, slug, and spider—some of her students were initiating the shift from the aesthetic riddle page to the more efferent diagram reading event by calling out body parts: "head," "eyes," "male," "eight legs." This scaffold became so strong that, in one instance, Mrs. Mack changed it by moving abruptly away from the diagram labels and symbols into the paragraph description. Immediately her students interrupted her and continued calling out labels and symbols that they had not finished reading on the diagram. Thus, her students pulled her back into the diagram for its proper completion.

Within the concept of scaffolding, Bruner (1983) maintained that mothers systematically change their speech in order to "raise the ante" or alter conditions they impose on their children's speech in different settings. Mothers support their children only when they need help. Likewise, mothers don't allow their children to slide backward. This kind of shift was seen on the second day and over subsequent days as Ms. Mack continued to scaffold her students' readings of the diagrams. However, she raised her ante and began to insist that they read the diagram by posing direct questions about insect characteristics. For example, she said: "Does it have a head?" "How many legs?" "Does anyone find the male or female part?" "Does it have any kind of change?" "Does it have an antennae?" "Does it have a thorax?" Thus, her students had to search the diagram for labels, symbols, and body parts. Students often pointed to and/or touched the diagram to show Mrs. Mack where they had found the information. In one instance on day three, a boy stood up and drew the male scientific symbol on the chalkboard to prove he knew the answer to her question requesting the sex of an insect. A second boy immediately followed by writing the female symbol to demonstrate the difference between these two symbols.

Within the context of the diagrams, Mrs. Mack used three supportive materials to maintain her efferent stance: the chalkboard,

World science magazines for children, and final assignments. Because Mrs. Mack possessed a natural artistic ability, she took any opportunities she could to further elaborate the diagrams. For instance, while studying the diagram of the slug, many children identified the extended eyes as antennae. Mrs. Mack then redrew the slug on the chalkboard and demonstrated through her own larger drawings how the eyes were positioned on the ends of two extensions called tentacles and not antennae, which she drew as shorter protrusions from the head between the tentacles.

Also, Mrs. Mack made use of her extensive collection of *World* magazines published by the National Geographic Corporation. Often, after completing a diagram, she searched through several *World* magazines to find photographs of the insect under study. If found, she would hold up an often magnified photograph of the same insect in its real environment for the children to compare to the book diagram.

The final and only project Mrs. Mack requested at the conclusion of the book *Bugs* was that children volunteer to diagram and label the insect characteristics listed in the picture glossary at the end of the book. The five children who volunteered to complete five important pieces of information copied one of the bug facts from the book. However, depending upon which fact they copied, they illustrated an insect diagram and labelled the diagram to match the bug fact. These bug facts closely matched Mrs. Mack's own insect information that she emphasized in discussions about the diagrams.

Paragraph Descriptions

The final reading context in *Bugs* consisted of the two insect names and a paragraph containing concise factual information. The predominant stance here was again efferent. Mrs. Mack usually read the sentences in chunks. She did not read the paragraph straight through. Rather, she would read two to four sentences and stop for various reasons:

1. To make her own comments on the information provided (i.e., "I didn't know that!").
2. To define vocabulary (i.e., venom means poison).
3. To elaborate the facts with her own knowledge (i.e., how to remove ticks with oil).
4. To answer children's questions (i.e., "How can you tell?").
5. To allow children's comments (i.e., "I got bit by one!" "That's true!" "And carry eggs too!")

No scaffolding was used in this reading context, so Mrs. Mack did not expect that all of the factual information in these paragraphs would be retained. (See Figure 7–3, which presents an extract from the transcript on the discussion of the centipede.) Rather, her approach seemed to be one of discovering interesting new bits of knowledge. "Basically, I believe *my* main aim was for them to experience the joy of learning information, in this case, about bugs" (personal correspondence with Mary Lou Mack about this chapter).

One final clue concerning Mrs. Mack's emphasis upon the efferent stance, especially within the contexts of the diagram and paragraph description, was reflected in the predominant functions of language used within these contexts. Halliday (1975) identified seven functions of language universally used by people to communicate meaning to others: Instrumental, regulatory, interactional, personal, imaginative, heuristic, and representational. Mrs. Mack primarily used representational language and heuristic language throughout her interactions with her students while reading *Bugs*. More than seventy percent of the utterances were representational (i.e., using language to convey information to others) and heuristic (i.e., using language to find out more, to ask questions, and to seek information).

THE AESTHETIC STANCE

During and after her read-aloud of *Bugs*, the aesthetic stance appeared in three ways. Her students found opportunities to focus on what they were experiencing, thinking, and feeling during the readings. These aesthetic responses appeared in the following ways: body language, oral language, and written language.

Body Language

Hickman (1979, 1981, 1987) discovered that children of preschool and primary ages often use their bodies to respond aesthetically to literature they hear read aloud. In this study, both second and third graders did not hesitate to use their bodies to express their feelings about the topic under study. The emotions they most often expressed were disgust, fear, excitement, and amusement.

When a bug was observed through illustration (as in Figure 7–1), given its common name, or explained via detailed information, children who did not like the bug would either assume a closed body stance and cower in fear or recoil in disgust away from the book and Mrs. Mack. Examples of these body movements were seen when Mrs. Mack read about the tick, slug, spider, centipede, cockroach, lice, and dragonfly.

In contrast to their expressions of fear and disgust, the children used their bodies in an open way and moved forward toward the book and Mrs. Mack when they felt excited or amused. Examples of this behavior were seen when Mrs. Mack read about ants, mosquitoes, termites, crickets, and fireflies. Children knelt and moved

---

(Teacher reads all but last sentence of paragraph about house centipedes and their speed, number of legs and places to live.)

DONNY: I saw a centipede under a rock!

CHERYL: What's a leaf mold?

TEACHER: Um, in a rock, yeah?

DONNY: Cause I, cause I dropped it, dropped something—I forgot what
it was. And I thought is was under the rock. And I picked up the rock
and saw one of those and I slammed the rock back down again!

TEACHER [laughs]: Oh, the poor thing! (The teacher then reads from the
text about many centipedes that are not dangerous.)

TEXT: Most centipedes are not dangerous, but the poison—

CHILD: Ooh!

CHILD: So, I don't know!

(Teacher reads from the text about the poison given off when a centipede bites.)

CHILD: Ooh!

TIM: How can. How could—

(Teacher then reads about the pain caused by a centipede's bite.)

TIM: Oh! How can they tell?

CHILD: I'd kill it!

TIM: How can they tell?

TEACHER: It doesn't poison you, but it does cause some pain.

TIM: How can you tell? How can you tell?

TEACHER: Tell what?

JOSE: You can tell because—

TIM: That they poison you and can't—

DONNY (to other children): Sit down!

FIGURE 7–3   *Paragraph description of the reading on the centipede*

forward, waving their hands excitedly, when the firefly was first
seen. The ant and mosquito, too, were responded to with laughter
and excitement, perhaps because the students recognized these
insects as common in their own experiences.

When the louse and cicada were shared, the children responded
differently. The cicada received no apparent active aesthetic
response—just quiet, still listening. This insect appeared to be
unfamiliar to the students. Likewise, when Mrs. Mack read the
riddle and identified the louse, she was met with dead silence. It was
not until she pluralized the name to lice that children recognized it
and backed away in fear and disgust.

Another way that these second and third graders used their
bodies to convey what they were experiencing and thinking during
Bugs occurred when Mrs. Mack read about the centipede, mosquito, and cricket. Children heard Mrs. Mack convey information
about the insect and used their bodies to dramatize their thinking.

TEACHER: Well, they would have known. Like, say, if you were poisoned from a centipede bite, you would go to a doctor and tell him what the bite was and he would report it, ah, to the health agency in [name of city]. And they'd say we had one poisonous bite by the centipede and it caused these reactions. The person had a fever. He was sick for four days. He broke out into a sweat. He, he had a stomach, he vomited.

CHILD: Yuck!

TEACHER: He didn't feel good. And they'd say that it was a poison, but all this bite does is just cause a sting and hurt you. It doesn't do anything to your body. It doesn't poison you in any way.

JOSE: But it does suck your blood!

TEACHER: But no person has ever reported, evidently nobody has ever told the health people that this bite is from this bug made them poisoned. See?

TIM: Nobody ever did?

JOSE: But it does suck blood. It does suck blood.

TEACHER: It sucks, well, it does. Well it does. It bites you and when it does it puts some poison in you or it puts in this thing that causes pain. All right! It doesn't, but sometimes.

JOSE: It sucks blood.

CHERYL: Some of them suck blood.

TEACHER: I'm sorry. It does. But the poison released can cause pain, but it doesn't do—

CHILD: Stop it, Skip!

TEACHER: Any harm, any big harm. Okay? All right. (The teacher concludes by reading the last sentence of the paragraph about centipedes that tells about the number of species found in the United States and around the world.)

For example, Mrs. Mack read that "Male crickets make chirping sounds by rubbing their wings together" (p. 27). Children not only made chirping sounds with their voices, but also put their arms in bent wing positions and rubbed them together. Likewise, when Mrs. Mack read about mosquitoes biting people, children scratched or slapped their arms and legs. And when the riddle illustration showed the centipede leaving three puffs of smoke behind it as it raced across a rug and Mrs. Mack emphasized its "astonishing speed" (p. 23), children use their hands to indicate the centipede zooming across the floor.

All of these aesthetic body language responses did not appear in one reading context; rather, they appeared across all three— riddle, diagram, and paragraph description.

Oral Language

Another type of aesthetic response that occurred was oral language which appeared in three ways: single utterances, comments, and personal narratives. Children used oral language as a way of conveying what they were experiencing, thinking, and feeling.

Single utterances Single utterances occurred across all three reading contexts. These emotional utterances were usually, but not always, tied to some body language. For instance, children who expressed disgust made such utterances as "Ugh!" "Yuck!" "Eoow!" "Ooow!" and recoiled away from the book. The emotion of fear was often accompanied by "Oooh!", widened eyes, and a cowering stance. In one instance, two girls hugged each other. In another, a boy shook his whole body as if to get the bug off it. Excitement had utterances such as "Oh!" "Wow!" "Yeah!" "Cool!" "Yeah!" Of course, amusement was expressed through laughter and giggling. These emotions of excitement and amusement were often accompanied by open and forward body movement toward the book and teacher. One last type of oral utterance occurred when Mrs. Mack showed the picture of a bug or read about the sounds a bug made. Children often began making the bug's sounds, such as humming, chirping, and buzzing.

Comments During the four days of read *Bugs,* children made 150 comments independent of teacher inquiry. These self-initiated, spontaneous comments occurred in all three reading contexts. The majority of these comments either concerned feelings or personal experiences. Examples of comments expressing feelings were: "Oh my God!" "I hate crickets!" "I was surprised by them!" "I like the firefly!" and "I hate these things!" Examples of comments concerning personal experiences were: "I killed one!" "A bee came by. It bit me. But it didn't die." "I got one of those on my leg right here and it sticks. It sticks real hard, man! And takes your blood away fast." "I caught one!" and "We have those at our house!" Other comments appeared less frequently and concerned observations and comparisons. Examples of comments that shared observations were: "I didn't know mosquitoes looked like that!" "That is a big bug!" and "That thing's ugly!" Examples of comments that concerned comparisons were: "They look like butterfly wings." and "The ones I saw looked like the wings like the first one. That's what they looked like."

Personal narratives These second and third graders shared twenty-three personal narratives throughout the four days Mrs. Mack took to read *Bugs.* These personal narratives were shared less frequently on days one (four stories) and two (one story) than on days three (eight stories) and day four (nine stories). Fourteen stories occurred during the paragraph reading context, while two took place during the riddle and four were told during the diagram context. Also, three narratives were shared during the last day when the picture glossaries at the end of the book were being read aloud and discussed. While personal narratives occurred in all three reading contexts, it appears that these students felt most comfortable telling them during Mrs. Mack's reading of the paragraph description in chunks. Examples of personal narratives from all four days are detailed in Figure 7–4.

The personal naratives in Figure 7–4 are examples of what White (1954) described and Cochran-Smith (1984) called "life-to-text" events, in which listeners make sense of a text "by bringing to light the extra-textual information they needed in order to make inner-textual sense" (p. 173). Life-to-text information came from listeners' broad areas of knowledge and life experiences and was seen as the "most important type of interaction around storyreading" (p. 173). Mrs. Mack adamantly felt that her students' personal narratives were crucial to their understanding of and connection with any fiction or nonfiction book. She encouraged her students to share their own life experiences and knowledge through narratives with her when she read aloud books. Also, she did not just hear the personal narrative and move on to the next item. She actively interacted with the child and the story through comments and questions.

Written Language

Since Mrs. Mack's hour with these second and third graders was a writing workshop, after the story-reading time, the children got their writing folders and worked on their written stories. Mrs. Mack encouraged her students to select their own topics. However, if she heard a good oral narrative, she encouraged the student to write it down during writing workshop time. Students were not expected to write stories based on literature read aloud. Hickman (1979, 1981, 1987) found that children in transition out of the primary grades often borrow from children's literature to complete their writing. Characters, settings, plots, and illustrations were used freely by children in Mrs. Mack's writing workshop (Holland, Bloome, & Solsken, 1991; Solsken & Holland, 1990). However, in the case of *Bugs,* only four children completed written responses to this book.

Jose and Jerry borrowed heavily from *Bugs* on the first day. Jose wanted to compose riddles and Jerry wanted to complete labelled diagrams. Since this was a collaborative effort, they argued with each other about which way to go. Finally, they went to Mrs. Mack with their dilemma: Should they make a riddle book or a diagram book? Mrs. Mack suggested they share the same book but make opposite pages. The drawings in Figure 7–5 show the result of their collaboration.

In this first draft, Jerry followed the efferent stance and used diagrams for the sex, length, and metamorphosis of each insect. On

Day one In connection with hearing Mrs. Mack read part of the paragraph description about ants in a rotten log that a boy sat on:
CHERYL: Ah, when I was in Florida we went by, um, this, um, pond and
  it had a um, alligator in it and holes with red ants in it, and I stepped
  in it and I got bit with red ants.
TEACHER: Oh, yes, several of them like to take nice bites! But they were
  living there, weren't they in that log?
CHERYL: Yeah, but I didn't know.
TEACHER: And that what [the authors of *Bugs*] say. Don't sit on a rotten
  log at a picnic because you know you could get a bite.

Day two In response to Mrs. Mack's inquiry, "How many people have
ever seen a flea on a dog or cat?"
JOSE: And, like, we went on a field trip. We went on a field trip in first
  grade, right? And we went to the apple orchard. There was [some
  students are making noise that masks his conclusion].
TEACHER: Excuse me. Jose is telling something very interesting and I'd
  like you to be listening. [to Jose] Go on.
JOSE: Um.
TEACHER: You went on a trip. When? In first grade, yeah?
JOSE: First grade, yeah. And to the apple orchard and this dog got, had
  fleas all over him.
MANY CHILDREN: Ooh! [surprise]
TEACHER: How many people saw that dog with the fleas? [Many hands
  are raised.] Oh my goodness! And you remember him, too!

Day three As Mrs. Mack begins reading this paragraph description
  about the cricket, Timmy finally gets to share his story about the
  cockroach, which had been the previously discussed insect:
TIMMY: Um, when I was a little boy—
[Lots of giggles]
JOSE: I, I found a cockroach!
DONNY [with *World* magazine]: I got to look for something else to eat!
TEACHER [to class]: All right! [to Donny] Later on we'll talk about that, but
  now I want to know what Timmy said. [to Timmy] What, honey?
TIMMY: Well, I went in my pool yard—

FIGURE 7–4   *Personal narratives from four days of reading*

the other hand, Jose followed the aesthetic nature of the book
riddles and made up his own ant riddle question, which lacked a
rhyme. He used a riddle question close to the book's ("What ran
over Grandma's brooch?" p. 24) but again dropped the rhyme.
However, in their second effort (Figure 7–6), Jerry's diagrams are
closer to the book's, while Jose's still doesn't rhyme and uses classmates and Mrs. Mack in his riddles.

Another written response to *Bugs* appeared first as a personal
oral narrative. Sonia told the following story about her own experience with cockroaches:

TEACHER: Pool?

TIMMY: Yard. And, uh, I went in my pool yard and there was this big stump and all. I picked this big stump up and there were all these cockroaches on it. And I picked it up high and I slammed it on 'em!

MANY CHILDREN: Oh! [Surprise]

TEACHER: Are you sure those were cockroaches? Because they live more in house, it said. Are you sure those weren't termites?

TIMMY: No!

Day four Told as Mrs. Mack finishes reading the termite's paragraph description:

DONNY: Um, when they were taking down, when they, when, were, um, building a new house next door. Their house is made out of wood. Well, my, when I was going over there to see my friends—

TEACHER: Yeah?

DONNY: There was a whole bunch of termites under there. They were on the trees.

TEACHER: Wow!

[Lots of giggling]

DONNY: And me and my friends, and me and my friends we took, we took, like, we took a spray and we, and we sprayed 'em and they died. And then when the spray ran out, we, we took a pail of water and there was like a sewer—

TEACHER: [laughs]

DONNY: And there was a sewer and they went down the sewer!

TEACHER [laughing]: Oh, gross!

DONNY: And we took some water and swept them under.

TEACHER: Well, what did you learn after the water all went away? Did they come back?

DONNY: No! 'Cause we killed them all!

TEACHER: You really did?

DONNY: Yeah, and my mother likes—

TEACHER: Do you think?

DONNY: And my mother let us have an empty can and there was a little bit of deodorant left and we sprayed it on them.

SONIA: My, my sister, I said to my sister, I say to my sister, "Dolanda, don't do nothing because cockroaches bite."

TEACHER: She doesn't, huh? All right, well, should we find out?

JERRY: They tickles.

SONIA: And then, um, my sister she sees a big one. She screams and I say, "Why do you scream?"

TEACHER: How old is she, Sonia?

SONIA: Six. The other one is five years old and she's little.

TEACHER: Does she mind the cockroaches, the little one?

SONIA: She kill them, too!

FIGURE 7–5   *Jose and Jerry's riddles and illustrations of an ant and a roach*

TEACHER: She's like you!
ERIC [pointing to book]: Look it!
TEACHER: You two are braver than—what's your sister's name who is six?
SONIA: Juanita.
TEACHER: Juanita is the one who is a scardy cat, huh?
SONIA: [laughs]

After Mrs. Mack encouraged Sonia to write down this oral story, the initial draft looked like this:

MY SISTER JUANITA SAER OF CACAROACH

[Page 1:] Wen we was sleeping
  something was
  bathring my sister
  and she trn on the
  lingt and she saw
  the cacaroach
  and she jump up
   and donwe

[Page 2:] and she want
  up to my bed

FIGURE 7–6 *Jose and Jerry's riddles and diagrams of a tick and a mosquito*

and she screm
at my ear and I
siad why you
screm in my era

[Page 3:] and she siad
becaus there are a
cacaroach in my
bed.

[Page 4:] and I saind am
cana cal that cacar
OK and went doawe
and I cal that cacaach
and my sister stay
in my bed

[Page 5:] and we sleep
faind and thre
was a cacaach
in my bed and
I screm in my sister
era

[Back cover:] the end

A parent volunteer who typed copies of children's written work for Mrs. Mack went over the preceding draft with Sonia and typed a final copy:

MY SISTER JUANITA IS SCARED OF A COCKROACH
by Sonia
Grade 2

When we were sleeping, something was bothering my sister, and she turned on the light and she saw the cockroach, and she jumped up and down.

She went up to my bed, and screamed in my ear, and I said "Why are you screaming in my ear?" And she said "Because there is a cockroach in my bed." I said "I am going to kill that cockroach." "O.K." she said. I went downstairs and I killed that cockroach, and my sister stayed in my bed.

And we slept fine. And then there was a cockroach in my bed and I screamed in my sister's ear.

The end

Sonia shared this story with her classmates at a later author's circle. After hearing it, Eric, a Korean ESL student, borrowed Sonia's "scardy cat" story idea and composed his own about his younger sister:

MY SISTER IS A SCARDY CAT

She is six years old.
My sister is a scardy cat.
My sister's name is hannah.
She is scared of flies because
the fly is gross.
My sister hates the flies.
And she went to throw out the
garbage and she saw
flies and she screamed
and she heard flies
and I saw her at the window and

I screamed because she heard
flies and called my Mom
and my Dad and my
grandmother and
my family screamed too
and my sister ran fast
and she went home.

The end.

Eric wrote two other insect stories on ants and bees about his own experiences with ants and his family's experiences at the beach with bees (see Figure 7–7). The personal aspects of these narratives especially showed in his writing. Eric did something he had never done before in Mrs. Mack's writing workshop: he wrote in both Korean and English on the first page of both stories.

CONCLUSIONS

During the four days she took to read aloud *Bugs* to her students, Mrs. Mack employed three ways to signal the predominance of the efferent stance. First, she used a procedural display that delineated three different reading contexts in this book: the rhymed and illustrated riddle page; the diagram, complete with insect body part labels and scientific symbols; and the paragraph, containing the common and scientific insect names as well as detailed factual information. The riddle page usually involved secondary aesthetic responses; however, the diagrams and paragraph descriptions predominantly involved efferent responses. Secondly, this predominance was further supported by the extensive use of informational and heuristic language within these two reading contexts. Finally, Mrs. Mack conveyed the predominance of the efferent stance within the diagram context by using scaffolding techniques to guide and support her students' foci upon specific insect body part labels and scientific symbol reading.

The appearance of the secondary aesthetic stance occurred in all three reading contexts in the form of body language, single utterances, comments, and personal narratives. The language function (Halliday, 1975) used for these aesthetic responses was personal, or language used to express individuality, personality, strong feelings, and opinions. While the first three forms listed previously spontaneously took place across all three reading contexts, the personal narratives appeared twice as much during Mrs. Mack's chunk reading of the paragraph description. The last type of aesthetic response occurred outside of the read-aloud context. Two children, Sonia and Eric, wrote personal narratives about their own experiences with

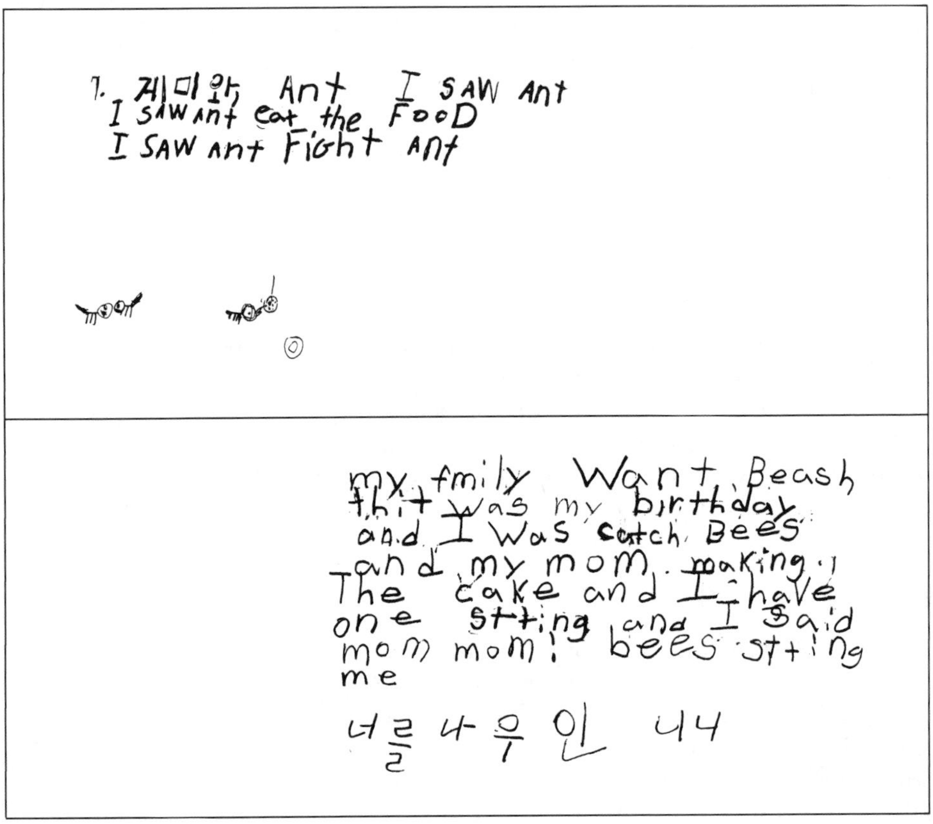

1. 제미있는 Ant   I SAW Ant
I saw Ant eat the FooD
I SAW Ant Fight Ant

my fmily Want Beash
thit was my birthday
and I Was catch Bees
and my mom making
The cake and I have
one stting and I Said
mom mom! bees stting
me

너를 나 우 인   나나

FIGURE 7–7   *Eric's first pages, with Korean written language, on ants and bees*

insects. Two boys, Jerry and Jose, collaborated within the aesthetic stance to write humorous riddles. However, Jerry maintained an efferent stance when he drew and labelled insect diagrams to go with their riddles.

Rosenblatt (1991) has suggested that any linguistic activity has both public or efferent (i.e., lexical, analytic, abstracting) components and private or aesthetic (i.e., experiential, affective, associational) components. In this case study of Mrs. Mack's reading of *Bugs,* the predominant public and efferent stance coexisted with the private and aesthetic stance. However, this read-aloud experience was not an evenly balanced display of both stances. Rather, in reading, teaching, and discussing *Bugs,* Mrs. Mack tilted her emphasis in favor of the efferent stance. Nevertheless, she did not rule out or neglect the aesthetic stance. She allowed its varied appearances among her students, but to a lesser degree than the efferent stance. Rosenblatt (1991) challenged teachers to clarify their sense of purpose while sharing literature with children.

> Confusion about purpose of reading has in the past contributed to failure to teach effectively both efferent and aesthetic reading. Why not help youngsters early to understand that there are two ways of reading? We do not want to give them theoretical explanations, nor do we need to. We communicate such understandings by what we do, by the atmosphere and the activities we associate with the kinds of questions we ask and the kinds of tests we give. (p. 447)

The critical choreographer in this dance between stances was the teacher. Only through her procedural display, her use of heuristic and informational language, and her scaffolding for instruction was she clearly and persistently able to keep her students within the efferent stance. However, she did not overdo this efferent slant by continuously staying with the facts. Rather, she encouraged her students to dance between stances and engage in their aesthetic responses. By allowing her students to use personal language and connect this text to their lives, Mrs. Mack developed their emerging meanings and feelings about insects in a variety of aesthetic ways both during and after reading. By choosing to allow these personal interjections and by not repressing their aesthetic responses, Mrs. Mack achieved her goal of encouraging the joy of learning.

IMPLICATIONS

First, the crucial role of teachers and their abilities to clarify purposes for books shared with children is apparent and necessary. When reading aloud to their students, elementary teachers might consider the types of language necessary to accomplish their purposes, the procedures used with books and discussions, and what they might be able to focus instruction upon through repeated scaffolding.

Second, the response choices given to students and assignments could connect strongly with the predominant stance. Students could be guided to elaborate and explore further whichever stance—aesthetic or efferent—is being emphasized through various response modes: oral language, drama, art and media, and writing.

Third, in this case study, Mrs. Mack demonstrated within the read-aloud context of one children's information book how she maintained and signalled the predominant efferent stance to her students and how she allowed the secondary aesthetic stance to appear. We need more investigations of how teachers convey a predominant stance to their students while sharing children's literature. One case study is not enough evidence to explore this movement between stances. Teacher-researchers, doctoral students, and academic researchers need to further turn their attention to this dance between stances.

PROFESSIONAL RESOURCES

Bloome, David (1986). Building literacy and the classroom community. *Theory into Practice, 25* (2), 71–76.

Bruner, Jerome (1983). *Child's talk: Learning to use language.* New York: W. W. Norton.

Calkins, Lucy (1986). *The art of teaching writing.* Portsmouth, NH: Heinemann Educational Books.

Cochran-Smith, Marilyn (1984). *The making of a reader.* Norwood, NJ: Ablex.

Graves, Donald (1983). *Writing: Teachers and children at work.* Portsmouth, NH: Heinemann Educational Books.

Halliday, M. A. K. (1975). *Learning how to mean—explorations in the development of language.* London: Edward Arnold.

Hickman, Janet (1979). *Response to literature in a school environment, grades K–5.* Unpublished doctoral dissertation, The Ohio State University.

Hickman, Janet (1981). A new perspective on response to literature: Research in an elementary school setting. *Research in the Teaching of English, 15* (December), 343–354.

Hickman, Janet (1987). Understanding children's response to literature. In Charlotte Huck, Susan Hepler, & Janet Hickman (Eds.), *Children's literature in the elementary school* (4th ed.). New York: Holt, Rinehart, and Winston, pp. 45–93.

Holland, Kathleen, Bloome, David, & Solsken, Judith (1991). *Responses of low-achieving students in writing process instruction in elementary and junior high school classrooms.* Research report completed for the Springfield School District, Springfield, MA.

Rosenblatt, Louise (1991). Literature—S.O.S.! *Language Arts, 68* (6), 444–448.

Solsken, Judith, & Holland, Kathleen (1990). The social construction of "writing process" in elementary classrooms for low-achieving students. Paper presented at the National Reading Conference, Miami, FL.

White, Dorothy (1954, 1984). *Books before five.* Portsmouth, NH: Heinemann Educational Books.

CHILDREN'S LITERATURE

Parker, Nancy Winslow, & Wright, Joan Richards (1987). *Bugs.* Illustrations by Nancy Winslow Parker. New York: Greenwillow Books.

8

The Evolution
of Response Through
Discussion, Drama, Writing,
and Art in a Fourth Grade

Lynda Hobson Weston

The origins and uses of ideas and literary concepts that children gain through a literature study can be seen in several ways. The literary piece that served as the basis for this study (Weston, 1989) was Mollie Hunter's *A Stranger Came Ashore* (1975), based on a Scottish Selkie transformation legend. Many of the events in my fourth-grade classroom began with an idea I presented to the students through reading aloud and related thematic study. Initially, the story representations conformed to my modeling; however, in most cases this starting point they were only the beginning of many divergent representations. Once the children had practiced the basic techniques or had discussed the original ideas, many new personal understandings evolved. They were asked to take ideas and information from the thematic study, clarify and extend their understanding through writing, artwork, or drama, and ultimately share their knowledge with the entire class. The children responded along the continuum Rosenblatt (see Chapter 1) identifies as efferent at one end to aesthetic at the other. In this chapter many of these responses are described. I believe that the aesthetic pleasure of hearing a high-quality children's book was one of the most important experiences of the children in my fouth grade.

During the first month, along with large group events, the children worked in small groups on projects predetermined by the entire class through the webbing of ideas (brainstorming). The children had the choice of one of four projects, but sign-up places were limited, so some children worked on second-choice projects.

137

Eventually, several weeks into the study, additional projects were undertaken. By then, groups were completely self-chosen and the projects came from the original web of ideas or new ones that surfaced later.

This chapter examines four events. Data was gathered through teacher-researcher qualitative methods. With the help of research assistants from two nearby colleges who took observational field notes over a period of two months, I looked closely at what the 9- and 10-year-olds in my class were doing with the ideas they shared from literature through artwork, writing, a science study, and interactive dramatics.

ART CONNECTIONS: MARBLEIZED PAPER

To provide background knowledge for the children, I shared several picture books based on the Scottish Selkie legends. In each tale a seal, known as a selkie, emerges from the ocean, sheds its fur coat, and transforms into a human. The selkie's coat is stolen and that prevents it from returning to its ocean home. One of the first was Yolen's *Greyling* (1968), illustrated by William Stobbs. Because this illustrator's technique reminded me of marbleized paper, I showed the children how to marbleize paper. The day after the picture book was shared I gathered the materials needed to make marbleized paper: colored chalk, a cookie sheet filled with water, paper, and scissors. I had originally planned to share the technique with a small group of students. Donald, Jason, and Melissa were chosen because they were all ending other projects. Together we experimented first with tempra paint, but eventually we switched to scraping colored chalk onto the surface of the water in the cookie sheet. Eventually the children were able to create a lovely swirl of colors on a sheet of paper by placing it gently on top of the water so that it picked up the colored chalk. The wet sheets were hung on a clothesline suspended between light fixtures.

This activity attracted many other students, who eagerly wanted to try making the paper. Julie, who had been out of the room, spotted the hanging papers as soon as she entered. She walked up to the papers, earnestly examined them, and then commented about various swirling waves she could see in the paint. She said, "This is kind of like looking at clouds when you see lots of different things!" She and several other students stayed in during recess and tried to create more sheets. Karrie and Sarah looked at the colors used by the illustrator in the Yolen book and chose those colors when making their own marbleized paper.

It quickly became apparent that everyone wanted to make some marbleized paper, so I incorporated the activity into my plan for work time the next day. The papers were very attractive, and seeing them hanging on the clothesline gave me another idea.

To help the children personalize the story, I asked them to construct a first-person narrative about the Selkie tales. I asked the children to assume personal vantage spots and draw what they saw on the marbleized paper using a black marker. All of the children had made at least two sheets of paper, so in some cases they experimented with one and used the other piece for a final picture. As they drew, they discussed with each other the events of the stories as the swirling waves on the paper suggested to them the water setting of the tales.

The art activity had already gone further than I had originally planned, and it had turned into more story dialogue among the children and also into an interesting writing experience for them. Sarah, reflecting in first person on Cooper's *The Selkie Girl* (1986), wrote:

> I once lived by the sea and one day I was looking at the sunset. But there was a rock in the way. But something was on it. I couldn't tell what, so I got a little boat but I didn't go close to the rock. But then I watched, I saw a man come up and take something of the woman's. Then I noticed it was a seal skin coat. Then I thought, I knew that he had taken something of herself away.

Sarah's account continued to retell the story from her personal vantage point. The children shared their first-person narratives and artwork in the classroom and then hung them on a mural sheet that read: SELKIE TALES: I WAS THERE.

During the course of the Selkie tales, the students independently initiated several more projects involving marbleized paper. Donald and Jason created a three-dimensional model of the underwater city mentioned in several of the Selkie tales. They made marbleized paper to line the box they used and give the effect of the ocean setting. Karrie and Sarah marbleized a small piece of paper to use on the Scottish "kollie" (lamp) they made for their Shetland Islands' museum. They used it for the lamp, they said, because they liked the pretty patterns it made.

The students were asked to find a poem that reminded them of the Selkie tales. After the poems were found and they had written explanations of how they thought the poems related to *A Stranger Came Ashore*, they were asked to mount their poems and connection pieces in any way they felt appropriate. Five of the students used marbleized paper to mount their poems and the pieces they had written describing the connection between their poems and the book. Three of the boys wrote about "Old Man Ocean" by Russell Hoban (1980):

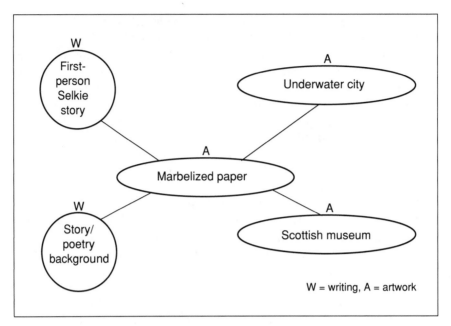

FIGURE 8–1 *Tracking an artistic technique*

Old Da [a character] tells stories like Old Man Ocean. A shipwreck was in the story *A Stranger A Stranger Came Ashore.* We chose "Old Man Ocean" because it says: Fog in the storm and the long bell tolling, Bones in the deep and the brave men gone and the part about the brave men being gone goes with the part about the shipwreck in the book *A Stranger Came Ashore.*

The selection of a mounting was the last step in making a poetry–story connection, but it showed that some children continued to link the story, its seaside setting, a poem, and an illustration.

Making marbleized paper served as a purposeful, but small core event around which the students chose to weave several other activities (see Figure 8–1). The activity functioned as a jumping-off point for them.

A GROUP WRITING EXPERIENCE: AN OBITUARY

Starting from a writing experience I initiated, the students showed that they could transfer ideas from a fictional story and create a newspaper article—in this case, an obituary. Using this experience, students made news writing personal as they created their own newspaper for the book. One student became so intrigued with the obituary writing and funeral scene that he researched the inscriptions on old gravestones and tried to write epitaphs appropriate to the time period of the read-aloud chapter book. Two other students demonstrated knowledge of the funeral scene in the story by creating a model. These interactions also generated a news drama in which the entire class participated. This drama reflected their knowledge of many aspects of the book. Students showed knowledge of the characters and the effects of setting, and they made many inferences based on book knowledge, research knowledge, and world knowledge.

When Old Da Henderson died in *A Stranger Came Ashore,* a discussion ensued that drew on the children's background knowledge about funerals in their own cultures. An obituary from the local newspaper was discussed. Several of the children shared their personal experiences of funerals. The students talked about the events in Old Da's life that probably would have been a part of his obituary. Andy wrote:

> Old Da Henderson died in Black Ness on July 5, 1888. He was
> 73 years old. He died in the bed-end of the croft at 7:30. He was
> born in 1815 in Black Ness. He was a farmer and a fisherman. He
> died of old age. His surviving relatives were Robbie, Elspeth,
> Peter, and Janet Henderson.

The discussion on Old Da brought out characteristics about him that connected to other events—character trait studies. This event blossomed into the creation of the Black Ness newspaper and a model of a graveyard with appropriate epitaphs on the gravestones.

Based on the obituary writing, Lance decided to make a graveyard for the town in the chapter book. The research assistant interviewed Lance concerning his project and made the following record in her journal:

> Lance is making a Scottish graveyard for his project. He has written down the names of all the characters from *Stranger, Selkie Girl,* and *Seal Mother.* He is going to write down things they've done, when they've died, etc. He's then going to write the information down on rectangular pieces of cardboard, then somehow place them upright on a brown piece of cardboard in graveyard fashion.

He looked up epitaphs in the library and began writing some of his own, and he returned to the book chapter to find events and characters to use for the cemetery. He also looked through some of the books about Scotland in the classroom so he would have appropriate names for the tombstones. Composing epitaphs gave him experience writing in a new style. The artistic part of his extension project did not work as well as he had hoped, but the writing was successful for him.

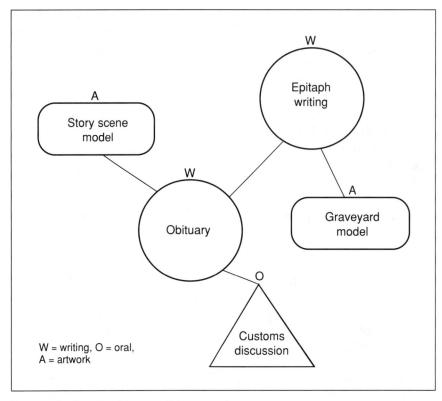

FIGURE 8–2   *Tracking a writing experience*

Also related to these events was the extension model built by Bobby and Tim. Their original purpose had been to make a model that would encourage other children to read *A Stranger Came Ashore*. When they finished, they presented a model of two events: the Selkie entering the ocean and the funeral scene where Elspeth walks in the ashes to compare her footprints to those left in the ashes of Old Da. Tommy said that he made the funeral scene because, "It was neat and scary when she [Elspeth] walked in the ashes and her feet fit." He made the ashes out of pencil sharpener shavings.

Obituary writing served as the beginning of several writing experiences, and as their curiosity grew, several children chose to explore the customs surrounding funerals presented in the book chapter (see Figure 8–2). The original obituary encouraged some students to write other types of news articles.

AN INTERACTIVE DRAMA: THE BLACK NESS NEWS

As an outgrowth of their obituary writing, several children in the class decided to create a town newspaper for Black Ness. John,

Kyle, and Jim were working primarily with sporting events when I decided to help them divert to other news writing topics. I talked to the boys about pretending to be reporters and interviewing class-mates pretending to be citizens from the village of Black Ness.

Early on the morning of the news conference drama, the day's work directions included choosing a name and profession as a member of the Black Ness community. Name tags were available and the children wrote names and professions for themselves. The following preliminary events were described by the research assis-tant in her journal:

> Lynda reminds the students that the reporters are coming this morning from the Black Ness News. For their journals this morn-ing, Lynda wants the students to write who they are in the Scottish town, what they do for a living, and any memories they have from their days in the town. The students will put name tags on to identify themselves to the reporters.
>
> Jason tells Lynda his character plays for the Black Ness football team. Jason writes in his journal that he's 19 years old. Jim, Kyle, and John prepare for the interview. John practices by focusing his camera as if to take a picture of Kyle. They all have their clip-boards and writing utensils out and ready. They sit on the couch in the den discussing their strategy.

I pretended to be Janet Henderson, a minor character in the chapter book. I introduced the reporters, and they began asking questions concerning events in the story. The answers began slowly. When Carl referred to the book, he was quickly questioned about what book. He caught on and quickly joined in the play acting. According to the research assistant "The children were very inven-tive, making up happenings, feelings, and situations. The interview was calm and controlled, but the students' participation was high."

The interviewing lasted forty-five minutes and could have gone on longer. As villagers, the children took on new views of the story and presented them. Julie pretended to be a dog trainer and added her perspective on why the Henderson's dog, Tam, had acted oddly toward the stranger, Finn Learson, who came ashore. She said:

> Last night I was taking my Sheltie dogs for a walk and we went past the Henderson's house. I was really surprised to hear Tam making such a racket. Tam was a dog I trained and I know him very well. He never used to behave like that. I really think something awfully strange must be going on for him to put up such a howl.

This dramatic event involved knowledge of many aspects of the story and additional background information gained through work projects and research. The reporters asked two boys, who said they were on the same team as the main character Robbie, if they had noticed any change. R. J. and Jason thought a while, and then R. J. said, "Robbie just hasn't been himself lately. He is usually our highest-scoring player. Ever since that man from the shipwreck came to live with his family, he just hasn't acted the same. He's lost his concentration!"

At various times later in the day, children were heard having conversations in their roles. I was called Janet and asked further opinions concerning the story events. Several new articles were created from some of the information shared during the drama. Melissa expanded upon the original obituary writing and created this news article, which was followed by John's sports page article:

> Old Da Henderson, 83, died of illness several days ago. The relatives surviving are his grandchildren, Elspeth and Robbie. At the funeral they took footprints to find out whose death would be next. When they read the footprints they found out that the next victim to die in the family would be Elspeth. Old Da had told Robbie that Elspeth would die. Robbie is reported to be stunned by this information.
>
> The local Black Ness boys' soccer team has been in a slump. The Seals leading scorer, Robbie Henderson, has not been able to make any goals in the last games. His teammates hope that he will be back to his old self soon.

Haine (1985) states that enacting a drama allows children to engage with it, struggle with its unfamiliar concepts, associate experiences with it, and let it shape personal interpretations. This drama brought about such experiences for these fourth graders as they struggled with creating characters whose traits fit the pattern established by the book author within the general theme and setting of the story (see Figure 8–3).

A SCIENCE STUDY: AN OCEAN FLOOR MODEL

Through their involvement with a science study on oceanography, my students learned about many aspects of the ocean. I presented several lessons on the ocean (e.g., currents, ocean floor, resources) as they were included in the fourth-grade curriculum. I also brought several films on oceanography to the class and provided many books on the topic from the school and public libraries. The children were interested in the study and many chose to pursue aspects of it during their work time. The connections between the scientific study and the fiction books were sometimes part of the

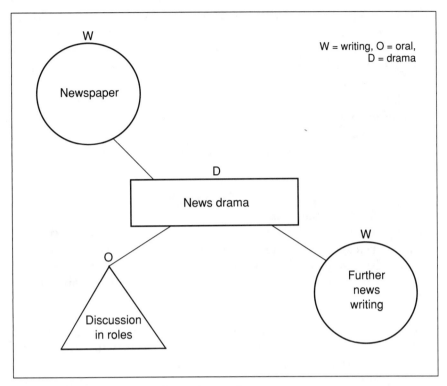

FIGURE 8–3   *Tracking a dramatic experience*

class read-aloud discussions. When the students discussed the coastal setting of the book they were able to make comments from their nonfiction book knowledge. Not only did the students study basic information, several groups chose to learn more about it through small group projects.

One group developed an ocean floor model made from salt dough. The group closely examined the formation of the ocean floor through their research and subsequent model. From this event two boys built a volcano to demonstrate the formation of islands in the ocean. These models inspired other groups to use the same artistic techniques; in particular, the salt dough was used in a farmhouse model. Another outgrowth of the science study was the model fishing setting that showed the "sixareen" fishing boat from the fiction story. This extension experience combined both the fiction study and the nonfiction oceanography study. The children working on the farmhouse model and the fishing boat model also learned about building to scale in their projects.

The project to create an ocean floor model chosen by a group of boys at the beginning of the study did not draw them back to the fiction book. However, they were drawn to many of the nonfiction books I had brought into class about oceanography. They studied several of the books as they formed the ocean floor model from salt dough. The following excerpt from the research assistant's journal describes this group as they began their ocean floor project:

> Raoul asks, 'Can we work on our salt map?' Raoul, Vincent, and one other boy move over to the art table where I am sitting. I help them staple some cardboard together. Mrs. Weston comes over and tells them that they have to read up on the ocean before they can start the salt mixture. Raoul, Donald, and Jason all get oceanography books and begin searching for drawings of the ocean floor. Lance is working on consolidating the two containers of salt. 'Look at that, this is neat,' Raoul exclaims upon finding a new picture in a different book. Now Vincent, Donald, Lance, and Raoul are eagerly digging through a brown bag filled with books about fish, plants of the sea, weather, and other ocean related subjects. Donald finds a picture of the ocean floor and is praised by Mrs. Weston.

As they learned about the ocean floor, they shared the information informally with other members of the class who stopped to check the most recent additions to the model. Community interactions were strong as this group negotiated its work assignments.

As a result of this extension project, Jason and Donald developed an interest in volcanos. They spent time reading about ocean volcanos and eventually asked if they could make an exploding model. Created out of papier-mache and covered with brown tissue paper, their model showed the outside of a volcano on one side and a cut-away view on the other. They carried it to the playground when they had finished the modeling and added vinegar and soda. They presented their understanding of active underwater volcanoes to their classmates and explained how volcanoes form islands in the ocean.

Another group of children, who were creating a Shetland Island farm called a croft, often worked beside the group using salt dough for modeling. Melissa, Kyle, Sara, and Karrie experimented with a wide variety of materials for their model, and they eventually borrowed some of the salt dough mixture to cover their small posterboard house. This material furnished the rough stone-like siding that their research had shown them to be appropriate to the setting.

Another exploratory learning event that resulted from the oceanography study dealt with the creation of a fishing boat. This extension project combined both the fiction study and the science study. The men of the village in *A Stranger Came Ashore* spent the summer at the "haaf" (ocean fishing). A group of boys, John, R. J., Andy, and Jim, decided to create a model of the "sixareen" boat the villagers used for fishing. While skimming through the collection of library books in the classroom, they came upon a picture of a whaling boat and decided that the sixareen might have been similar. Through their work, they learned how to read a blueprint and then created one of their own. They worked with building the boat to scale. An adult classroom volunteer, Kevin, brought a saw and some wood glue and helped the group build a lap-sided boat. As they worked, they discussed the number of fishermen needed to row the boat. Before they presented their model to the class, they decided to create an ocean scene around it and looked through more books to discover what kinds of fish might live in the North Sea. They made models of sea creatures from clay.

In conjunction with their study of scale model building, they taped the outline of a life-sized model on the classroom floor. After they had explained to the class the information they had gleaned, they drew attention to the life-sized model and discussed the relationships. A few weeks later they drew another model on the playground with chalk so their classmates could have the feeling of being in a small boat on the ocean. When the models were presented to the class, an impromptu story reenactment took place as the extension group talked about the roles of the various people in the boat (e.g., helmsman). The children sitting in the outlined boat spoke to one another as the story characters logically might have. They were drawn into a discussion of the fishermen in *A Stranger Came Ashore,* and they clammered for turns at pretending to row and steer the boat. The experience helped the group to become involved in woodworking, researching ocean vessels, identifying ocean fish, working to scale, studying some geography of the setting, and inferring information from the fictional story.

In some thematic studies, scientific and mathematical events come more naturally than in this one, which was somewhat contrived; however, this artificiality did not detract from it. The study supported an interest in the geography of the Shetland Islands. While maintaining a link to the story, the study also led the students into nonfiction books that taught them about oceanography and many other related topics (see Figure 8–4). Carl and John's original group had created the sixareen boat model, which was surrounded by an assortment of underwater fish made from clay. This activity prompted the boys to make a further study of sharks. Using nonfiction source books, they researched the topic of sharks, wrote a report, and shared their knowledge with the class.

Jim and Kyle built an iceberg model that depicted its above-water and underwater exposures. They made light-blue and dark-blue backgrounds in a shoebox, set the box up vertically, and suspended a stuffed white paper bag inside it to represent the iceberg. A blue piece of yarn divided the portion of the iceberg above water from

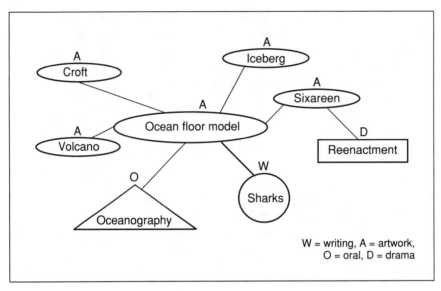

FIGURE 8–4   *Tracking a science study through an ocean floor model*

that below the surface. Both Jim and Kyle had worked on the ocean floor model and continued their nonfiction study through research on icebergs.

CONCLUSIONS

The descriptions in this chapter show how events frequently are linked to other events. Some of these ideas can be generated by a teacher-directed experience. For example, creating marbleized paper, writing an obituary for a story character, giving information about oceanography, and proposing a news-gathering drama were activities that I initiated. By interacting and sharing with each other, the children were able to borrow ideas for uses of artistic media, such as salt dough for the croft, marbleized paper for an underwater city model, and others. One student's dramatic inter-pretation often spawned another's response, such as when Julie replied as the dog trainer to John, Jim, and Kyle's questions as news reporters.

I may have tracked some ideas incorrectly or attributed them to the wrong event; nonetheless, few events took place in isolation and the atmosphere of sharing contributed to the richness observed in the classroom. The dramatic events drew more deeply on the stu-dents' world and story background than any other single event. The first-person story narratives allowed the children to personally identify with the characters and the plots of stories. These and other pieces of writing served as places to form and manipulate their ideas. The student's depth of identification with the stories made the dramas very rich in knowledge both taken directly and inferred from the chapter book. These experiences strengthened the children's versatility in expressing ideas and supported many divergent responses. As the teacher, I deepened my appreciation of how children need to act on what they have learned. Ideas find new meanings and uses when children have the opportunity to explore ideas instigated through stories.

IMPLICATIONS

As I worked through this study with the children in my fourth grade, my focus on control changed. I wanted the thematic study to go well and I began it in the role of director. By its end, I found myself in the role of facilitator. At first I led, but the children had choices. As they gathered information from the read-aloud sessions, they began brainstorming to create an idea web that incorporated some of my ideas with many student-generated ones. Ideas were added to the web throughout the sharing of the book. Ultimately, as I shifted to facilitating, I followed their lead. More ideas cropped up as initial work projects were completed and, most importantly, were shared with the entire class.

The children in my class constantly showed me ways in which they were working along the continuum between efferent and aesthetic response stances (see Chapter 1). Their aesthetic responses were demonstrated through their questions, comments, and references to other story and life connections. Raoul, for example, insisted that he had to get the book out of the library so he could find out how it ended more quickly than it could be read aloud in class. Another instance was Andy's moving recollection of the death of his grandfather and primary caregiver when the grandfather character (Old Da) died in *A Stranger Came Ashore*.

Many extension projects were completely efferent (e.g., the ocean floor model). Some began with an aesthetic experience and moved toward the efferent (e.g., the sixareen model project), while others moved from efferent to aesthetic (e.g., the model of Finn Learson, the antagonist of the story, coming ashore, which the creators insisted would entice people to read the book).

Wonderful and rich experiences can result in a classroom as the teacher becomes comfortable with taking personal risks and supporting the risks taken by the children. The children did not simply do anything that struck their fancy. They were involved in making meaning for themselves and their classmates. This mode of education centers around giving children choices, helping them develop creatively, interacting with them as they explore, and helping them find information and materials. This approach changes the concept of how time is used in the elementary classroom. The children only began to manipulate materials and ideas when they were given large blocks of time over several months.

PROFESSIONAL RESOURCES

Duke, Leilani (Ed.) (1985). *Beyond creating: The place for art in America's schools.* Los Angeles: J. Paul Getty Trust.

Goodman, Ken (1986). *What's whole in whole language.* Portsmouth, NH: Heinemann Educational Books.

Haine, Gano (1985). "In the labyrinth of the image": An archetypal approach to drama in education. *Theory into Practice, 24,* 187–192.

Newman, Judith (1985). *Whole language: Theory in use.* Portsmouth, NH: Heinemann Educational Books.

O'Neill, Cecily (1985). Imagined worlds in theatre and drama. *Theory into Practice, 24,* 158–165.

Rosenblatt, Louise (1978). *The reader, the text, the poem: The transactional theory of literature: Points of departure.* Norwood, NJ: Ablex.

Tarlington, Carole (1985). "Dear Mr. Piper . . .": Using drama to create context for children's writing. *Theory into Practice, 24,* 199–204.

Wagner, Betty Jane (1988). Research currents: Does classroom drama affect the arts of language? *Language Arts, 65,* 46–55.

Weston, Lynda Hobson (1989). The evolution of the literature study in a fourth grade across four modes: Oral, written, artistic, and dramatic. Unpublished doctoral dissertation, The Ohio State University, Columbus.

CHILDREN'S LITERATURE

Bang, Mollie (1983). *Dawn.* New York: Morrow.

Cooper, Susan (1986). *The Selkie girl.* New York: Macmillan.

Gerstein, Mordicai (1986). *The seal mother.* New York: Dial.

Hesslewood, Juliet (1983). *Tales of sea and shore.* Oxford: Oxford University Press.

Hoban, Russell (1980). Old Man Ocean. In John Foster (Compiler), *A second poetry book* (p. 48). Oxford: Oxford University Press.

Hunter, Mollie (1975). *A stranger came ashore.* New York: Harper.

Irvine, Georgeanne (1987). *The true story of Corky the blind seal.* New York: Scholastic.

Smith, Iain Crichton (1982). The sea. In John Foster (Compiler), *A third poetry book* (p. 52). Oxford: Oxford University Press.

Watson, William (1984). The ballad of Semmerwater. In Edward Blishen (Complier), *Oxford book of poetry for children* (pp. 81–82). New York: Peter Bedrick.

Williamson, Duncan (1985). *The broonies, silkies and fairies: Travellers' tales of the other worlds.* New York: Harmony.

Yolen, Jane (1968). *The Greyling.* Illustrations by William Stobbs. New York: Philomel.

9

Children's Responses to Poetry in a Supportive Literary Context

Amy A. McClure

"I finally finished 'August'!" Jennifer told me triumphantly one day in late April. "Hooray!" I told her. "You've been working on that poem a long time." And so she had. Since early February, Jennifer had played with words, manipulated lines, and experimented with different images—all to get just the effect she wanted.

Jennifer had originally titled the poem "April" and had written it in response to hearing Marcia Masters' poem "April" read aloud. Her rough draft consisted of a series of images that she associated with that month:

April
(*Revision 1*)

April is a child to March.
April is a daisy opening up into the world.
April is a daisy opening.
April is a daisy.
April is a mother to May.
April is a daisy opening up.
April is a lamb, baaing down to sleep.
April is a bird singing in May.
April is a bird chirping to wake up it's child.

A more detailed discussion of this study can be found in *Sunrises and Songs: Reading and Writing Poetry in an Elementary Classroom* by Amy McClure, Peggy Harrison, and Sheryl Reed, published by Heinemann in 1990.

For weeks Jennifer periodically returned to the poem, trying out different images she associated with April and experimenting with various line patterns. Although she was intrigued by the subject, she was not yet satisfied with the ideas she was associating with it. Then, one day in early April, she crossed out everything except the lines "April is a child to March" and "April is a mother to May." She decided to focus on the idea of months as succeeding generations. But April somehow didn't seem to be the best month to sustain this metaphor.

"I think August is better," she told me, "because everything gets kind of older and dies after August."

She started over. Using August as the central focus and the idea of successive generations as the theme of her piece, she once again experimented with ideas, images, and patterns. When she finally showed the piece to me, she was elated to have conveyed a unique idea in just a few short lines:

> August
> (*Checkmarked version*)
>
> *August is a*
> *child of July.*
>
> *Mother*
> *To September*
>
> *Grandmother*
> *to October.*
>
> *And a faded memory*
> *to November.*
>
> JENNIFER
> Grade 6
> from *Sunrises and Songs* (1990)

I was struck by the fact that Jennifer had been given the time, opportunity, and encouragement to pursue this piece until she reached a satisfying conclusion. How unusual to have such freedom in school!

In Jennifer's classroom, children loved poetry: they read and wrote it daily. They eagerly helped other children find just the right word or rhythm to make a poem sing, and they were willing to subject their own pieces to similar scrutiny. They pulled poetry books off the shelves and snuggled in a corner with a friend to savor several of their favorite pieces.

Unfortunately, these positive attitudes are not typical of most children. Research suggests that they heartily dislike poetry, invariably ranking it in preference at the bottom of the list along with literary criticism, speeches, and letters (Matanzo & Madison, 1979; National Assessment of Educational Progress, 1981; Norvell, 1958). When children do demonstrate a liking for poetry, their preferences for specific elements and forms are strikingly similar, even when viewed across age, sex, demographic data, and time (Fisher & Natarella, 1982; Ingham, 1980; MacKintosh, 1924; Simmons, 1980; Terry, 1974). Generally, children tend to prefer poetry that includes elements of humor, nonsense, familiar experiences, imaginative story lines, animals, holidays, and people. In contrast, they dislike poems like Longfellow's "The Children's Hour" or Hughes's "April Rain Song" that they perceive as didactic, meditative, serious, or "difficult to understand." Narrative and limerick forms are enjoyed, while more abstract forms such as haiku and free verse are generally disliked. Favorite poetic elements include rhyme, rhythm, sound, and repetition. Figurative language is not particularly enjoyed.

When I reviewed these findings, I was dismayed. Where was the love of language, the enjoyment in the "gradual unfolding [of a poem] revealing its rich inner self" as Naoshi Koriyama describes in his beautiful poem "Unfolding Bud"? Could poetry be a lost and dying genre of literature?

When I visited the classrooms of Peg "Sheryl" Reed and Peggy Harrison in Mt. Victory, Ohio, I found a refreshingly different environment. Rather than viewing poetry as the literary equivalent of liver, their children loved it. As a leafed through poetry journals and listened while children eagerly shared their current pieces, I was struck by the creativity and thought so evident in their poems. As I listened to them talking with each other about poems they and their teachers read with each other, I was amazed by the perceptiveness of their comments as well as their enthusiasm for the genre. Something different was happening here, and I wanted to document what it was.

I decided to conduct an ethnographic, participant-observer study because I felt that conducting research in an environment that offered many continuous opportunities to observe response and teacher–child interactions would provide rich insights and demonstrate that children may be capable of developing quite complex understandings of poetry when their efforts are continually supported over time. Additionally, I was guided by Rosenblatt's ideas (1965, 1978), which suggested that response to literature is tempered by the reader's experiences and perceptions and, thus, is individual in nature. Further, I was convinced that response is also social; interactions with both peers and teachers in which meanings are negotiated through language can affect response. The ethnographic methodology seemed the best way to explore the children's responses as well as how the social context of the classroom influenced and shaped these responses. In this way I hoped to arrive at insights that more quantitative studies may have missed.

The study thus extended previous research on children's responses to poetry by continuously examining these responses in an environment that nurtured and supported them. Further, the study was designed to provide additional insights into the teaching practices that seemed to support the development of more complex responses than had been documented in previous studies.

FINDINGS

After spending a year in this classroom, tape recording talk, scribbling notes, talking to teachers and children, and then sifting through all this data, I began to see patterns and common threads running through the fabric of life as it relates to poetry. By the end of the school year, the teaching of poetry merged with the teaching of writing. When the children wrote, they saw themselves as part of a community of writers that included the poets who had created pieces they read over and over again. When they read poetry together, their own experiences as writers made them aware of the struggle involved in creating a meaningful piece.

These discoveries are described in two sections. The first details the general classroom context that shaped and supported children's responses. The second describes children's responses to poetry, focusing particularly on the social network they created and their emerging understandings of poetic elements. Although each aspect is described separately to facilitate clarity, in reality they formed an interrelated network. Figure 9–1 summarizes the findings.

CONTEXT

Classroom Events in Poetry

Throughout the year, these teachers orchestrated the classroom context so that many events relating to published poetry and poetry written by the children occurred. These events comprised the "poetry curriculum," as what transpired with poetry did occur within the broad parameters of these events. This curriculum was composed of three interrelated parts. In the first, children participated in activities designed to build their familiarity with the work of professional poets. Thus, through large group sharing sessions with teachers as well as small group and partner sessions with peers, children developed constructs about the characteristics of good poetry by reading fine examples of it to each other.

The second component complemented the first. As children acquired experience with poetry, they experimented with their ten-

Context	Response
A. *Poetry-related events:*	A. *To peers:*
1. Reading/discussing poetry	1. Peer reading/writing communities
2. Writing poetry	2. Support for the less able
3. Extensions	3. Providing ideas
	4. Clarifying meaning
B. *Teacher values and beliefs:*	5. Supporting the struggle
1. Role as facilitator	
2. Commitment to poetry	B. *To poetry:*
	1. Sense making
C. *Classroom climate:*	2. Poetry must reflect reality
1. Peer interaction sanctioned	3. Selecting the best word
2. Support for experimentation	4. Look and sound of poetry
3. Sanction frustration and small steps	5. Poetry is unique
4. Focused praise and feedback	6. Awareness of form
5. Freedom within limits	
D. *Communicating understandings about poetry:*	
1. Sense-making	
2. Clarifying meanings	
3. Poetry must reflect reality	
4. Selecting the best word	
5. Look and sound of poetry	
6. Poetry is unique	
7. Awareness of form	

FIGURE 9–1   *Findings of the study*

tatively constructed understandings of poetic elements by trying them out in their own daily poetry writing. As they wrote, they were encouraged to go beyond the obvious, to play with ideas in order to revise their pieces. Critiquing sessions with both teachers and peers helped them improve their initial efforts.

The third component, artistic extensions, complemented as well as extended the insights acquired through the first two. In this phase, children were encouraged to extend their poetic under-standings through art. The close attention to meaning and content that is required to illustrate a poem often forced them to think more deeply or even reconceptualize their original thought.

Within these broad activities, the teachers functioned in the man-ner described by Rosenblatt (1978) and later refined by Rosen and

Rosen (1973) and Hepler (1982). They endeavored to help children examine meanings in their lives and then supported them in the process of linking a poem with these individually constructed understandings. Emphasis initially was always on enjoyment. Eventually enjoyment was deepened through closer scrutiny of a poem's meanings, composition, or purpose.

The Classroom Teachers

Both teachers held certain philosophical convictions about teaching and learning that supported their subsequent organization of the environment. Their espoused convictions concerning the teachers' role could be summarized as viewing the teacher as a facilitator of a developmental process rather than as an agent of remediation or transmitter of knowledge. Similarly, these teachers advocated a perspective on language that was compatible with this view of the teacher's role. They believed that children learn best when encouraged to interact with peers and adults as they negotiate meanings through language.

The teachers held equally strong opinions on poetry's central role in life and the school curriculum. They believed poetry not only helps children become more sensitive, observant, and thoughtful, but also better writers. In addition, poetry was perceived as a useful tool for studying various content-area topics. The following examples, written respectively for units on milkweed and time, reflect the teachers' emphasis on helping children link curricular experiences with poetry.

Past and Future

Flying in the wind
A milkweed passes by.
The milkweed like a
*   fluttering flying bird*
Meets a cloud in the sky

MANDY
Grade 5

People change with time
Like days grow into weeks
The past is grandfather to
*   the future*
But I am now.

JOHNNY
Grade 6

Classroom Climate

The emphasis on a nondirective teaching role and an active, exploratory, self-directed role for the learner contributed to the creation of a classroom climate that supported children's tentative, exploratory responses. Several aspects of the environment seemed particularly conducive to fostering this climate.

Sanctioning of peer interaction These teachers perceived peer interaction as a valuable and integral part of life in their classroom. They firmly believed that collaborative learning, in which children explored and negotiated their tentative understandings through language, was an essential part of the response process. Thus, they would often directly suggest that talk be an integral part of children's interactions around poetry. For example, children were often invited to attend a group critiquing session or urged to work with specific children.

Support for experimentation The teachers tolerated and supported experimentation and divergent thinking. However, flexibility had its limits, particularly with published poetry. Both teachers recognized the parameters of meaning inherent in particular poems and continually communicated this to the children. Thus, although they encouraged children to explore various potential meanings, they did not encourage interpretations that were clearly unsupported by text.

Supporting the struggle Similarly, the teachers also acknowledged the difficulties inherent in writing and understanding poetry. Thus, when one child complained that her poem wouldn't "come out right," a teacher responded:

> Do you know that's a plague of every poet? Or every writer? Everyone who tries to write poetry that plagues them . . . trying to get down what is in your head. Because oftentimes it's an image or a picture, an idea. Then when you try to write that down . . . you can't find the words to say what you are feeling or thinking. Don't get discouraged because I tell you when you first start to write sometimes it is very difficult . . . but it will come—don't despair.

This recognition seemed to reassure children that it was permissible to feel frustrated and anxious about their work.

Focused praise and feedback The teachers offered praise and criticism in an honest, focused manner. Comments were directed specifically to what the child had done and also included suggestions for what might be changed. Thus, a teacher would say, "When you revised, you lost the best part of your original poem . . . the part that was unusual. Go back to your original and work with that idea," or "You need to expand the last line—think about how the leaves crackle and crunch when you land." Although the teachers' comments were quite direct, their attitude seemed to be more supportive than intrusive, confirming rather than critical.

Freedom within limits: Establishing expectations The teachers articulated clear, explicit expectations for both appropriate behavior and task completion. Using direct statements, peer modeling, and consistent monitoring of student activities, they created certain parameters within which children could exercise much choice.

Understanding about Poetry

The teachers sought to build understandings about how specific elements contribute to the overall meaning or poetic image. These understandings were built through interactions occurring with both professional poetry and that written by the children. However, no clear causal or sequential relationships could be discerned. Rather the relationship was transactional; children seemed to draw simultaneously from all sources in order to develop their constructs of poetry. Similarly, the teachers used all available opportunities to communicate these ideas. Several recurring themes that seemed to guide these interactions emerged from the data.

Sense-making The teachers communicated the attitude that poetry must make sense, that there is a logical connection between the real world and the world created by the poem. Not only was a viable meaning available to readers, but several meanings could be generated in relation to one poem.

Clarifying meaning The teachers asked questions that helped children clarify, refine, and extend meanings so they went beyond surface sense-making to a more complex awareness of how sense is conveyed in poetry.

Poetry reflects reality Teachers continually developed children's awareness of the notion that poetry must reflect they true essence of an event or object. Thus, they first developed an awareness of how professional poets do this and then helped children make their own poems true-to-life.

Selecting the best word The teachers frequently developed children's awareness that each word in a poem must express just the right shade of meaning for the context. This was initially conveyed through comments on the ability of professional poets to select the perfect word. Children then were encouraged to experiment with this element in their own writing.

The look and sound of poetry The teachers endeavored to show children how poets pay particular attention to the way the words sound together as well as the particular form the words take on the page. Children were introduced to elements of rhythm, rhyme, alliteration, line pattern, and shape through their use by professional poets. They were then encouraged to make their own pieces look and sound poetic by paring away unnecessary words.

Poetry is unique Teachers continually helped children appreciate how poets go beyond the obvious and try to make their poetry unique. As the children gained experience with writing poetry, they were encouraged to say something new or something old in a new way in their own work.

Awareness of form The teachers built awareness of poetic form through exposure to many types of poetry. With the exception of haiku, discussion of form was secondary to discussion of meaning. Eventually children experimented with creating poetry that exemplified a particular form.

RESPONSE

Various facets of children's responses to poetry were examined, beginning with the ways children supported each other in constructing and refining their understandings. Next, emerging understandings of various poetic elements were documented to describe how the children gradually acquired formal awareness of literary constructs.

Response to Peers

In this classroom, children built a strong social network among themselves within which they supported each other's tentative responses to poetry. The following variables were identified as the significant aspects of this peer-constructed social context.

Peer reading/writing communities Children regularly selected friends to whom they read poetry and submitted their own poems for critiquing. Because they worked closely on a continuing basis, a sense of rapport and trust was built among group members. These shared activities created a group history that, in turn, supported subsequent activities. Thus, if a poem critiqued in the past was mentioned, group members understood the reference and perceived its relationship to the poem currently under group scrutiny. It seems these communities provided the opportunity to try out ideas in a supportive setting. This, in turn, nurtured the development of more complex, thoughtful responses than might be generated alone.

Support for those less able Often able children provided assistance in the form of extensive scaffolding for children who were experiencing difficulty with response. They provided a model of appropriate response as well as guided the less able child's initial efforts so they conformed to expectations. The following comment by one child illustrates how useful this assistance was:

> Last year I used to write just three-line poems, you know. But this year I started writing poetry with meaning. Just coming to groups and getting to talk with friends . . . watching other people write poetry . . . talking with the guys in the morning. . . . Well, we'd get some crazy ideas and some good ideas about poetry and someone might pick up on different subjects and we'd make a poem.

Provide ideas Peers frequently served as a source of ideas for both reading and writing poetry. For example, during poetry sharing sessions, children would suggest ideas to each other on what to read and for the activities that transpired during these sessions. Peer suggestion was even more influential during the process of writing poetry. Often topics, titles, words, and ideas for extending a poem's focus or meaning were offered to a friend. Sometimes a child would model an entire poem after a friend's piece. It seemed that peers played a critical role in helping each other extend beyond the obvious to think in more complex, divergent ways than might be possible when relying solely on individual resources.

Clarifying meanings Peers frequently helped each other clarify the meanings of their written pieces. Sometimes the focus was on clarifying the use of one word that might not effectively convey an intended meaning. At other times the focus was on clarifying a line or the meaning of the whole poem. This mutual collaboration produced additional ideas and refinements that children might not have perceived on their own. The result was usually a more imaginative, meaningful piece.

Supporting the struggle Just as the teachers provided praise and honest criticism concerning children's tentative efforts with poetry, peers offered similar support. At the beginning of the year, these comments were invariably positive and relatively unfocused. When one child asked a friend, "Listen to this" or "Does this sound right?" the listener usually showed only minor interest, responding with "That's good" or "I like that." Occasionally, more negative comments, like "That sounds more like a story than poetry," were offered.

As the children became more used to each other and more familiar with the critiquing process, the tenor of these comments changed. They became more focused, addressing specific aspects of a poem, while recognizing the writer's struggle in creating it. Thus, comments such as "I really like that poem, you really showed me about spring" or "That's a good poem—the words just roll around in my head" were heard. Critical comments were also focused, often specifying particular modifications. In this way initial understandings were refined and modified in an environment of mutual trust and support.

Understanding of Poetic Elements

Through their extensive experiences with poetry, these children began building constructs about the meaning and use of various poetic elements. This development was not linear but, rather, transactional. Awareness, which evolved initially through repeated encounters with professionally written models, influenced the children's subsequent experimentation with these elements. This experimentation, in turn, deepened awareness and appreciation for their skillful use by professionals.

Within this interdependent cycle of awareness and experimentation, children's responses evolved along a continuum ranging from no understanding of an element to a concrete, literal awareness to a rather abstract conceptual level. By May, few children could be classified as at the "no awareness" level for any element. Yet not all advanced to the more complex levels. Those children who did seem to have acquired more formal understanding had progressed through levels that were eventually exhibited by the others; this observation lends further credence to a continuum model for analysis. Their understandings are described in the following section.

Poetry is sense-making By the year's end, most children viewed poetry as something that could be understood by making use of insights from teachers or peers. Few could construct interpretations of professional poetry on their own; sense-making was essentially a social activity. Children also frequently helped each other clarify and extend the meanings of their own pieces.

Poetry must reflect reality In their selection of topics, critiquing comments, and subsequent revisions, most children seemed to realize that a poem must faithfully reflect the world as they knew it. Thus, they increasingly selected topics and refined meanings to reflect their perceptions of the world.

Selecting the best word The children began acquiring an increasingly refined understanding of how words can complement and extend a poem's meaning. Initially, their understandings were unfocused; any word that seemed to fit was used. However, most children moved to a level at which they selected words that were both unusual and appropriate to the poem's meaning. Some children were even able to play with various possible word choices.

Poetry must look and sound poetic Children at both grade levels developed increasingly complex understandings of how poetry's sound is conveyed through rhythm, rhyme, and alliteration. Initial understandings were rather unfocused and literal. However, many progressed to a level at which they could appreciate skillful integration of these elements with the poem's meaning. These understandings were then applied to their own pieces.

They also gradually acquired a sense of how poetry looked. Most passed through an initial stage of unawareness to a conscious understanding of how shape affects and extends meaning. Some became skillful at manipulating multiple lines or stanzas within one poem.

Poetry is unique The children began noticing how poets go beyond the trite and obvious to make their poetry unique. Then they attempted to say something new or something old in a new way in their own pieces. Initially, little attention was given to how the unusual word or image contributed to the poem's meaning. However, many were eventually able to introduce unique elements that contributed to the overall sense.

Poetic form The children began developing an awareness and appreciation of various kinds of poetry. They became skilled at identifying different forms, and many attempted to make their own poems conform to the characteristics of acrostics, limericks, haiku, and nonsense.

Awareness of Figurative Language

In order to provide more specific evidence as to how teachers built these understandings and how children responded, their interactions with the elements of figurative language will be described in some detail. Through reading professional poetry and critiquing the children's own work, these teachers sought to extend the children's understandings of various aspects of figurative language including simile, metaphor, onomatopoeia, and personification. In this way they helped children construct a critical framework for discussing figurative language and heightened their appreciation for the complexity of its use. This encouragement did not mean that children were expected to formally identify such constructions. Rather, the terms were used naturally in conjunction with many examples and as part of a general discussion of the poem. The emphasis was always first on enjoyment and then on deepening enjoyment through close examination of how a poet orchestrates this element to create a coherent image.

Similes and metaphors were most often the focus of these discussions. The emphasis usually was on helping the children become aware of what was being compared and then realize how this comparison helped them view the phenomena differently. The following discussion, held by the sixth-grade teacher in conjunction with a reading of Merriam's "From the Japanese" illustrates how this occurred:

TEACHER: What's it mean—"the night is a dark blue hammock sitting between the white pillars of day?"

JOHNNY: I think the poet is in a hammock and he's writing about the night.

BRANDON: Yeah . . . it's talking about how this poet is in a hammock at night.

TEACHER: What do you think? Anybody got a different idea?

BECKY: I think it's talking about day against night.

TEACHER: What do you mean?

STACIE: It's between the end of one day and the beginning of another. You know . . . one day is one white pillar and the next day is the other pillar. The hammock is like the night. You know . . . it's dark.

TEACHER: Why do you think the poet called it a dark-blue hammock?

DEON: Because dark blue is like the night's color and white is for day.

TEACHER: That's a really different way to show it, isn't it? Would you have thought to show it like that? That's really different.

Most children began at a stage of concrete, literal awareness in which they realized the poet was comparing. Yet they had little understanding of the purpose of this comparison or how it related to a more abstract, complex meaning. Some remained at this level the entire year, always viewing a comparison from this literal perspective. Thus, for example, when the sixth-grade teacher read aloud Thurman's "Breaking Through" (a poem comparing a plant breaking through the ground to morning breaking through night and spring breaking through winter), Matt could not see the poem as anything more than "a seed coming out of its shell." Similarly, when the fifth-grade teacher organized a small group of her students to discuss "Warning," a poem about a middle-aged woman longing to be as spontaneous as a child, Tiffany insisted that the speaker was a child. She maintained this stance even when others showed her lines that indicated the woman was addressing her children.

Some children moved beyond this level to a more complex awareness of the deeper meaning inherent in metaphorical language. This development was not confined to sixth graders; fifth graders who read a great deal of poetry and regularly experimented with the use of figurative language in their own writing also could express these more abstract understandings. Thus, during the previously mentioned discussion of "Breaking Through," Becky disagreed with Matt, stating:

> I had a different view of that, I was kind of thinking it was comparing spring and the day to a seed breaking through the ground. . . . You know how everything has to fight through to get out . . . when they're first beginning . . . all three verses have this alike.

In the discussion of "Warning," Earnie, in contrast to Tiffany, understood the allusion to an adult "thinking about the future and how she wanted to change."

The children demonstrated similar patterns of understanding in the use of metaphor in their own poetry. This awareness was initially implemented quite literally. Comparisons would be created with little attention to the uniqueness of the image or to how the rest of the poem functioned in relation to the metaphor. The following poems illustrate this level of understanding:

Rain

Rain is like thunder
That can't stop itself
Then it stops to rest.
            DOLLY
            Grade 5

Windmill

As the windmill
Spins and spins

It cuts the wind
Just like cutting a pie.
JIMMY R.
Grade 6

Winter

Winter snow falls in my
mitten, like rain on
A Cloudy day falling in
A puddle.
DEON
Grade 6

Many children, however, went beyond the literal level to a more abstract understanding of how a poet can manipulate various elements to maintain the use of figurative language throughout the poem as well as select just the right words and phrases to precisely convey the intended image. The following are a few examples (created after many drafts) of this more advanced use of figurative language:

Midnight Express

Fast as a speeding bullet
Whistling through a moonlit night
Silver lightning strikes ahead,
Searching for its journey's end.
JEREMY
Grade 5

Balance Scales

Twin brothers sit side by side
One no higher than the other
Until one is filled with hate
And sinks lower than the
*   better brother.*
EARNIE
Grade 5

Autumn Masterpiece

The wind brushes
Warm colors
On a turquoise sky.
Capturing a fall day.
JOHNNY
Grade 6

Pencil Sharpener

A sharp jawed monster
Awaits a long-leaded meal.
With its mouth of metal,
It chews and spits
*   splinters of wood,*
Makes its point,
Then satisfied, it rests.

EARNIE
Grade 5

Nature's Gallery

Carved wooden puddles
Crystal canvas springs
Splatter painted brooks.
Make Nature's children
*   believe*
They too can become pieces
*   of art.*

JENNIFER
Grade 5

Those who used more advanced metaphors in their pieces were usually assisted in their efforts by both teachers and peers. It was generally through comments offered in large and small group critiquing sessions that the children were able to refine and extend their metaphorical constructions.

ANGELA'S "SUNRISE"

To provide a fuller account of how context interacted with the children's developing responses to various poetic elements, a typical poetry cycle is presented. The example was selected because it incorporated a wide variety of contextual and response elements. The evolution of many poems did not always occur over such an extended period of time. However, the basic components in this cycle occurred at some point in most other cycles, making the example a valid synthesis of what frequently transpired.

Angela got the original idea for her poem from an ordinary event in her life: an early Saturday trip to Columbus in October. As the sun rose that morning, Angela became intrigued by the interplay of shadow and color. She jotted down her initial impressions and later that day created the following rough draft:

Sunrise
(*Rough draft*)

The sun is slowly rising
Over the horizon.
A bird chirps its song
While the other birds join in.
As the sun rises higher,
The world wakes
To sun rays in
their windows.

Angela initially asked her mother and sister for reactions. Both agreed the line "While the other birds join in" didn't quite fit. Angela decided to eliminate it, later stating that "it didn't sound poetic." Her teacher indicated that the poem "had possibilities" so Angela decided to work on it further.

The poem was next submitted to several friends for help. Their comments focused mainly on refining the words. Thus, after looking through the thesaurus, they suggested that Angela change slowly to gradually, higher to greater and rises to grows. These selections "made the meaning better," in their opinion.

The poem was then taken to a teacher-led critiquing group. At this point a major reconceptualization occurred. The group first talked extensively about the phenomena Angela was trying to describe: what really happens, what the sun looks like at that time of day, and other issues to ensure that she remained "true to her subject." They also decided to compare the sun to an animal stalking its prey. Several children commented that the word gradually was too ordinary. Using the thesaurus, they generated many words, including explodes, pops up, sneaks, peeks, strikes, and creeps; they finally decided that sneaks upon the night was the best word to convey the metaphorical image of the sun eating night as analogous to an animal eating its prey. One child, casually passing by the table, commented, "Well, if you're making it sound like an animal, why not use preys?" The group enthusiastically concurred with his choice. They also played with various ways to line the poem. The poem now looked as follows:

Sunrise
(*Revision 3*)

The sun preys
Upon the night
As it steps across the horizon
The sun grows greater
At the crack of day.

Angela once again returned to an informal peer-critiquing group. However, this time she received much less assistance. Rather, she was observed muttering aloud, "I don't like steps, I like peeks over the horizon better" and "crack is like what you do with an egg . . . that don't sound right." Shelli, a sixth grader, was the only one to provide substantive help by suggesting that Angela substitute tiptoes for peeks. After experimenting with more words and lining patterns, Angela's poem now looked as follows:

Sunrise
(*Revision 4*)

The sun preys
Upon the night
    ~~*peeps*~~
As it ~~steps~~ across the horizon
    tiptoes
The sun grows greater
At the crack of day.

Angela then decided she needed more help with constructing an ending for her piece. She thus initiated a blackboard critiquing session with Angie and Becky in late December. The girls first suggested that Angela describe the sun's colors. They brainstormed pink, yellow, red and blue before deciding that yellow was the most realistic color. They next experimented with several words, substituting peeks around for preys (later rejected because it broke the rhythm) and adding swallows to describe what the sun does to the night.

The sixth-grade teacher then asked several focused questions to help extend the metaphor. She pretended to eat, asking the girls to describe her actions. They responded, "Biting," then Angela observed thoughtfully, "Big biting, big biting." "Does that fit with your metaphor?" asked the teacher. Next, the teacher questioned them about the title, which they had changed from "Sunrise" to "Devouring Sun." Again, she asked them to think of a new title that aptly crystalized the metaphor. The poem finally evolved into the following:

Breakfast

The sun preys
Upon the night
As it tiptoes to the horizon.
Big, yellow bite; by big, yellow bite,
The sun swallows the night.

Britton (1982) states that "the poet draws on his own experience in order to create fresh experience." Angela did this. She took a simple everyday experience and created a unique image that is fresh and imaginative. This was not accomplished independently. Rather, she was supported by an environment in which her initial ideas were nurtured and valued.

CONCLUSIONS

My tentative hunches about this classroom were confirmed. The children not only manifested a wide range of enthusiastic and informed positive responses to poetry, but their understandings were in many cases at a level of complexity that is more typical of much older students. Yet they were not particularly gifted, nor did they have a strong interest in or affinity for poetry before becoming a part of the class. Rather, the supportive context provided by the teachers seemed to make the difference. Repeated opportunities to discuss and savor poetry and then to experiment with the ideas they had acquired through writing their own poems seemed to create the willingness to take risks and experiment with more abstract responses.

These findings have several important implications for the teaching of poetry. First, children need to be immersed in reading and writing poetry if they are to develop complex responses to it. Neither a short-term poetry unit nor an occasional poetry read-aloud session on a rainy Friday afternoon is sufficient. These activities don't allow for the evolution of carefully considered responses, which need time to evolve. Continuous, sustained exposure to many kinds of poems and regular opportunities to write poetry seem to be the critical variables. Such activities provide children with models for how poetry looks, how other poets have described a particular phenomena, and how various poetic elements complement and extend meaning. More importantly, however, constant exposure can lead to a more informed appreciation of poetry's place in literature and in life.

Thus, teachers need to regularly read poetry aloud and help children deepen their enjoyment through discussions, choral reading, and other group activities. Children should also be encouraged to examine poetry on their own, without teacher direction. Teachers can also coordinate poetry with science, social studies, and mathematics to provide a valuable aesthetic perspective on these subjects as well as the sense that poetry permeates all aspects of life.

A regularly scheduled poetry writing time is important. Children in this classroom wrote poetry every day. While replicating this practice might be difficult, I cannot stress enough the importance of regularly exercising one's "poetry muscle." Children get over their trepidation of the writing task. Writing a rough draft that was not expected to be perfect was very freeing to the children in this study. Having time to play with and work on a piece further lessened their anxiety. As anxiety decreased, fluency increased.

In addition, children should be encouraged to experience a poem personally and aesthetically before they are asked to respond efferently, to analyze or dissect it. Nothing kills delight faster than instance on one meaning that is accessible only to the skilled, sophisticated reader. There are many ways to interpret meaning, with each person's perception tempered by a personal view of reality as well as by prior experience with literature. Thus, children first should be encouraged to take delight in a poem and then supported in the process of linking their perceptions of the world with those in the poems. They can discuss what a poet did to create an intriguing sound or enjoyable image. Then, within this context, teachers can informally yet deliberately introduce more technical terms. Using the terms in conjunction with many examples seems to build deeper understandings than when those terms are introduced in more formal, decontextualized lessons. Heightened enjoyment and awareness of structure, form, and other poetic elements then naturally evolve out of such repeated satisfactory experiences with poetry.

Similarly, the major emphasis in writing poetry should not be on the development of technical perfection like the perfectly balanced rhythm or correctly spaced rhyme scheme. Instead, the focus should be on creating a feeling or image that satisfies the writer.

Children should be allowed and encouraged to talk with each other about poetry. I discovered that children strongly support and shape each other's responses and frequently turn to each other for ideas and assistance with various response activities. Some of this is deliberate, but much occurs spontaneously as a result of shared needs and interests. Their mutually constructed responses were usually more imaginative and complex than if each participant had worked alone.

Teachers need to value and utilize this social network. Not only should talk be encouraged, but children should be shown how to help each other in a focused, constructive manner. However, teachers should be careful not to classify peer assistance as productive or unproductive. Sometimes seemingly irrelevant comments can lead to surprising insights.

Finally, an atmosphere of support and freedom to take risks is critical to generating thoughtful, more complex responses. Recognition and approval for seemingly insignificant yet positive efforts in this classroom seemed to engender willingness to tackle increasingly more difficult and more abstract responses. The teachers in this classroom did not expect children's oral responses to resemble those of adults. Nor were all expected to produce poems like Angela's "Sunrise." Rather, small steps were celebrated and seen as important milestones for the eventual acquisition of more sophisticated behaviors. Teachers need to scaffold initial responses and help children link what they already know to new ideas and concepts. Thus, teachers can make links between poets or poems with similar themes; they can ask questions in critiquing sessions that help children link their understandings about what professional poets do with their own struggles to create meaning; and they can sanction frustration so that children sustain their efforts.

Tolerance for divergence and experimentation can also support children's responses. The children in this study did quite a bit of experimenting with poetry, often making false starts and considering many possibilities before eventually expressing a viable or original meaning. They expected to revise several times, knowing their first attempt rarely yielded the best idea. Freed from the necessity to get the right answer, children can take risks and explore several alternatives in order to discover the best one for their purpose. This combination of support and freedom was significant in generating the imaginative, fresh responses offered by the children in this study.

PROFESSIONAL RESOURCES

Britton, J. (1982). Poetry and our pattern of culture. In Gordon Pradle (Ed.), *Prospect and retrospect: Selected essays of James Britton.* London: Boynton/ Cook.

Fisher, C., & Natarella, M. (1982). Young children's preferences in poetry: A national survey of first, second and third graders. *Research in the Teaching of English, 16,* 339–355.

Hepler, S. (1982). *Patterns of response to literature: A one-year study of a fifth and sixth grade classroom.* Unpublished doctoral dissertation, The Ohio State University.

Hickman, J. (1979). *Response to literature in a school environment, grades K–5.* Unpublished doctoral dissertation, The Ohio State University.

Ingham, R. (1980). *The poetry preferences of fourth and fifth grade students in a suburban school setting in 1980.* Unpublished doctoral dissertation, University of Houston.

MacKintosh, H. (1924). A study of children's choices in poetry. *Elementary English Review, 1,* 85–89.

McClure, A. (1985). *Children's responses to poetry in a supportive literary context.* Unpublished doctoral dissertation. The Ohio State University.

McClure, A., Harrison, P., & Reed, S. (1990). *Sunrises and songs: Reading and writing poetry in an elementary classroom.* Portsmouth, NH: Heinemann Educational Books.

Matanzo, J., & Madison, J. (1979). A poem-a-day can make a difference. *Connecticut English Journal, 10,* 410–430.

National Assessment of Educational Progress (1981). *Reading, thinking and writing: Results from the National Assessment of Reading and Literature.* Denver, CO: Education Commission of the States.

Norvell, G. (1958). *What boys and girls like to read.* New York: Silver Burdett.

Rosen, C., & Rosen, H. (1973). *The language of primary school children.* New York: Penguin.

Rosenblatt, L. (1965). *Literature as exploration.* New York: Barnes and Noble.

Rosenblatt, L. (1978). *The reader, the text, the poem: The transactional theory of the literary work.* Carbondale: Southern Illinois University Press.

Simmons, M. (1980). *Intermediate-grade children's preferences in poetry.* Unpublished doctoral dissertation, University of Alabama.

Terry, A. (1974). *A national survey of children's poetry preferences in the fourth, fifth and sixth grades.* Unpublished doctoral dissertation, The Ohio State University.

CHILDREN'S LITERATURE

Hughes, Langston. (1968). April rain song. In Nancy Larrick (Ed.), *Piping down the valleys wild.* New York: Dell Publishing.

Joseph, J. (1971). Warning. In *Modern poetry.* New York: Lippincott.

Koriyama, N. (1967). Unfolding bud. In S. Dunning, E. Lueders, & H. Smith (Eds.), *Reflections on a gift of watermelon pickle . . . and other modern verse.* New York: Lothrop.

Longfellow, H. (1927). The children's hour. In *Poems for the children's hour.* New York: Bradley.

Masters, M. (1967). April. In S. Dunning, E. Lueders, & H. Smith (Eds.), *Reflections on a gift of watermelon pickle . . . and other modern verse.* New York: Lothrop.

Merriam, E. (1976). From the Japanese. In *Rainbow writing* by Eve Merriam. New York: Atheneum.

Thurman, J. (1976). Breaking through. In *Flashlight and other poems* by Judith Thurman. New York: Atheneum.

Part III

Literary Responses in Late Childhood

10

Responding to Literature Through Journal Writing

Joanne M. Golden
& Elaine Handloff

Reader response to literature has been examined in a variety of ways, including analyses of children's discussion of literature, dramatic interpretation, interviews, and written essays. Few studies, however, have specifically explored reader response through journal writing. Research on reader response to literature and on the writing process suggests that journal writing may provide an excellent vehicle for students to articulate and develop their responses to literature.

The journal, perhaps in contrast to other modes of response, lends itself to capturing what Rosenblatt (1976) referred to as the intensely personal and active experience of reading literature. Since readers may write in journals both during and after reading a particular work, it is possible to see how the text unfolds for the reader. Thus, the role of the reader in making sense of literature is illuminated in journal writing. Because students choose the focus of their entries, the journal provides insights into what the student thinks is interesting or significant about a work.

This chapter examines the journal responses of readers in one fifth-grade class to determine patterns of reader responses. The goal of the teacher, one of the authors of this chapter, was to gain insights into areas of particular concern to her as a reading teacher. First, it would be useful to know if the responses of students at a particular age and developmental level form any consistent patterns for the group as a whole and, if so, what those patterns are. Second, analyses of individual students' patterns of response would offer a new avenue by which to approach and direct their unique reading experiences. This knowledge of the characteristics of both group and individual responses would enable the teacher to tailor a reading program to meet the needs of the students.

RELATED RESEARCH

One use of journals that has been systematically researched is the dialogue journal. In this type of journal writing, students write daily entries on topics they choose. The teacher writes back to each student on a regular basis, focusing on the content of the entries. Analyses of dialogue journals show that they increase students' self-knowledge, improve students' language abilities, and develop students' cognitive abilities (Staton, 1989). In addition to these benefits, Bode (1989) found that reading achievement improved with dialogue journal writing because students were learning about literacy in an integrative fashion.

Fewer studies have explored the use of journals as a vehicle for exploring reader response to literature. Tashlik (1987) had students experiment with writing both fictional journals and response journals. Students generally preferred writing the fictional journals, but they felt the response journals better helped them to understand the literature they were reading. Crowhurst and Kooy (1986) explored the use of response journals in teaching the novel. Responses were analyzed according to comments about structure, hypotheses, personal responses, and comments about style. They found that ninth graders were more likely to respond to structure and less likely to respond to style than twelfth graders.

Atwell (1987) used journals as an integral part of her reading workshop. In studying student-to-student writing as part of her program she found marked differences in the kinds of writing that resulted. Students in this situation, for example, wrote more affective descriptions and tended to ask more often for recommendations of other books to read. Using this same reading workshop technique with learning disabled middle school students, Oberlin and Shugarman (1989) found that the use of the program had positive effects on the students in terms of reading attitudes and an increase in the level of book involvement. These students, on average, had read one book a year prior to the study, but that average increased to twenty during the eighteen weeks of the study.

In general, research on reader response journals suggests that it is a promising approach for capturing reader response. Further studies are needed to investigate the nature of students' responses to literature and their development of these responses through journal writing. The present study addresses this need, as described in the following section.

DESCRIPTION OF THE STUDY

Background

In the year prior to this study, the teacher had implemented a journal writing program in her class as a means to establish links between reading and writing, to learn about how students who did not participate in class discussion responded to literature, and to establish an accountability for reading. From this intuitive base, the teacher sought to undertake a systematic study of journal responses in the second year. While the procedures for journal writing remained essentially the same, perspectives on the nature of reader response and ways of analyzing the responses were developed.

The program is based on a number of objectives related to journal writing as a teaching and learning technique. These objectives include helping students to develop a conscious awareness of how they feel and react while reading, increasing opportunities for writing within the reading curriculum, tracking the independent reading of individual students, providing more one-to-one dialogue between teacher and students, and providing a vehicle for teacher analysis of individual reading styles.

Procedures

During the second week of class, the teacher introduced the independent reading program. Students were told they could choose whatever material they liked, with the stipulations that the material should be appropriate for their reading level and that cartoon books, comic books, and magazines were not acceptable. Time for independent reading was provided regularly during class, and homework was not assigned to insure that students had adequate time to read regularly.

In a second session, the teacher introduced the students to the journal writing project. In the first part of the lesson, students discussed prior experiences with journals. The teacher then introduced the reader response journal and emphasized the importance of responding to the story rather than retelling it. The point was made that what happens in a story is only one aspect of a piece of literature and that students' entries should address some other aspects of the literary experience. The teacher stressed that she could easily find out what happens in a book by reading it herself. The purpose of the journal entries was to record students' unique reactions to their books. This basic function of the journal writing task was stressed repeatedly throughout the lesson. Students were encouraged to discuss their reactions to the book or parts of it, to express their feelings and opinions, to look for ties to their own lives, and to think about how the author's style of writing affected their responses to the book. They were also encouraged to use examples from the literature to illustrate a point or to support an opinion. The teacher shared an entry she had written and pointed out various aspects that met the requirements of the task. The final component involved sharing samples of previous students' work to show the variety of types of responses and ways to write about those responses. During this stage of the lesson, students could sometimes identify the book being discussed in the entries; sometimes they could not. The teacher pointed out that had the writer simply retold the story, the books would have been easy to identify and it was because of the personal nature of the response, which is so unique to each reader, that the books were not easy to identify. Students were told that someone other than the teacher was interested in reading their journals, but that their permission was required. Thus, students were assured that their journals could be private if they chose. Following the introduction, students wrote in their journals. In subsequent classes, students were given the opportunity to write in their journals for fifteen to twenty minutes at the beginning of the class period three times a week.

The teacher responded to the students' writing approximately once a week. These responses basically included questions and comments. The questions generally performed two functions: requesting clarification of unclear responses and stimulating students to expand a thought or to support a statement more fully. Comments were used to reinforce good writing and original thinking as well as to direct students when their entries were off track or did not meet the criteria established at the beginning of the program. Comments were also used to respond to questions or statements that appeared to be directly addressed to the teacher. Students were free to choose to respond to the teacher's responses.

Analysis of Journal Entries

To see how the journals would work with average readers, one class of average readers was selected. The journals of nineteen students in the class were analyzed. Each journal entry from each student was segmented into responses that were defined in accordance with Squire (1964) as the "smallest combination of words which conveyed the sense of a single thought" (p. 17). Each response was then labelled independently by two raters (and cross-checked) in terms of the response categories identified in Squire (1964), with minor modifications. The label "personal" was added to Squire's category of associational in order to emphasize the personal aspect, and the category of personal character identification replaced Squire's category of self-involvement in order to reflect the students' responses more fully. The narrational response category was expanded to include statements that were generally descriptive rather than interpretive. The literary judgment category was extended to include statements in which students linked the book to a particular genre. The categories (and their codes) include: literary judgment (LJ), interpretive (I), narrational (N), personal (P), prescriptive (PR), personal associational (PA), and miscellaneous (M). In addition, an "S" was added to indicate whether a statement was used to support an idea. For example, the codes were assigned as follows: I like the book (P) because the author writes well (LJ-S). The categories and their definitions are presented in Figure 10–1.

To ascertain individual patterns, a percentage of statements reflecting each category was determined for each individual. To identify group patterns of response, a percentage of total statements reflecting each category was determined.

FINDINGS

Whole Group Pattern

The pattern of the percentages of responses in the journals is presented in Figure 10–2. The most frequent response was narrational (.32), followed by literary judgment (.26), personal (.17), and interpretive (.15). The personal associational and prescriptive categories had fewer responses (.04 and .01 respectively). In general, the group pattern suggests that children were responding in a variety of ways to the range of books they were reading, though the most frequent responses were narrational and literary judgment.

Patterns of Response Within the Group

When we looked at children's responses within the group, different patterns emerged among subgroups of children. That is, certain children wrote responses that reflected a dominant pattern in terms of their two most frequently used response categories. Seven students, for example, wrote responses that were predominantly narrational and literary judgment. (One of these wrote literary judgment responses most frequently and miscellaneous as the second most frequent category.) These patterns were evident in the journals of children who read a range of books as well as those who read a more limited range. One of the girls read Brink's (1935) *Caddie Woodlawn*, Bruce's (1964) *Death in Albert Park*, Cleary's (1975) *Ramona the Brave*, White's (1969) *Charlotte's Web*, and Martin's (1988) *Babysitters on Board!*, among other books. Her response to Pascal's (1990) *The Ghost of Tricia Martin* shows her orientation toward narrational as the most frequent response and literary judgment as the second most frequent response:

Category Name	Definition	Examples
Interpretive (I)	Making inferences and/or predictions; explaining or relating the work to something else; expressing the theme of the work; discussing characters, setting, or other literary elements	"I think the rats will escape in time." "Marcy probably won't win the election because she is a snob." "Jim knows now that friends are important." "I think the main character is funny." "What will Steve do?"
Literary judgment (LJ)	Assessing or rating the author's and/or illustrator's style; genre classification; pointing out use of language and/or literary devices; evaluation of the work	"This book is scary and exciting." "The author is very creative." "The illustrations are beautiful and really go with the text." "This is a great book." "This is a humorous mystery." "It made me feel like I was in the story."
Narrational (N)	Literal retelling of the story; listing literal aspects of the work, such as names of characters	"This story is about a ten-year-old boy named Steve who has to move to a new neighborhood." "The book I'm reading is *The Secret Garden.*"
Personal (P)	Statements about how the student felt while reading; statements expressing personal interest; what book the student wishes to read next	"I'm glad the kids were able to get out of the house in time." "I like this book." "I wonder what will happen next." "I am going to look for the sequel to this book to read next."
Personal associational (PA)	References to ties to the student's life; references to how the student would feel or react if in the character's place	"I'm a lot like Jason because I hate math and I have a bratty brother." "If I were Jane, I would be really scared."
Prescriptive (PR)	Statements regarding what the character should do or have done	"His parents should let him choose his own friends."
Miscellaneous (M)	Unrelated matters, such as number of pages read	"I am on page 61." "I saw the movie."

FIGURE 10–1   *Response categories used in the study*

Interpretive	.15	Personal associational	.04
Literary judgment	.26	Prescriptive	.01
Narrational	.32	Miscellaneous	.05
Personal	.17		

FIGURE 10–2   *Percentages of types of responses for the whole group*

> This story might sound spooky (LJ) but it is not (LJ). It's not as
> good as you think it would be (LJ). The story is about a girl (N).
> It was her first year (N) and nobody knew she was a ghost (N).

One of the boys also wrote predominantly literary judgment and
narrational responses with literary judgment as the most frequent
response. He read a variety of books, including Dahl's (1977) *Charlie and the Chocolate Factory,* Dygard's (1986) *Halfback Tough,* and
Sachar's (1987) *There's a Boy in the Girl's Bathroom.* His response to
Donnelly's (1988) *Titanic: Lost and Found* illustrates a preference
toward literary judgment and narrational responses:

> This book is a really good story (LJ) because it tells who the peo-
> ple were saying it couldn't sink (N-S) and then how it sunk (N-S)
> and how the scientist found it and just left it alone (N-S). This
> book tells you all about it (N). It's just like you were right there on
> it (LJ). It has a magnificent picture of it when it was sinking and
> how it was sunk and how it was found (LJ).

A second pattern was evident in the responses of three children
who wrote primarily literary judgment responses, but who also frequently wrote personal responses to the books. Another boy read
books such as Asimov and Greenberg's (1982) *Mutants,* Blume's
(1980) *Superfudge,* Schwartz's (1981) *Scary Stories to Tell in the Dark,*
and Kalmus's (1960) *101 Simple Experiments with Insects.* His response to *Charlie and the Chocolate Factory* illustrates his orientation:

> This is a very funny book (LJ). It also makes you hungry when
> you think about all the chocolates (P). Roald Dahl writes some of
> the best ever read by human eyes (LJ). I have read most of his
> books including *The BFG, The Witches* (P) and I am still trying to
> find *Boy* at the local library (P).

One of the girls wrote journal entries in response to books that
included Pascal's (1990) *Ghosts in the Graveyard,* Hickok's (1958) *The
Story of Helen Keller,* and Juster's (1961) *The Phantom Tollbooth.* Her
responses include a number of personal reactions as well as literary

judgments. A portion of an entry in response to Bellairs's (1989) *The Treasure of Alpheus Winterborn* reflects her focus:

> I said he's [John Bellairs] an awesome writer (LJ). As I read this book it gives me a tingle up my spine (P). He's pretty scary (LJ) but he's really scary when I'm reading at night in my room alone (P).

A third pattern was evident in five children who wrote responses reflecting the two categories of narrational and personal. One read books such as Bulla's (1988) *Pocohontas and the Strangers*, O'Dell's (1960) *Island of the Blue Dolphins*, Montgomery's (1935) *Anne of Green Gables*, and Clark's (1989) *Freedom Crossing*. Her response to Burnett's (1963) *A Little Princess* shows her use of the narrational and personal categories:

> Sara has just met Lottie the baby of the school (N). She's only four years old (N). I think that is very young for boarding school (P). Now Lottie throws tantrums a lot (N).

Another student also responded with narrational and personal reactions to books, including Babbitt's (1975) *Tuck Everlasting*, Corbett's (1977) *The Hangman's Ghost Trick*, and Littke's (1989) *Prom Dress*, among others:

> But this book isn't what I thought it would be like (P). I thought that this book was about sixth or seventh graders (P) but it's not (N). It's about fifth graders (N). I don't really like stories about fifth graders (P) because there's not much action (LJ-S).

While these narrational and personal responses reflect the most frequently used categories, these children also used interpretive responses to discuss the books.

The fourth pattern was reflected in the journals of four children whose most frequent response was interpretive. Three of these also wrote narrational responses frequently, while the fourth also wrote personal responses frequently. One girl primarily read realistic stories, such as Cleary's (1951) *Ellen Tebbits*, Cavanna's (1987) *Banner Year*, Burnett's (1963) *A Little Princess*, and Fenner's (1989) *Summer of Horses*. In one of her several responses to Stearns's (1984) *Breezy*, she wrote:

> I think Robin was so mad when the horse she wanted had already been taken (I). She was so steamed (I) I'll bet she wanted to punch someone's face in!!! (I) But then she saw the mare of the bunch that the stallion stayed around (N). She thought she was a great horse . . . (N)

Another student in this group read fantasy, such as Cleary's (1970) *Runaway Ralph* and O'Brien's (1982) *The Secret of NIMH*, and sports stories, such as Halecroft's (1990) *Breaking Loose*. His responses primarily reflected interpretive and personal levels. His response to *Runaway Ralph* illustrates this orientation:

> I sure am glad that boy can talk to Ralph now (P). I hope the boy understands that Ralph got to be let free (P). I think in the end Ralph will go home and let all his brothers and cousins ride his bike or push them (I). Then Ralph will have learned a lesson (I).

CONCLUSIONS

Several conclusions can be drawn from the analysis of children's journal responses in the independent reading program. First, the journal provided a valuable means of engaging children in literary response. The journal was valuable for the children in providing them with a forum for sharing their opinions about books and exploring their own feelings in response to literature. The journal enabled children to engage in a dialogue with another person about the books they read and to receive feedback and encouragement about their responses. Thus, the journal offered children a means of articulating, exploring, and extending their responses to literature. The private nature of the journal allowed children another avenue of expression that is not normally available in the classroom. The journal was valuable for the teacher in that it provided a means of observing how children were responding to literature as well as what kinds of books they were reading. The teacher could also see how children utilized reading strategies for predicting, modifying, and extending information; established intertextual connections; and identified genres. In addition, the journal served as a vehicle for the teacher to monitor children's reading activities and to interact with children about the books they read.

Second, the group analysis of the journal entries offered insights into how a group of average fifth-grade readers responded to books as well as the kinds of books they read. While the predominant response was narrational, the analysis showed that children were engaging with literature in a variety of ways, including making literary judgments, connecting personally with the literature, and interpreting the literature.

Third, the analysis of patterns within groups indicated that different children were oriented toward specific types of response patterns, such as narrational–personal, narrational–literary judgment, personal–literary judgment, and interpretive–narrational. These patterns were evident across a range of books.

Fourth, the analysis showed that children often used supporting statements to elaborate on their responses by sharing specific examples or reasons for their response. This practice was related to the teacher's initial lesson, which stressed the importance of supporting one's opinions. A second lesson was given in November because the teacher felt that the students needed to develop and support their responses more fully. In a future study, the influence of the teacher's lessons and comments in the journal will be examined to determine their role in the journal-writing process.

Fifth, the analysis revealed the kinds of books that children were reading. Although this was not a focus of the analysis, the journals indicated that children read books from a variety of genres and by a variety of authors. Genres included poetry, nonfiction, historical fiction, contemporary realism, and fantasy and science fiction. Some children wrote several entries in response to three or four books, while others wrote a different entry on each book. Some responses occurred during the reading of the book and others after the book. In some cases, children indicated they were looking forward to reading a book.

The observations in this chapter are based on one class of average readers during the fall semester. Future analyses will focus on the development of responses over the period of the school year and, in addition, the journals of other levels of readers.

IMPLICATIONS

This exploration has several implications for the classroom. One implication is that the response journal is an effective tool for gaining insights into what Rosenblatt terms the reader's transaction with literature. Through the journal, we can learn about readers' responses as the text unfolds during and after the reading process. Students' responses show us how they interpret text and whether the text holds a personal significance for them.

A second implication is that the journal not only provides insights into reader response but offers information about how the child is developing as a reader in terms of reading interests and reading strategies and as a writer who learns to articulate thoughts and feelings for an audience.

A third implication is that the journal is an effective means for the teacher to monitor children's reading in an independent reading program. The teacher can observe which books the children are reading and, in some cases, offer suggestions that confirm and/or expand the child's choices. In addition, knowledge of how children respond to literature and what books children like to read provides a basis for the planning of more structured transactions with literature (e.g., guided book discussions).

A fourth implication is that the journal, in conjunction with other modes of response (e.g., discussion groups), provides a less restricted way to respond to literature than other forms (e.g., a traditional book report). Children, for example, choose not only the books they read but how they respond to the literature.

PROFESSIONAL RESOURCES

Atwell, Nancie (1987). *In the middle: Writing, reading, and learning with adolescents.* Portsmouth, NH: Boynton/Cook.

Bode, Barbara (1989). Dialogue journal writing. *The Reading Teacher, 42,* 568–571.

Crowhurst, M., & Kooy, M. (1986). The use of response journals in teaching the novel. *Reading-Canada-Lecture, 3,* 256–266.

Oberlin, Kelly, & Shugarman, Sherrie (1989). Implementing the reading workshop with middle school LD readers. *Journal of Reading, 32,* 682–687.

Rosenblatt, Louise M. (1976). *Literature as exploration* (3rd ed.). New York: Modern Language Association of America.

Squire, James (1964). *The responses of adolescents while reading four short stories.* Urbana, IL: National Council of Teachers of English.

Staton, Jana (1989). An introduction to dialogue journal communication. In Jana Staton, Roger Shuy, & Joy Kreeft Peyton (Eds.), *Dialogue journal communication: Classroom, linquistic, social and cognitive views,* pp. 1–32. Norwood, NJ: Ablex.

Tashlik, Phyllis (1987). I hear voices: The text, the journal and me. In Toby Fulwiler (Ed.), *The journal book.* Portsmouth, NH: Boynton/Cook.

CHILDREN'S LITERATURE

Asimov, Isaac, & Greenberg, Martin (Eds.) (1982). *Mutants.* Milwaukee, WI: Raintree Publishers.

Babbitt, Natalie (1975). *Tuck everlasting.* New York: Farrar, Straus & Giroux.

Bellairs, John (1989). *The treasure of Alpheus Winterborn.* New York: Bantam.

Blume, Judy (1980). *Superfudge.* New York: Dutton.

Brink, Carol Ryrie (1935). *Caddie Woodlawn.* New York: Macmillan.

Bruce, Leo (1964). *Death in Albert Park.* New York: Scribner.

Bulla, Clyde R. (1988) *Pocahontas and the strangers.* New York: Scholastic.

Burnett, Frances Hodgson (1963). *A little princess.* New York: Lippincott.

Cavanna, Betty (1987). *Banner year.* New York: Morrow.

Clark, Margaret G. (1989). *Freedom crossing.* New York: Scholastic.

Cleary, Beverly (1951). *Ellen Tebbits.* New York: Morrow.

Cleary, Beverly (1970). *Runaway Ralph.* New York: Morrow.

Cleary, Beverly (1975). *Ramona the Brave.* New York: Morrow.

Corbett, Scott (1977). *The hangman's ghost trick.* Boston: Little, Brown.

Dahl, Roald (1977). *Charlie and the chocolate factory.* New York: Bantam.

Donnelly, Judy (1988). *Titanic: Lost and found.* New York: Random House.

Dygard, Thomas J. (1986). *Halfback tough.* New York: Morrow.

Fenner, Carol (1989). *Summer of horses.* New York: Knopf.
Halecroft, David (1990). *Breaking loose.* New York: Penguin.
Hickok, Lorena A. (1958). *The story of Helen Keller.* New York: Grosset.
Juster, Norton (1961). *The phantom tollbooth.* New York: Random House.
Kalmus, H. (1960). *101 simple experiments with insects.* New York: Doubleday.
Littke, Lael (1989). *Prom dress.* New York: Scholastic.
Martin, Ann M. (1988). *Babysitters on board!* New York: Scholastic.
Montgomery, L. M. (1935). *Anne of Green Gables.* New York: Grosset.
O'Brien, Robert C. (1982). *The secret of NIMH.* New York: Scholastic.
O'Dell, Scott (1960). *Island of the blue dolphins.* Boston: Houghton Mifflin.
Pascal, Francine (1990). *The ghost of Tricia Martin.* New York: Bantam.
Pascal, Francine (1990). *Ghost in the graveyard.* New York: Bantam.
Sachar, Louis (1987). *There's a boy in the girls' bathroom.* New York: Knopf.
Schwartz, Alvin (1981). *Scary stories to tell in the dark.* New York: Harper.
Stearns, Helen M. (1984). *Breezy.* Camden, ME: Cricketfield Press.
White, E. B. (1969). *Charlotte's web.* New York: Harper.

11

Exploring Literature with Children Within a Transactional Framework

Margaret Anzul

Throughout most of my teaching life I have been working with children in literature discussion groups. My earliest attempts along this line were inspired by my own love of literature and my memories of literature discussions in college classes. As I became aware of the growing body of research in readers' responses to literature (Applebee, 1978; Cooper, 1985; Holland, 1975; Purves & Beach, 1972; Rosenblatt, 1978), however, I began to attend more carefully to the personal responses of my students and to provide a context in which they could respond more spontaneously and at greater length. I became less concerned with formulating questions that would lead my students to reasoned analysis and more interested in their experiences as they "lived through" (Rosenblatt, 1978, p. 70; 1983, p. 277) the stories they read. Taping some of the literature discussions allowed me to document the children's responses and insights and, in time, to reflect on and modify my own teaching.

The transactional theory of literature of Louise Rosenblatt provided the ideal conceptual framework within which data such as I had been gathering informally could become the stuff of formal research. The resultant study was based on two years' work with children in literature discussion groups throughout their fifth- and sixth-grade years (Anzul, 1988). The events that are described and analyzed in the study illustrate what can happen when students read and discuss literature with one another and with a teacher who is working toward implementing the implications of transactional theory in the classroom.

THE CONTEXT AND METHOD OF THE STUDY

The teaching and research activities documented here were conducted in a small K–6 school in a suburban community. There were two sections at each grade level. I had been newly assigned as the librarian to this school, and most of the students were strangers to me. At that time, it was customary to schedule members of the top reading groups to meet with the librarian for a literature discussion "enrichment" program that met weekly. I started with two groups, one of seven students and one of nine students, from the fifth-grade classes.

It is characteristic of the transactional nature of the qualitative research process (Anzul, 1991) that changes will inevitably occur in the research setting. During the course of the fifth-grade year, the students were regrouped, and I worked for a time with one of the classes as a whole. During the sixth-grade year, participation in the literature discussion groups became voluntary. One of my goals as a teacher had been to make participation in the literature program more open and flexible and to include some voluntary aspects. However, a core of fifteen students remained with the program throughout the two years, and the segments of data selected for close analysis are those in which they were involved. Altogether, there were nine boys and six girls. One of the girls was African-American; two of the boys were of Asian descent, and one of them was still attending English as a second language classes. The ethnic designations are given here to make the point that although minority groups are small in this school, children from them were proportionately represented in the group of student participants. The names of the students have been changed to preserve anonymity.

PLANNING WITHIN A TRANSACTIONAL FRAMEWORK

In *Literature as Exploration* (1983) and *The Reader, the Text, the Poem* (1978), Rosenblatt sets forth transactional theory in detail and outlines many implications for teaching within a transactional framework. She points out that "language is at once basically social and intensely individual . . . it must be internalized by each human being with all the special overtones that each unique person and unique situation entail" (1978, p. 20). All reading is a transactional process in which the reader and the text both influence and are influenced by each other. Reading processes can be understood as occurring along a continuum. At one pole is efferent reading, in which the reader's attention is directed solely toward grasping meaning. At the other pole, in aesthetic reading, each reader's attention is directed as fully as possible to all aspects, both cognitive and affective, of the experience the text evokes. Out of this aesthetic involvement, readers shape for themselves the personal, lived-through literary experience that each knows as the novel, play, or poem. Throughout Rosenblatt's writings, she has insisted that the experiential nature of aesthetic response is the essence of the humane nature of literature (e.g., 1983, pp. 5–9).

Rosenblatt advises teachers to make sure that activities in the literature class primarily support aesthetic reading. Students should be encouraged and helped to experience fully their own evocations of a literary work and then guided to reflect self-critically on these experiences. As they voice their individual responses, they may then be directed to consider what in the text and in themselves evoked these responses. The discussions provide a means of furthering insights into alternative interpretations and divergent points of view, out of which each reader may fashion a new and richer synthesis of the work (Rosenblatt, 1983, pp. 280–290).

CREATING A SETTING FOR SPONTANEITY

"The problem that the teacher faces first of all . . . is the creation of a situation favorable to a vital experience of literature" (Rosenblatt, 1983, p. 61). If readers are to become sensitive to their own personal responses to literary works, the classroom setting must encourage the free and spontaneous expression of these responses. For most of us, this means a restructuring of the classroom environment.

The students with whom I worked were accustomed to the more traditional type of classroom interactions in which all student remarks are addressed to the teacher. It was necessary to encourage them to speak directly to one another. In the beginning, I did this overtly: "Charles, if you don't agree with Steven, talk to him directly." The students were quick to respond to nonverbal cues as well—my quizzical look from one to another or a gesture inviting someone to speak up. In line with transactional theory, I saw this open exchange as a "necessary condition" (Rosenblatt, 1983, p. 75), but it was only the beginning. Students next had to be encouraged to become aware of their responses to a work of literature, and, finally, to reflect critically on those responses.

TILTING TOWARD AN AESTHETIC STANCE

As the students became more independent in their discussions and more comfortable and trusting in this classroom context, I focused on strategies that would guide them to an awareness of their personal transactions with and responses to the texts we were reading. Rosenblatt (1983) reminds us continually that "the teacher of literature, especially, needs to keep alive this view of the literary work as personal evocation, the product of creative activity" (p. 280). Several strategies were used to tilt the emphasis toward aesthetic reading.

First, time for reading from the work of literature featured in the discussions was allowed in class. Rosenblatt (1978) states that "the poem must be thought of as an event in time" (p. 12). I hoped to make the literary passages we were about to discuss exist for us as an event in our time. The decision whether to read in class or not was often made as the students entered and arranged themselves. If they were obviously ready to talk about the book, or even had already started to do so on their way downstairs, I usually went with their interest. If they entered tepid or if some were unprepared, I wanted to make sure there was some fresh experience of the work before we began to talk. The reading in class might be individual and silent. More often, however, when a book was new to the students, had unfamiliar names, a particularly poetic cadence, or underlying notes of humor, sarcasm, or melodrama, I found it most effective to read aloud to the class.

Another strategy was to include an opportunity for students to write, and sometimes to draw, whatever was uppermost in their minds during the discussion periods. As the findings show, not all children spoke as fluently as they wrote, and some participants did not wish to share their personal responses with a group. A great deal of latitude was allowed in this regard. Often, a student reluctant to share in the beginning would come around to wishing to do so by the end of the period or on another occasion.

Also, class sessions often began with an open-ended question like "talk about what touched you the most." After opportunity for all to share freely was offered, questioning and instruction were based on material from students' opening remarks.

Students were encouraged to be aware of what they were experiencing as they read. This was often done through an opening question or writing assignment phrased to focus on the experience. Sometimes it was "What touched you the most?" at the end of a book. Again, they might be asked to start a new book with paper and pencil at hand, read as long as they liked, and when they had something to say, stop and write about the point where they felt they had really become hooked into the story. Sometimes I would ask them to form small groups and decide what was most important to talk about in a particular book or passage and plan how they might lead a discussion of it.

Attention was directed back toward the text during the discussions to see what had evoked particular responses or what could support a reader's interpretations or predictions. Rosenblatt (1983) frequently stresses that not all interpretations are equally valid. She also stresses the importance of encouraging readers to become aware of what in themselves gives rise to responses that seem highly idiosyncratic or out of relation to what the text seems to present (pp. 277–287).

Rereading of texts and future returns to a text were encouraged. On occasion, I assigned the students to reread a passage before going on because I felt the class discussion had enlightened what was previously obscure for them. As can happen with such a group, occasionally some students already had read a text that was being newly assigned. They were expected to reread it as necessary so that it would be fresh for them. I was, of course, always rereading the texts I was using with them. I discussed this with the children and drew on the experiences of those in the class who were already confirmed rereaders. Gradually, the students began to refer freely to what they had missed the first time and to express pleasure at the prospect of savoring a favorite work again. This response was especially true with *Bridge to Terebithia* by Katherine Paterson, when child readers who had been somewhat numbed by the shock of Leslie's death in their first reading found new richness in the story before and after that climactic episode on their second reading.

Finally, the accumulation of literary experiences over time was provided for. Rich experiences in aesthetic reading in childhood provide a seedbed out of which literary knowledge can grow naturally. Such growth did begin in our classes, and the students began to refer spontaneously to books previously read and to compare one book with another.

EVIDENCE OF AESTHETIC READING

Rosenblatt (1983) makes the distinction that, although the experience of reading literature is aesthetic, the language of discussion about literature probably is not. The public and supportive aspects of a literature class may therefore be studied more easily than the primary but private act of reading. From the beginning, however, a guiding focus of this research was to look for evidence of aesthetic reading that a teacher might discern in a classroom. Several behaviors were observed recurring often over time.

Absorption in the act of reading whenever time was given for silent reading during class sessions was perhaps the most common and easily discernible sign of involvement in a story. On numerous occasions, students were reluctant to leave such periods of silent reading and join in the group or to leave their reading to go to their next daily activity. On one occasion, while reading Katherine Paterson's *The Great Gilly Hopkins* with the girls in the sixth grade in a voluntary noontime session, Rachel came in with the book, sat down to read while she was eating her lunch, and continued reading right through the discussion carried on by the other girls.

An easing of position, relaxing, sprawling, or sitting on the floor often accompanied absorption in the story. In the spring of the year, while working with the books of Madeleine L'Engle, the students began asking if they could sit on the floor while we were talking. Generally when this happened, I joined the students on the floor. Over the years, in many teaching situations I have noticed this spontaneous move toward relaxed posture as a group begins to take ownership and literally as well as figuratively gets down to earth with the work at hand.

Strong verbal expressions of feeling experienced during a story are certainly the most easily identified signs of involvement in a literary experience. With children at this age level, these remarks tend to be rather sweeping: "This is the best book I've ever read." "I loved this book." "I couldn't stop reading it." "I cried so much when I was reading this book." Children are often not very articulate about their reasons for "loving" a book. A major purpose of the group discussions was precisely to help readers tease out, name, and explore such responses. During the course of any particular class session, after attention was focused on one or another passage or episode in a book, the students became more articulate as the discussion became more specific. In the following segment of transcript, the students were discussing their strong feelings of identification with Sara and Charlie when Charlie was lost in *Summer of the Swans* by Betsy Byars.

TEACHER: What has the author done that makes us feel that *I* was the one . . . that makes us look as though . . . that *I* was looking for him?

SHARON: When Charlie got that gash in his chest, you could almost feel that it happened to you.

RACHEL: Yeah . . . ow . . . it was real . . . like . . . I was very upset.

TEACHER: Let's find that section. If it's that strong, then let's find it and see why.

STEVEN: I know that Sarah was confident. She said that, "I know he's there. I can feel it inside me."

TEACHER: How has the author made that so strong?

SHARON: Lots of details.

TEACHER: Look at it carefully. Try to see what's there.

STEVEN: It says, "threw him back"—threw! It was like an exaggeration.

RACHEL: It could have . . . It could.

STEVEN: I mean not actually throw him back.

RACHEL: It's like a trampoline effect. He ran into it with such force that he just sprang backwards.

ALL: [Everybody talking at once]

SHARON: When I was in Michigan, I ran into a cable and I got a big red mark and it threw me back.

STEVEN: Suddenly.

RACHEL: The surprise of it.

STEVEN: His bare chest . . . and he is gasping.

Aesthetic involvements do not invariably produce pleasant or positive responses. While reading *Bridge to Terebithia,* students commented that they "couldn't believe" that Leslie had died and that they could "hardly stand to read it." Not only this group but others I have worked with have denied the implied ending of *The Bears' House* by Marilyn Sachs. Although Fran Ellen is given the Bears' house to keep and her teacher is seeking help for the sick baby sister, an adult reader experienced in the ways of social agencies might expect that the children would be sent to foster homes, perhaps separated. Most of my students fantasized that the absent father would return home and the mother would then get well, although there is more in the text to suggest the opposite. When the children became emotionally involved with texts, in general they went more with the strength of their own inner construct of what they felt the story should be than they did with a close reading of the text. The same tendency was observed at the end of *The Great Gilly Hopkins.* Once the student readers realized that Gilly's mother really did not love her, they anticipated Gilly's return to her foster mother, Maime Trotter, even as Trotter, in the words of the text, is strengthening Gilly to remain with her grandmother.

The desire to share responses and the ability to explore them in extended discussion became another hallmark of aesthetic reading in this class setting once an atmosphere of trust and openness had been established. I would like to note, however, that in my experience the lack of such exchanges need not necessarily indicate to a teacher that aesthetic reading is not taking place. I have worked with several groups in which the personalities or interpersonal relations were such that discussions were disappointing, but individual students privately expressed strong aesthetic responses.

Identifying with and playacting a situation can often be observed as readers become absorbed in a discussion of a passage meaningful to them. While reading *The Summer of the Swans* as fifth-graders, some of the students became aware of their own movements while reading:

STEVEN: When he put the watch up to his ear, I put my watch up to my ear, too.

SHARON: When you read something that's unusual in a book, you feel like it's really you.

EDWARD: He's limping . . .

SHARON: Yeah, and you walk . . .

EDWARD: You walk with a little shuffle.

Rachel was a week later than the other girls in starting to read *The Great Gilly Hopkins,* and she was vehement in her appreciation of it as she entered the library that noon for a lunchtime discussion period. The rest of us were talking about the early chapters. As Rachel settled down at the table where we were eating and talking, she opened her book and commenced to read to catch up. She had obtained a piece of bubble gum, like the heroine in the story, and while she read she chewed and blew bubbles until the rest of us noticed her likeness to the picture of Gilly on the cover of the book Rachel was holding up before her face.

Making connections between literature and other life situations became increasingly common for the students as they became more deeply absorbed in the stories. Rosenblatt (1978) writes about how during the literary experience "the boundary between the inner and outer world breaks down" (p. 26) under the intensity of the aesthetic reading experience. Consequently, this was an aspect of aesthetic reading that I was on the alert for, and I observed it manifest itself in many different ways. Notice how Steven and Mark, in the following passage, drew on another life experience to illustrate Sara's emotions, which they were attempting to name during a discussion of *The Summer of the Swans:*

CHARLES: Maybe she was really, really worried, and she didn't want to show it, and she kept telling herself that . . . oh . . . that she was going to find him . . . because she *had* to find him. She was worried about what would happen if she . . .

STEVEN: I think that she was really worried, but she was confident, and she didn't want to show it because she would get everyone panicked.

TEACHER: Now you are saying confident, Steven, but I'm not hearing Charles say confident.

STEVEN: She is worried and she knows if she says it . . . like in a bus accident, if you say, "I want to get out, I want to get out," you'll cause a lot of problems. You just stay calm yourself.

RACHEL: I wouldn't . . .

MARK: You've got to keep your worries to yourself or you'll cause all sort of more trouble. If you panic and you try to get out and you're yelling that everybody should get out of your way . . . you have to keep calm and wait.

As the children worked when challenged by another student or, as here, by the teacher, they refined their insights as they drew on other life experiences. In the preceding segment, Steven moved from the word confident to the word calm, with the connotation of calm under stress. A few moments later, the students went on to contrast Sara's behavior with that of Aunt Willie, who was "being so hysterical." The sensitivity of Mark's insights throughout this discussion may be noted again as he continues to say that "maybe she was being so hysterical because she thought it was her fault for asking Sara to take Charlie to see the swans."

On another occasion, toward the end of the sixth-grade year, Cynthia recognized in herself the same anger she was reading about in the life of Gilly Hopkins. When we were discussing what made Gilly "mean or different," to use Cynthia's words, she continued, "Well, I mean, like, sometimes I'm really mean to my step-dad just because I want my dad better than I want him . . . I do that a lot. . . . Well, Gilly doesn't have either parent. I've got one parent." When one of the girls responded in a soft tone of support for this last statement, "And at least you see your dad," Cynthia replied, "Once a year or so, so I do see him."

"The English classroom, if it is a place where literature really resides, becomes the arena for a linkage with a world of the student" (Rosenblatt, 1983, p. 288). Literature's essentially experiential nature allows these linkages to occur. Because of these connections, readers may be able to turn from the literary experience to other life experiences with broader understanding and increased sensitivity.

GROUP TALK, LEVELS OF THINKING, AND THE EXTENSION OF INSIGHT

As the months went by and the proportion of student talk increased, I noted that the students were spontaneously achieving and sustaining higher levels of thinking. By November of the first school year of the study, I found that I was pointing out these advances to other teachers, the principal, the children's parents when I saw them, or anyone who was interested in the sometimes messy and excited discussions going on in my room. I had been working with the taxonomies of Hilda Taba (Taba & Elzey, 1964) and Benjamin Bloom (1954) for some time and found that practice had given me an ease in detecting and charting changes in levels of thinking. Taba emphasized the role of the teacher in bringing about lifts in thinking. When she charts such lifts in her work, they are in a context of controlled interactions, usually with the teacher and a student taking alternate turns. I had for some time been aware that children were able to start independently or lift spontaneously in an atmosphere arranged by the teacher to provide them greater freedom in initiating topics and more direct student interaction. Now I had the documentation to verify my perceptions.

To show student growth over time, I selected the segment of transcript that showed the highest number of student turns of talk without teacher intervention in the fall, winter, and spring quarters. The segment for the winter quarter, presented in Figure 11–1,

Page and line numbers		Levels of thinking			
		Recall	Compre-hension	Appli-cation	Analysis
P. 3, 26	Mark: It's like if something goes wrong . . . like your mother would take you in with her open arms and this is like the same thing. The meadow took Kit in.			•	
	June: She doesn't even have a mother.	•			
27	[M: It's like an old, old saying, "Mother Earth" . . . precisely.]			•	
28	Rachel: She didn't have a mother or a father or grandfather; she just had herself and her aunts.	•			
30	June: Her aunts?	•			
	Rachel [reading from text p. 91]: "Thee did well, child, to come to the Meadow. There is always a cure here when the heart is troubled."	•			
32	Mark: Sometime I always wonder if Hannah is really a witch because that thing that was always magic to everyone else was . . . the blueberry cobbler.				•
35	Steven: No, I don't think so: she's been through so many hardships that she's understanding a lot of problems of everybody else.				•
37	Rachel: Like her with her husband when they first came to that town, they wouldn't take her in.				•
39	June: Blueberry cake.	•			
40	Miranda: No. Blueberry shortcake.	•			
41	Rachel: So she knows what it's like to try to make good and everything.	•			
42	Steven: Yeah, and rejected and everything.				•
43	Mark: Yeah, she's been rejected before and she knows what it . . . understands it so when somebody is like that she tells them . . . not trying to mean . . . like she was treated.				•

FIGURE 11–1 *Excerpts from the transcript of the group talk, January 24*

Page and line numbers		Levels of thinking			
		Recall	Compre-hension	Appli-cation	Analysis
	Steven: And also, she was good, she takes her mind off what her problems are and she'll discuss something else.				●
48	Edward: She's just like the meadow. She, like . . . she soothes.			●	
49	Steven: I think she is the meadow, or something, because she lives there and Kit said that the meadow took her in the so like . . . so did Hannah Tupper. She came in and she said, "Here . . . have some blueberry pie," and she was really nice to her and I think that Hannah was a better mother to her than anybody.			●	
P. 4, 4	Miranda: Except maybe her grandfather, but—			●	
5	Steven: I mean anybody in the town.			●	
6	Mark: She's really getting to like Hannah. I mean Hannah was really like her grandmother or something or like a mother.		●		
8	Miranda: She was like that to Nat.		●		
9	Rachel: I agree that Hannah is like a grandmother, because some people can understand their grandparents better than their parents, and, or something like that, and . . . I forgot what I was going to say.			●	●
13	Miranda: When you get older, you're supposed to get wiser, and she's been through all the experiences.			●	
15	June: Not all . . . just some.	●			
16	Miranda: Yeah.	●			
17	Mark: Not all, but a lot of them, a lot of major problems.	●			
18	Edward: And she's really old.			●	
19	Rachel: She says, "The answer is in the heart; you can always hear it if you listen for it." [text p. 97]			●	

is taken from a discussion of *The Witch of Blackbird Pond* by Elizabeth George Speare. The students were discussing the passages in the story in which Kit first discovers the meadow and meets Hannah Tupper, the "witch."

Mark opened this segment of discussion by putting into his own words and interpreting the effect the meadow had on Kit. June picked up the word mother and made the factual statement that "she doesn't even have a mother." My interjection at that point was to validate the metaphoric interpretation. Rachel, however, continued with the factual listing of the relatives who had died, but with an expressive cadence that almost reads like a litany of Kit's losses and loneliness. June interjected with another factual correction, but Rachel by this time had returned to the text and was now reading aloud a passage to reinforce the metaphoric interpretation of the meadow as comforter. In the passage she chose, Hannah comes upon Kit sobbing in the meadow and begins to speak to Kit in the words Rachel was reading.

Mark's response to this passage was a question that lifted the discussion to an analysis of whether or not Hannah is really a witch. He supported his implied no with the reason that her magic is "blueberry cobbler." First Steven and then Rachel supported his position with additional arguments based on the text. There are several points to note here. In this passage, a lift in thinking to the analysis level was effected spontaneously by a student, Mark, rather than in answer to a teacher's question. Discussions such as this open a window for the teacher into the ongoing process of the students' interpretive responses and thence to consideration of ways in which the text comes to life as a literary work for student readers. In this instance, Hannah's character was unfolding for the child readers at the pace it unfolded for Kit in the story. When children are permitted to arrive at and defend their own insights, thinking at a much higher level is possible than if the teacher had told them "of course, we know Hannah isn't really a witch" based on her prior reading of this and other books and a more sophisticated understanding of witchcraft and the historical period.

The general intent of the response from the boys throughout is that Kit's coming to the meadow is most significant, and this for the meadow's metaphorical meaning. Seen in this context, the overall intent of the discussion is analytical. Mark was drawn to a discussion of the symbolic meaning of meadow. His analogy was "like if your mother would take you in with her open arms." Steven returned to the idea of mother by considering Hannah as mother to Kit and began an evaluation of Hannah's mothering that is extended by Miranda as she proposed the grandfather in Barbados as the best mother. Mark provided a further extension of the mothering concept by suggesting that Hannah was "really like her grandmother," and Miranda extended still further by contributing that Hannah was also like this to Nat.

Rachel, however, has been struck by the word grandmother, and rather than continue the discussion of the extent of Hannah's influence, she returned to an analysis of its quality. She remarked that grandmother was a better analogy for the relationship than mother and continued with a defense of this position. In the midst of her remarks, however, she forgot what her original point had been, and Miranda picked up with an additional point: "When you get older, you're supposed to get wiser." This statement in itself might be considered a lift in thinking within the overall passage, because a generalization is introduced, lifting from the specific of Hannah to older persons in general.

Looking at the segment as a whole, it is almost as if two discussions were continuing simultaneously. Mark and Steven, with contributions by Edward and Rachel, were pursuing the themes of meadow/mother/Hannah; June, Miranda, and to some extent Rachel, were exploring in a sort of counterpoint the details of Kit's relatives, who mothers her the most, and, in the case of June, the details of the blueberry cake.

THINKING IN AN EMOTIONALLY COLORED CONTEXT

In a chapter entitled "Emotion and Reason" in *Literature as Exploration* (1983), Rosenblatt examines the interplay between one's responses to a literary work and the action of reason in dealing with these responses. She contends that the processes of our responses to life situations and personalities are essentially the same as our responses to literary texts.

> Literature . . . may provide the emotional tension and conflicting attitudes out of which spring the kind of thinking that can later be assimilated into actual behavior. The emotional character of the students' response to literature offers opportunity to develop the ability to *think rationally within an emotionally colored context.*
> (pp. 227–228.)

As I watched the students in my groups, I saw again and again that the most fertile discussions grew out of emotional tensions. Often the students' discussions exploded into what we came to identify as "moments of passion" (Ely & Anzul, 1989). Among their characteristics are: an unwonted fluency, a momentum fueled by excitement over the ideas being discussed, joy and a sense of play that accompany the proliferation of building ideas, or, conversely, sudden moments of quiet or withdrawal. Topics of concern or interest may be brought up spontaneously by the students, often interrupting or overriding a previously stated agenda or line of discussion. This happened during the discussion of *A Wizard of Earthsea* by Ursula LeGuin when the students had been carrying on a debate in their classroom during the week over whether or not Ged should have left his master, Ogion, and gone to the School for Wizards. This topic had exploded during the previous discussion period, lasted through the week, and was still of passionate concern a week later.

It would be a mistake to conclude that thinking in the discussion groups always proceeded straightforwardly during these processes. The segments quoted in this chapter demonstrate the circular or erratic directions the discussions sometimes took. When viewing the progress of group discussion, the findings in this study indicate that students move through a succession of response modes and that their thinking is richer when they do so. In transactional terms, they move from their aesthetic responses to a text to an expression of that involvement and, through some mix of perception and interpretation, perhaps to evaluation. If students begin with an evaluative comment, as a teacher, I would generally direct them to the perceptive mode and hope that they would explore further what in the text inspired their original judgment.

Rosenblatt quotes John Dewey as she points out that constructive thinking usually grows out of some sort of tension and is colored by it. In education, therefore, it is not profitable to attempt to eliminate "the emotional, passionate phase of action . . . in behalf of bloodless reason. More 'passions,' not fewer, is the answer. . . . Rationality . . . is not a force to evoke against impulse and habit. It is the attainment of a working harmony among diverse desires" (1983, p. 228).

IN RETROSPECT . . . AND PROSPECT

It has been several years since this particular research project was designed and documented. Because so much has happened since in language arts education, I am aware that what seemed innovative then seems less so now. Influenced by the whole language movement, many teachers have turned from textbooks and worksheets to literature as the mainstay of their reading program. The principles of giving students responsibility for and ownership of their work are much more widely accepted. Children are seen clustered in small groups for independent discussion of their reading and their writing (Atwell, 1987, 1990; Calkins, 1986, 1991; Perl & Wilson, 1986). Many teachers are now engaged in research in their classrooms, whether independently, with colleagues, or in collaboration with university researchers (Goswami & Stillman, 1987; Jaggar & Smith-Burke, 1985).

Three metathemes that seem to run through my findings have been reinforced many times over in whole language and teacher-as-researcher literature. The first has to do with the power of the process of teacher research. My work as a teacher powered my research, and my work as a researcher cast new light on my teaching. I came to feel, in the course of those two years, as though I were in a "hall of mirrors" (Anzul & Ely, 1988) in which every aspect of my work reflected off of and enriched all the others.

Secondly, the multifaceted nature of student growth became quite evident. As I analyzed the lesson transcripts, I found that the segments showing higher levels of thinking also usually were those in which the emotions were the most involved. As children learned to take more responsibility for their own discussions, they also became more adept at marshalling reasons to explain their interpretations. As membership in the literature groups became more open, children not usually judged to be top readers saw themselves as capable of participating in this enrichment activity and in time were moved to a higher group in the classroom. Much of the growth that I documented and that their teachers also observed was not what standardized tests are designed to measure. The current movement toward alternative methods of assessment appears to be addressing some of these concerns.

The third metatheme has to do with the value of transactional theory as a framework in which to design educational programs. The power of this approach has become evident time after time during this project, in my teaching and research since, and in reader-response literature in general. I would like to single out the experiential nature of aesthetic reading to comment on here, however. Although literature is becoming a much more integral part of reading and language arts curricula, its transactional nature is not always understood and honored. Thus, workbooks designed to accompany sets of novels in paperback format, for instance, often support efferent rather than aesthetic reading.

As teachers of literature, we must continue to realize that the personal experience of literature, as of all the arts (Dewey, 1934), is the unique source of its value. "A work of art . . . is a mode of living . . . an extension, an amplification of life itself." Together with Rosenblatt, we can continue to urge that our students be given ample opportunity "to add *this* kind of experience to the other kinds of desirable experience that life may then offer" (Rosenblatt, 1983, p. 278).

PROFESSIONAL RESOURCES

Anzul, Margaret (1988). *Exploring literature with children within a transactional framework.* Doctoral dissertation, New York University.

Anzul, Margaret (1991). Reflecting. In M. Ely, et al. (Eds.), *Doing qualitative research.* New York: Falmer.

Anzul, Margaret, & Ely, Margot (1988). Halls of mirrors: The introduction of the reflective mode. *Language Arts, 65* (7), 675–687.

Applebee, Arthur N. (1978). *The chid's concept of story, ages two to seventeen.* Chicago: University of Chicago Press.

Atwell, Nancie (1987). *In the middle: Writing, reading, and learning with adolescents.* Portsmouth, NH: Boynton/Cook.

Atwell, Nancie (Ed.) (1990). *Coming to Know: Writing to learn in the intermediate grades.* Portsmouth, NH: Heinemann Educational Books.

Bloom, Benjamin (1954). *Taxonomy of educational objectives: Part I, cognitive domain.* New York: Longman.

Calkins, Lucy McCormick (1986). *The art of teaching writing.* Portsmouth, NH: Heinemann Educational Books.

Calkins, Lucy McCormick (1991). *Living between the lines.* Portsmouth, NH: Heinemann Educational Books.

Cooper, Charles R. (Ed.) (1985). *Researching response to literature and the teaching of literature: Points of departure.* Norwood, NJ: Ablex.

Dewey, John (1934). *Art as experience.* New York: Capricorn Books.

Ely, Margot, & Anzul, Margaret (1989). Moments of passion: On looking out of the corner of one's eye. *Language Arts, 66* (4), 742–748.

Ely, Margot, with Anzul, Margaret; Friedman, Teri; Garner, Diane; & Steinmetz, Ann McCormack (1991). *Doing qualitative research: Circles within circles.* New York: Falmer.

Goswami, Dixie, & Stillman, P. R. (Eds.) (1987). *Reclaiming the classroom: Teacher research as an agency for change.* Portsmouth, NH: Boynton/Cook.

Holland, Norman N. (1975). *5 readers reading.* New Haven, CT: Yale University Press.

Jaggar, Angela, & Smith-Burke, M. Trika (Eds.) (1985). *Observing the language learner.* Newark, DE: International Reading Association; Urbana, IL: National Council of Teachers of English.

Perl, Sandra, & Wilson, Nancy (1986). *Through teacher's eyes.* Portsmouth, NH: Heinemann Educational Books.

Purves, Alan, & Beach, Richard (c. 1972). *Literature and the reader: Research in response to literature, reading interests, and the teaching of literature.* Urbana, IL: National Council of Teachers of English.

Rosenblatt, Louise M. (1978). *The reader, the text, the poem: The transactional theory of the literary work.* Carbondale: Southern Illinois University Press.

Rosenblatt, Louise M. (1983). *Literature as exploration* (4th ed.). New York: Modern Language Association.

Schon, Donald A. (1983). *The reflective researcher: How professionals think in action.* New York: Basic Books.

Taba, Hilda, & Elzey, Fremont (1964). Teaching strategies and thought processes. *Teachers College Record, 65,* 524–534.

CHILDREN'S LITERATURE

This list of the books used during the two years of literature discussions that form the basis of this chapter is included here for the convenience of readers. In no sense does this list constitute a canon. It was determined by the interests and abilities of the particular students, by my own tastes, and by what I had available in multiple copies at the time.

Byars, Betsy (1970). *The summer of the swans*. New York: Viking.

De Angeli, Marguerite (1949). *The door in the wall*. New York: Doubleday.

LeGuin, Ursula (1968). *A wizard of Earthsea*. New York: Parnassus.

L'Engle, Madeleine (1962). *A wrinkle in time*. New York: Farrar, Straus & Giroux.

L'Engle, Madeleine (1973). *A wind in the door*. New York: Farrar, Straus & Giroux.

Lewis, C. S. (1950). *The lion, the witch, and the wardrobe*. London: Macmillan.

Paterson, Katherine (1977). *Bridge to Terebithia*. New York: Crowell.

Paterson, Katherine (1978). *The great Gilly Hopkins*. New York: Crowell.

Pinkwater, Manus (1975). *Wingman*. New York: Dell.

Sachs, Marilyn (1971). *The bears' house*. New York: Doubleday.

Speare, Elizabeth George (1958). *The witch of Blackbird Pond*. Boston: Houghton Mifflin.

Tolkein, J. R. R. (1938). *The hobbit*. Boston: Houghton Mifflin.

12

Puerto Rican Students Respond to Children's Books with Puerto Rican Themes

Ann Egan-Robertson

Despite the burgeoning interest in the field of reader response during the 1980s, there remains a dearth of research investigating the responses of children to books representing their own cultural experience. From the work of cognitive psychologists, anthropologists, and literary theorists and critics, educators have grown in awareness of the fact that the acquisition and learning of language—oral and written—occurs within specific sociocultural contexts. Negative cognitive consequences can result from a lack of appreciation and affirmation of the variety of linguistic and literary experiences students bring to their schooling (see Donaldson, 1979; Heath, 1983; Rosenblatt, 1978; Sims, 1982; Vygotsky, 1978, 1986). In the case of second language learners, when this perspective is neglected, the acculturation process, already stressful by nature, is exacerbated, all too often resulting in academic failure (Cummins, 1986; Nieto, 1992; Trueba, 1987).

Ethnographic research conducted from multidisciplinary perspectives indicates that the child should inform instructional content and practice (Goelman, Oberg, & Smith, 1984; Harste, Woodward, & Burke, 1984). Yet little research has been conducted documenting readers' responses to the representation of their culture in literature. Though limited in scope, the study described in this chapter attempts to address this gap by exploring the responses of Puerto Rican students to picture books written about the Puerto Rican experience.

THE SETTING OF THE STUDY

The field study site was an urban middle school of approximately 400 students. The New England community was among the earliest planned industrial cities in the country. Historically, the city has been populated by waves of immigrants. The newest group to struggle to establish themselves are Puerto Rican families. Sixty-five percent of the city's schoolchildren are of Puerto Rican heritage. During the 1988–1989 academic year, 200 students dropped out of the public school system; of these, 127 were Hispanic. Low test scores and a high drop-out rate among the city's students need to be understood within the sociopolitical context of schooling for minority students in this country (see Cummins, 1986; Nieto, 1992).

THE PARTICIPANTS

Maria, Edwin, Carmen, and José were my students in activity period during the first six weeks of school. All but Maria were also in my homeroom class. In both of these eighth-grade groups, my role was advisor, advocate, and homework assistant. Maria, Edwin, and Carmen spent this period every day reading avidly. We talked informally about books as time and interest allowed. Therefore, when it was time to conduct a research project through which I would gather within-culture reactions to books written about the Puerto Rican experience, I decided to invite these students to participate.

Desiring to have balanced gender representation and to include a student who was born and schooled in Puerto Rico prior to moving to the area, I invited José to participate in the research project. José is similar to Gilmore's (1986) informants in that he was comfortable reading quite complicated texts, as he demonstrated as an accomplished Dungeons and Dragons enthusiast; however, he performed poorly in English class. Gilmore argues that the contrast between literacy achievement in and out of classrooms results from the narrow definition of literacy and the nature of the instructional interactions in school.

THE CRITERIA FOR SELECTING TEXTS

Each of the four books selected for the study fit an extended category of Sims's (1982) culturally conscious books. That is, to quote Sims, "They are books that reflect, with varying degrees of success, the social and cultural traditions associated with growing up Afro-American in the United States. The author's intent is to speak to Afro-American children about themselves and their lives while remaining accessible to others" (p. 50.). In this study, I extended Sims's definition of culturally conscious books to genres other than realistic fiction and to literature that portrays the growing up experience within other cultural traditions. The books chosen for review all have Puerto Rican characters and themes: *Juan Bobo and the Pig* (Chardiet, 1973), *Flamboyan* (Adoff, 1988), *Yagua Days* (Martel, 1976), and *My Aunt Otilia's Spirits/Los Espiritus De Mi Tia Otilia* (Garcia, 1983). Nieto (1982) found *Juan Bobo and the Pig* and *Yagua Days* to be authentic in their representation of the Puerto Rican experience. According to Nieto, *Juan Bobo* "faithfully retells one of our traditional folktales," and among the fifty-six books reviewed, it is the only book intended for the young reader that "reflects the richness of Puerto Rican oral and literary traditions" (p. 9). *Yagua Days*, Nieto writes, provides positive role models for children, particularly in the richly portrayed character of the uncle who is a *jibaro*, a peasant. Wanting a response to *Flamboyan* and *My Aunt Otilia's Spirits/Los Espiritus De Mi Tia Otilia* from a Puerto Rican adult before discussing them with the students, I consulted with my colleague, Eva Silva. Besides sharing her response to the literature, she also answered questions I had about the cultural content of the books.

PROCEDURES

The response group met for four forty-five minute sessions in a small conference room off the library. I taperecorded each of the four sessions. The first meeting was an orientation during which I formally outlined my purpose and plan for the study. After hearing brief introductions to the books, each student chose one. They were encouraged to share the book with a child of the age for which it was written. My intent was to incorporate an interactional literacy experience into the research plan and to provide for an incubation period prior to the response session (Huck, Hepler, & Hickman, 1987).

I explained to the group that as a teacher-researcher, I am particularly interested in finding books that accurately reflect student's various cultural experiences. I also told them that my intent was to share their responses with educators committed to becoming more knowledgeable about the cultural and linguistic heritages of their students. I discussed the objective of my research project: to gather cultural responses to four books, each of a different genre, intended for the young reader. I wanted to know whether in their opinions these books accurately and fairly represent the Puerto Rican experience. I was interested in finding books they would recommend to teachers for use in their classrooms and also in informing teachers of the kinds of cultural information that the participants have as members of the culture. I wanted answers to questions such as: What is there about this book with which you really identify? What makes it a special experience for you as a Puerto Rican to read this story? What did you or didn't you like about the book and why? And, in particular, what is it about how the culture is represented that you do or do not appreciate? If a reader is not Puerto Rican, what important cultural information or misinformation could the reader take away from the transaction with the text?

In the response group, the students shared their reactions and the reactions of their young friends or siblings and then read the book to the group members, who subsequently discussed their responses to it. I invited the students to suggest any alteration to my project plan that they felt would help meet the project goal. While no suggestion emerged in the introductory session, Maria and Carmen involved their parents in the analysis of the books, thus adding another set of informants and an intergenerational layer to the research. The acceptance of this invitation led the research in very interesting directions, particularly to an exploration of the significance of intergenerational interactions around text.

JUAN BOBO AND THE PIG, PREPARED BY JOSÉ

Several response themes that emerged from the interaction around the Puerto Rican version of the universal simpleton folktale are captured in the following excerpts from the transcripts of the discussion of *Juan Bobo and the Pig.* José read the story for the group with obvious familiarity and dramatic interpretation. Throughout the reading, the other group members responded with laughter and exasperation to the character of Juan Bobo. The animated response of the group signals the joy of recognition that emerged for the participants upon revisiting a favorite folktale. The students' recollections of relatives relating various versions of the Juan Bobo tale resound with clarity, strength, and poignancy.

JOSÉ: Juan Bobo is a stupid kid; the more he thinks, the dumber he gets.

TEACHER: You began, José, by saying you grew up hearing Juan Bobo stories. Is that true for everybody else too?

CHORUS RESPONSE: Yes.

TEACHER: Have you heard this version before? When? Where? Did it differ at all?

JOSÉ: The same. It is like I heard it when I was a little kid growing up in Puerto Rico.

TEACHER: Did you hear it at home, at school?

JOSÉ: It was at home. My grandfather used to tell it to me.

MARIA: When my father would tell it, the pig ended up in church. The pig would start running around in the church [laughter] and the mother would figure out it had to be Juan Bobo and she would chase him with the broomstick.

EDWIN: I heard it the same way. [Told brief church scene with enthusiasm.]

TEACHER: Are there other versions of Juan Bobo?

EDWIN: His mother sent him for a carton of milk and someone sold him a dead cow and he brought it home, thinking it would have milk.

[Group laughter.]

In the transcript, the voices of the participants' family members are heard in the recounting of their experiences of the events and interactions during which they all learned the Juan Bobo folktale. Maria and Edwin each heard the tale narrated by their fathers. Listen to the echoes of Maria's father's voice in her words: "When my father would tell it, the pig ended up in church. The pig would start running around in the church and the mother would figure out it had to be Juan Bobo and she would chase him with the broomstick." And, hear the resonance of Edwin's father's voice in Edwin's own: "His mother sent him for a carton of milk and someone sold him a dead cow and he brought it home, thinking it would have milk." For José, his grandfather had been the storyteller: "I heard it when I was a little kid growing up in Puerto Rico. My grandfather used to tell it to me."

The students' responses underscore the social nature of experience. Throughout this study are reminders of the Vygotskian tenet that language is a dynamic sociocultural institution, the vehicle by which one becomes integrated into the life of the community. Vygotsky describes how this occurs through his cultural law of development: the dialogue accompanying activity (interpsychological functioning) over time becomes inner speech (intrapsychological functioning). All thought processes appear on the social level before appearing on the individual level. Learning occurs within the zone of proximal development: "the distance between the actual developmental level, as determined by independent problem solving and the level of potential development, as determined through problem solving under adult guidance or in collaboration with more capable peers" (1978, p. 86).

Again and again in the discussions of the books, the theme of the family emerged, and the voices of various relatives resounded loudly through the talk and interpretations of the students. What made the reading of *Juan Bobo and the Pig* special for these Puerto Rican students was the memory of learning the tale and its lesson from their families.

MY AUNT OTILIA'S SPIRITS/LOS ESPIRITUS DE MI TIA OTILIA, **PREPARED BY EDWIN**

Commenting that he needed a book written in Spanish for his four-year-old neighborhood friend, Jorge, Edwin chose *My Aunt Otilia's Spirits/Los Espiritus De Mi Tia Otilia* because of its bilingual presentation. The book tells of the main character's aunt's visit from Puerto Rico. Early in the response session I questioned Edwin about his reading process:

TEACHER: Okay, so I assume you read the book just in Spanish, or did you read both sides of the page?
EDWIN: Both sides.
TEACHER: So how did you do that? Did you read it through in Spanish first?
EDWIN: I read it in English first and then I read it in Spanish.
TEACHER: And why did you choose the English first?
EDWIN: I know that so much better. . . . I read the English first so that then I might know what it said in Spanish. I can read Spanish, but I can't understand it well. I read the English first to understand what the Spanish said.

What made reading this book particularly special for the participants was its bilingual format. They felt that this type of book works to build literacy in both languages. The consensus of the group about the value of bilingual books is expressed well by Edwin in this excerpt from the transcript:

EDWIN: If someone doesn't know Spanish, it's not hard to figure out if the words are in English on the other page. Okay, this is the English, so this is what those words are in Spanish.
TEACHER: You feel it helps a person analyze the meanings of words when you are learning to read in one of the two languages.

Both the nature of the task, to read the book with a child, and the bilingual format of the book validated the linguistic experiences of the students. Possibly for the first time, Edwin, who has received all of his formal schooling in English, was in a position to ask a teacher for a book written in Spanish. Typically, students are asked to leave their first language outside the classroom and little or no space is provided in school for celebrating their linguistic heritage and accomplishments. In constructing classroom contexts for learning in which a student's native language is ignored, we treat students as though they were invisible. Anthropologist Renato Rosaldo (1989, pp. 209–210) writes: "North American notions of the 'melting pot' make immigration a site of cultural stripping away. Seen from the dominant society's point of view, the process of immigration strips individuals of their former cultures, enabling them to become American citizens—transparent, just like you and me, 'people without culture.' . . . To become middle class in North America is purportedly to become part of the culturally invisible mainstream. The immigrants, or at any rate their children or grandchildren, supposedly become absorbed into a national culture that erases their meaningful past—autobiography, history, heritage, language, and all the rest of the so-called cultural baggage." Clearly, schools must replace such assimilationist practices with mechanisms that reflect and celebrate the rich diversity of students.

Another important theme that was addressed in response to *My Aunt Otilia's Spirits/Los Espiritus De Mi Tia Otilia* was the place for spirits in the cultural experience of Puerto Ricans. Richard Garcia explains the source of the idea for his book in an author's note. "Like all stories, this one is based on a kernel of fact—and that is that my Aunt Otilia was accompanied by bed shakings and wall knockings everywhere she went. However, this was not regarded as unusual in my family, or as a cause for much concern. The supernatural had a place in our lives" (1983, p. 24). None of the participants had had the experience of hearing stories about the spirits of dead ancestors. When I questioned the students about the phenomenon, two expressed skepticism and two had open minds about people being able to communicate with the spirits of deceased people.

I also asked about the place for dream interpretation that Garcia discusses:

MARIA: We don't have a dream interpretation book, but usually in my family my mother and father remember their dreams and talk about what they mean. In Puerto Rican families there are traditional interpretations: for example, if someone is dressed in white it means somebody is going to die.

While the group agreed that *My Aunt Otilia's Spirits/Los Espiritus De Mi Tia Otilia* is an enjoyable story that represents an aspect of the Puerto Rican experience, it is not an aspect with which the students had experience. The strongest response centered around the bilingual presentation of the book.

FLAMBOYAN, PREPARED BY MARIA

Maria read *Flamboyan* with her six-year-old niece Alicia, her sister's daughter. *Flamboyan* is a fantasy story poem in which the main character flies around the island of Culebra observing the events that occur there. In introducing the book to the group, Maria shared that Alicia liked the story because of the bright, beautiful pictures. Alicia asked questions about the book, such as: "What do you mean her name is Flamboyan? Is her hair on fire?" While Maria enjoyed the pictures, she stated that they reminded her more of Hawaiian than Puerto Rican culture because they were so bright and colorful.

After Maria read the story to the group, I asked her to share more of her reactions to the fantasy:

MARIA: It didn't seem that particular to Puerto Rican culture.
TEACHER: Tell me more.
MARIA: I don't think that any Puerto Rican would name their daughter Flamboyan, for example.
TEACHER: You don't think so? Tell us more about that, please.
MARIA: My mother said that not in her lifetime has she known a Puerto Rican to name their child Flamboyan. It just did not click with what I know of Puerto Rico in the background of my parents.
TEACHER: So you shared this story with your parents, too? And they were saying from their own experience that this just didn't ring true for them? Can you tell us more of what your parents said?
MARIA: Coconut candies were sold where the little shops were and not by people walking on the beach. When she saw the pictures she said, "We never carried baskets on our heads."
MARIA [after Carmen reacted negatively to the whole village coming to rest in the middle of the day]: Puerto Rican people are known to keep busy throughout the day; they come to rest at night, at the end of the day when they sit down and eat the dinner. . . . It looks more like Hawaiian culture. . . . That's one of the things my parents were telling me when they looked at the illustrations.

Based on their own experience, the students discussed a number of details that they found inaccurate, such as that the whole village does not rest in the middle of the day and that women do not carry baskets on their heads. Maria's parents noted several other details as inaccurate. Sra. Ramírez said that even in her youth, women did not carry platters of fruit or baskets on their heads in Puerto Rico. Also, in real life, people did not walk the beach road selling candies as the book depicts. There were concession stands at the beach where candies were sold. In addition, the Ramírezs found the illustrations to "look more like Hawaiian culture" than Puerto Rican, citing as an example the brightness of the illustration of the fisherman on page 6. In reference to the name of the main character, Sra. Ramírez remarked "that not in her lifetime has she known a Puerto Rican to name their child Flamboyan."

I raised Sra. Silva's criticism of the book with the students. She was concerned that the book's setting, the Puerto Rican island of

Culebra, was noted only on the jacket and in the inscription on the bottom of the copyright page. The reader could get the impression that the setting is any Caribbean island or archipelago. The students talked about the influence of the genre on their response. While acknowledging that the opening line, "One sunshine morning in the month of July, on a small green island in the blue Caribbean sea, a baby girl is born," specifically characterizes the genre as fantasy, the students expressed concern that it might reinforce among some readers inaccurate concepts of homogeneity across Caribbean cultures.

While each of the four books included in this study fit an extended category of Sims's culturally conscious books, *Flamboyan* was the only book criticized as being inaccurate in many details, particularly in the illustrations. It is interesting to note that the book jacket remarks indicate that the illustrator had not been to Puerto Rico. The response of the group and one group member's family reflects the types of concerns that can arise for authors and illustrations of culturally conscious fantasy books.

YAGUA DAYS, PREPARED BY CARMEN

Yagua Days is a realistic fiction book about a young Puerto Rican child's first visit to Puerto Rico. When Carmen read *Yagua Days* to her eight-year-old brother Ricardo, who was just a few years younger than the main character in the book, he liked it very much. "He especially liked the sliding down the hill on a big leaf." Carmen felt this was her favorite part, too. A marvelous example of what Rosenblatt (1978) calls a poetic transaction is provided by Carmen in response to her reading about *yagua* days, which refers to riding a huge palm frond down a steep hillside on rainy days: "It reminds me of our sixth-grade trip to Mount Tom. When I was reading this, it reminded me of the water slide we went on there."

Maria brought the book home to share with her parents. As in the earlier transcript from the discussion of *Juan Bobo*, Maria's responses reflect the power of the parental voice. This observation underscores the evidence of the importance of the parents' experience in the child's construction of meaning around text. Maria does not have firsthand knowledge about *yagua* days, but she constructs her cultural identity through the intergenerational interaction and dialogue accompanying events. In this particular literacy event, the evocation of her father's childhood memories of growing up in the countryside are captured poignantly in the following excerpt from the transcript:

MARIA: My father felt the illustrations were really effective, particularly of the mountains [pp. 9–10]. He said, "They look just like where I grew up. The cluster of houses is typical." At the picture of the grandfather, my mother commented that the picture looks just like my father, the same build, same hat, just the style of his favorite old hat [p. 8].

When they read the part about the plantation, my father became homesick. This portion of the book in particular brought back a flood of memories of his childhood: climbing trees to harvest fruit, bringing the fruit down from the hills [reference to pp. 15–20].

This he really liked: the pictures of *yagua* days [pp. 23–24]. When I read this part of the story, he said it reminded him of what they used to do in Puerto Rico. He described the experience of riding down a wet hill on a huge leaf. He loved it: he went "Yahhhhhhhh!!!"

Knowing Maria's parents are not fluent English speakers, I asked about their reading. "Page by page is how I do it," Maria said in explaining her approach to translating books into Spanish. As noted in the earlier discussion about *My Aunt Otilia's Spirits/Los Espiritus De Mi Tia Otilia*, the rich linguistic and literacy practices of students all too often go unrecognized in the classrooms. The language and literacy stories of students (Harste, Woodward, & Burke, 1984) and Maria's and Edwin's explanations of their reading processes should inspire us anew to find ways to acknowledge and affirm the abilities of second language learners in our classrooms.

The following excerpt illustrates the students' responses to the theme of *Yagua Days*, expressed by Carmen as "finding out more about your roots." As Maria states, what makes reading *Yagua Days* special as a Puerto Rican is "the realistic portrayal of a Puerto Rican family, like when Adan meets the relatives he's never known." Both Carmen's and Maria's comments in the following excerpt reveal the anticipation and tension from the children's viewpoint surrounding the long-held tradition of meeting extended family members for the first time.

MARIA: The book is a realistic portrayal of a Puerto Rican family, like when Adan meets relatives he's never known. It usually happens in many Puerto Rican families because I have relatives in Puerto Rico that I don't even know.

TEACHER: And you've heard of them for years.

MARIA: And saw the pictures and I'm, like, "These are my family!" My grandmother has like ten stacks of albums of family I haven't even met.

CARMEN: This summer my aunt died and all my family came down the same day. I have, like, a lot, a lot of family. My grandmother has a small house; I mean, the house is packed. People you don't even know come up to you, squeeze you so hard, and they give you a kiss. And I'm, like, "Who are you? I don't even know you!"

MARIA: When she took my oldest brother Luis back to Puerto Rico, he really didn't know any of his family at that time. She says he thought he was going to be bored to death because he thought there'd be a lot of old people around, but he found that he enjoyed being at the beach, talking late into the night with his cousins.

Another topic the group discussed was the main character's naivete. In the story, the postman pulls Adan's leg about his lack of knowledge of Puerto Rico by telling the boy that fruits and vegetables were grown in vans in Puerto Rico. Maria's response captures the group consensus that the characterization of Adan was unrealistic: "Most Puerto Rican kids would know something of Puerto Rico from their parents, and he seemed not to have that knowledge." Their response was corroborated by Maria's mother, who said about Adan, "Well, he must have been dumb if he believed that mangoes and papayas are grown in vans!"

Edwin's voice is missing from the transcripts in this section because he became ill toward the end of the study. When he returned to school, I gave him a copy of *Yagua Days* as a token of appreciation for participating in the study. Upon finishing it, he remarked that it was a "good book" and that he had enjoyed it. A remarkable example of how the lived-through experience influences the transaction with a text was provided by Edwin months after this project ended. One's experience of a book changes as one's experience changes. Compare his earlier response to Edwin's reaction upon his return from a vacation trip to Puerto Rico. "This is my story! I'm just like the boy in *Yagua Days*. Well, my father doesn't own a *bodega*, but he's always told me about rainy days in Puerto Rico and now I know what he means!" Then he shared with me a draft of a piece of writing he had begun. The purpose of the piece, he explained, was to capture his first experience of *yagua* days.

INTERPRETATION

The responses of these Puerto Rican students, their friends, and their family members to books with Puerto Rican themes richly portray the transaction of reader and text that Rosenblatt (1978) calls a poem. Again and again in their discussions these students brought their cultural experiences to the reading process (Rosenblatt, 1978). José's recounting of learning *Juan Bobo* tales from his grandfather in Puerto Rico, Edwin's adroitness with the English and Spanish versions of *My Aunt Otilia's Spirits/Los Espiritus De Mi Tia Otilia,* the group members' challenge of the accuracy of *Flamboyan,* Maria's account of reading *Yagua Days* with her parents, and Carmen's evocation of a memory—meeting a houseful of relatives following her aunt's death—in response to Adan's experience in *Yagua Days* are particularly poignant poems.

These children draw on their collective cultural memories and frames of reference acquired from their own living that Sims (1982) writes about. Again and again the transcripts reveal the power of the parental voice in the students' responses. The importance of family and levels of experience in the construction of meaning around text is evident as one hears mother, father, brother, grandmother, grandfather, and extended family members, whose voices were included by the students in their analyses and interpretations of the books. One finds evidence that through the intergenerational interaction and dialogue accompanying family events, children construct their own cultural identity (Vygotsky, 1978, 1986).

IMPLICATIONS

The opportunities for creative multicultural curriculum development abound when teachers intentionally find ways of weaving familial and community literary experiences into the fabric of classroom literacy events. By inviting students and their parents to share their meanings and by listening carefully to their stories, educators can validate the linguistic and literary experiences students bring to their schooling. These kinds of conversations can provide the foundation for language and literacy learning in classrooms and counteract the tendency to negate these in the curriculum (Nieto, 1992; Trueba, 1987). This dialogue enhances the interactional patterns through which cognitive development occurs (Vygotsky, 1978, 1986).

Since 1980, the number of culturally conscious children's books that have been published has decreased dramatically (Nieto, 1991; Sims-Bishop, 1990). In a visit to our school, acclaimed Nuyorican poet Sandra Maria Esteves advised students to address this problem by doing as she did with her book *Tropical Rains* (1984): "I encourage you not to wait for someone to say they will publish your work. Publish your writing yourself!" Support for such action and opportunities to publish are evident in whole language classrooms, where innovations in the teaching of writing have flourished during the past decade (Calkins, 1986, 1991; Edelsky, 1986; Hudelson, 1989; Johnson & Roen, 1989). When completed works are published in both Spanish and English, students' first and second language literacies are recognized and celebrated.

Teachers can validate children's linguistic and literacy experiences by designing learning activities that encourage students to draw on their knowledge of community genres—folk tales, fantasy, poems, stories—and on the community voices of family members, friends, and neighbors (Moll & Diaz, 1987; Nieto, 1982, 1991, and

1992). Maria opened space for her parents to become involved as participants when she accepted my invitation to alter the project plan in any way. Involving students as researchers and their parents as research partners holds potential as a new horizon for educational research (Branscombe, 1987; Goswami, 1991; Heath, 1983; Heath & Thomas, 1984, Mercado, 1992; Mercado, Torres, & Students, 1991; Moll & Diaz, 1987; Walsh, 1991).

Significant benefits can result from connecting home and school through the kind of cross-age and intergenerational literacy events engaged in by the participants in this study. Asking students' and their parents' opinions about books that represent their cultural experience is one way of appreciating and affirming the variety of linguistic and literary experiences students bring to their schooling. Concern for the respectful representation of students' cultures in literature on the part of teachers conveys a message to families that diversity, rather than assimilation, is the goal in integrating the child into the life of the school community.

PROFESSIONAL RESOURCES

Branscombe, A. (1987). I gave my classroom away. In D. Goswami & P. Stilman (Eds.), *Reclaiming the classroom: Teacher research as an agency for change.* Portsmouth, NH: Boynton/Cook.

Calkins, L. M. (1986). *The art of teaching writing.* Portsmouth, NH: Heinemann Educational Books.

Calkins, L. M., with Harwane, S. (1991). *Living between the lines.* Portsmouth, NH: Heinemann Educational Books.

Cummins, J. (1956). Empowering minority students: A framework for intervention. *Harvard Educational Review, 56,* 18–36.

Donaldson, M. (1979). *Children's minds.* New York: Norton.

Edelsky, C. (1986). *Writing in a bilingual program: Habia una vez.* Norwood, NJ: Ablex.

Esteves, S. M. (1984). *Tropical rains.* New York: African Caribbean Poetry Theatre.

Gilmore, P. (1986). Sub-rosa literacy: Peers, play, and ownership in literacy acquisition. In B. Schieffelin & P. Gilmore (Eds.), *The acquisition of literacy: Ethnographic perspectives.* Norwood, NJ: Ablex.

Goelman, H., Oberg, A., & Smith, F. (1984). *Awakening to literacy.* Portsmouth, NH: Heinemann Educational Books.

Goswami, Dixie (1991). Learning to keep an open agenda: Three local inquiries. Paper presented at the University of Massachusetts Third Annual Ethnographic and Qualitative Research Conference, Amherst, MA.

Harste, J., Woodward, V., & Burke, C. (1984). *Language stories and literacy lessons.* Portsmouth, NH: Heinemann Educational Books.

Heath, S. B. (1983). *Ways with words: Language, life, and work in communities and classrooms.* New York: Cambridge University Press.

Heath, S. B., with Thomas, C. (1984). The achievement of preschool literacy for mother and chid. In H. Goelman, A. Oberg, & F. Smith (Eds.), *Awakening to literacy*. Portsmouth, NH: Heinemann Educational Books.

Huck, C., Hepler, S., & Hickman, J. (1987). Understanding children's response to literature. In C. Huck, S. Hepler, & J. Hickman (Eds.), *Children's literature in the elementary classroom*. (4th ed.). New York: Holt, Rinehart and Winston.

Hudelson, S. (1989). *Write on: Children writing in ESL*. Englewood Cliffs, NJ: Center for Applied Linguistics.

Johnson, D., & Roen, D. (Eds.) (1989). *Richness in writing: Empowering ESL students*. New York: Longman.

Mercado, C. (1992). Researching research: A student–teacher-researcher collaborative project. In A. Ambert & M. D. Alvarez (Eds.), *Puerto Rican children on the mainland*. New York: Garland.

Mercado, C., Torres, M., & Students. (1991). Learning about learning through collaborative research. Paper presented at the Twelfth Annual University of Pennsylvania Ethnography Conference.

Moll, L. (1989). Second language learning: A Vygotskian perspective. In D. Johnson & D. Roen (Eds.), *Richness in writing: Empowering ESL students*. New York: Longman.

Moll, L., & Diaz, R. (1987). Teaching writing as communication: The use of ethnographic findings in classroom practice. In D. Bloome (Ed.), *Literacy and schooling*. Norwood, NJ: Ablex.

Nieto, S. (1982). Children's literature on Puerto Rican themes. *Bulletin of the Council on Interracial Books for Children, 14*(1 & 2), 6–16.

Nieto, S. (1991). Creating a literature for the Puerto Rican community: A case study of Latinos in children's books. In V. Harris (Ed.), *Multicultural children's literature*. Boston: Christopher-Gordon.

Nieto, S. (1992). *Affirming diversity: The sociopolitical context of multicultural education*. White Plains, NY: Longman.

Rosaldo, R. (1989). *Culture and truth: The remaking of social analysis*. Boston: Beacon Press.

Rosenblatt, L. (1978). *The reader, the text, and the poem: The transactional theory of the literary work*. Carbondale: Southern Illinois University Press.

Sims, R. (1982). *Shadow and substance: Afro-American experience in contemporary children's fiction*. Urbana, IL: National Council of the Teachers of English.

Sims, R. (1983). Strong black girls: A ten year old responds to fiction about Afro-Americans. *Journal of Research and Development in Education, 16*(3), 21–28.

Sims-Bishop, R. (1990). Trends and themes: New books, new faces. Paper presented at the Society of Children's Book Writers' Conference.

Trueba, H. (1983). Forms, functions and values of literacy: Reading and writing as a jr. high student. Paper presented at the National Reading Conference, Austin, Texas.

Trueba, H. (1987). The ethnography of schooling. In H. Trueba (Ed.), *Success or failure? Learning and the language minority student*. Cambridge, MA: Newbury House.

Vygotsky, L. (1978). *Mind in society*. Cambridge, MA: Harvard University Press.

Vygotsky, L. (1986). *Thought and language*. Cambridge, MA: MIT Press.

Walsh, C. (1991). *Pedagogy and the struggle for voice: Issues of language, power, and schooling for Puerto Ricans*. New York: Bergin & Garvey.

CHILDREN'S LITERATURE

Adoff, A. (1988). *Flamboyan*. Illustrated by Karen Barbour. San Diego, CA: Harcourt Brace Jovanovich.

Chardiet, B. (1973). *Juan Bobo and the pig: A Puerto Rican folktale retold*. Illustrated by H. Merryman. Walker Publishing.

Garcia, R. (1983). *My Aunt Otilia's spirits/Los espiritus de mi Tia Otilia*. Illustrated by R. Cherin & R. Reyes. San Francisco, CA: Children's Book Press.

Martel, C. (1976). *Yagua days*. Illustrated by J. Pinkney. New York: Dial.

13

Beyond the Information Given: Response to Nonfiction

Maryann Downing

When we consider older children and the reading demands made on them, the question arises whether our knowledge about response to stories, poems, and films also applies to readers' responses to expository prose (Petrosky, 1985). Little research has been done to investigate response to nonfiction.

Rosenblatt's transactional model addresses fiction, but invites application to nonfiction. The readers' experiences with any text involve a stream of ideas, feelings, images, and associations that arise as they construct meaning under the guidance of the text. Readers may narrow their attention for the purpose of taking away information—efferent reading—or they may remain open to the intellectual and emotional associations set up by the diction, voice, and tone—aesthetic reading (Rosenblatt, 1978). What Rosenblatt implies is that the rich mixture of responses is available at the outset of the reader's transaction with nonfiction as well as with fiction. Particularly with texts that lie on the continuum between the poles of efferent and aesthetic, it is a question of the choice of stance. What happens when older children are invited to respond to nonfiction and not simply to take away information? Do they draw on what Rosenblatt calls the "experiential matrix," and how does such a response influence their subsequent reading and thinking? Finally, what do successful readers do that is worth demonstrating and fostering for less-experienced readers?

Concerned with understanding more about the reading processes of above-average junior high school readers, I asked a class of eighth graders to read and then write down their responses to nonfiction selections. I had also observed that the best readers frequently made reference to the author, and I had begun to wonder what role this awareness played in their responses. My questions evolved into an investigation of the reading process of older children through examining their responses to nonfiction, with particular focus on the role played by their idea of the author (Downing, 1989).

This chapter offers a sketch of the formidable activity of these older children in their transactions with nonfiction. It gives evidence that they shape texts distinctively, guided by the same printed words, yet each drawing from a unique reservoir of knowledge and experience. It shows their diversity of response to the versions they have evoked. I see in these findings important implications for reading across the curruculum.

THE READINGS

The four readings were a memoir, "Man Meets Dog" by Konrad Lorenz (1970); an explorer's observations, "The Psychology of Seals," by Vilhjalmur Stefansson (1980); an opinion essay, "In Cities, Who Is the Real Mugger?" by Kenneth Clark (1985); and a historical narrative, part of a chapter entitled "Inventing Resources: Ice for the Indies," by Daniel Boorstin (1965). The texts were chosen to represent varieties of nonfiction that might be met in school reading and to offer topics that had some potential for dialogue.

"Man Meets Dog" details the loyalty of a dog, expressed in her acute suffering and wildness when separated from her master. "The Psychology of Seals," first published in 1913, offers a close observation by Alaskan explorers of seals' sleeping habits—the object being to hunt the seals successfully.

"Ice for the Indies" narrates the development of the use of ice for cooling food and the role played by the ambitious Frederick Tudor of Boston, who succeeded in transporting ice to a hot climate. "In Cities, Who Is the Real Mugger?" argues that those who mug people in our cities have themselves been robbed of their humanity by an indifferent society.

THE READERS

The children involved in the study were students at the urban independent school in which I had been working for five years as a member of the Learning Center, a support service to assist students with learning difficulties. Teachers allowed me into their classes, where I asked 125 eighth graders each to read and contribute a written response to one of the readings. I met the three boys known here as Ted, Randy, and Kevin when they answered my request in the school bulletin for volunteers. They read and responded in writing to all four readings and participated in interviews about their responses. Interviews were taped and transcribed.

Brief descriptions of the three boys may help the reader to distinguish them. Ted, age fourteen, had always done well in school; his teachers considered him an excellent reader and thinker, unafraid in class discussions to maintain minority viewpoints. He claimed he had come to dislike reading and read little on his own. Negative feelings about his reading test results in comparison with others' loomed large, despite a score at the ninety-fourth percentile.

Randy, at 13½, was the youngest of the three. He, too, was an above-average student. Unlike Ted and Kevin, he loved to read and he was an avid reader of science fiction and mysteries. In class discussions he made original and thoughtful contributions.

Kevin, the oldest, was 14½. His grades were average or sometimes slightly above average. A mild learning disability made learning to read a struggle, and he had repeated first grade. His sixth-grade teacher observed that orally he was "superb: curious, questioning, inventive" but distrustful of his ability to learn through reading and "more competent than he believes himself to be."

DIFFERENT VERSIONS OF THE SAME NONFICTION TEXTS

Although they shared comparable educational and upper middle class backgrounds, these three students showed great variety in the way they viewed and comprehended the same texts. The notion that a literary text has a single meaning has been displaced in current literary theory by the idea of multiple interpretations. There was a comparable diversity in the three boys' readings of nonfiction. Their versions of the texts differed in organization, emphasis, and detail. Their writing and talk about "Inventing Resources: Ice for the Indies" ("Ice") demonstrates that what Rosenblatt calls the evocation of the text (1978) is an interpretation rather than a literal reproduction. The diversity belies the common-sense assumption that students come to class having read the same assignment.

As inferred from their writing and interviews, their organization reflects the way each reader chooses from the many possible cues in the text what are perceived as the top level ideas. Ted's version had five sequential chunks; Randy shaped his into two, problem and solution, and omitted the sections that detail the historical progression of the use of ice. Kevin divided the text into two discrete topics. These differences in organization reflect Ted's and Randy's dominant themes and Kevin's lack of a unifying theme. The differences in emphasis become even sharper if we look more closely.

In Ted's written summary, he emphasized how the luxury of ice was democratized over time:

> Ice was once scarce and a luxury. Without ice people did not have many foods, which we have now. Eventually several wealthy families shared or owned their own ice houses. Tudor increased the use of ice by others, and now, finally, ice is commonplace.

The original printed passage sketches the context up to the present before focusing at length on Frederick Tudor, but Ted reordered the sequence, downplaying Tudor's contribution and placing it in chronological order.

Randy, in his summary, emphasized the problem and indicated Tudor's solution as the centerpiece of the text:

> This story is about the problems of the world without ice on a regular basis, and how one ambitious man worked to help solve them.

Kevin offered a perfunctory summary; together with his spoken comments, it indicates that he found the organization confusing. (He mentioned India, but "Indies" refers to the West Indies.) He wrote:

> It is about the history of Ice and preserving it. Also of a man who tried to ship ice to India.

He did not view the first part as leading into and preparing for the second part; for him, the arrangement was seriously flawed and the promise of the title misleading: "I think the title was bad. 'Ice for the Indies' was only disguised [discussed] at the end."

Besides the differences in overall organization and emphasis, the three students differed in the number and kind of details they recalled. Ted's comments on the food came from earlier in the text than Randy's and were fewer and more vague:

> Probably a lot of the food wasn't as good, 'cause salt meat isn't nowhere near as good. And a lot of meat is a big part of everyone's diet. You know, most people eat it. Fruits and stuff.

When Randy was asked to comment on his reference to "the problems of the world without ice," he responded with specific information and precise language drawn from "Ice":

> It was warmer in North America than it was in Europe, even though they were on the same latitude line, and some of the things that European tourists had noted was that there's a lot

of Americans had—what was it—[he consults the text] "putrid
meat, . . . rancid cream, sour milk," and so forth.

Both Randy and Ted were able to offer additional details in response to questions probing areas of the text on which they had
chosen to focus. However, Ted could not say more about Tudor,
whom he downplayed, until he read the section about him for a
third time. Kevin, even with close questioning, could not retrieve
particulars. He seemed to think he should at least remember the
process of preserving ice, although the passage did not describe it,
and he spontaneously offered his theory about why he could not:

I don't even remember how they did it [preserved ice]. I think it
was because, it's one of those you're reading it, you're not really
there. You're reading every word, but your mind is elsewhere,
'cause it's just, it's uncaptivating.

The three boys demonstrate something that perhaps has not
been researched to any great extent, whether in studies of fiction or
nonfiction: how different the evoked text is for each person.
Kevin's minimal text, a mere nod to the topics; Ted's dutiful history, minus the drama and human interest; Randy's story of human
ingenuity triumphing over life's hardships (and these epitomes are
themselves interpretations) are recognizably about the same piece
of reading, but the interest lies in the vastly different transaction
each one had with it. The differences were firmly set. Even when
the boys reread and talked about the texts during the interviews,
they tended to consult the text as they had originally shaped it and
to ignore cues they had passed over in the first reading. We need to
consider the consequences of such varied constructions and to
value and utilize students' different perceptions.

If we accept the existence of many versions of the text, perhaps
quite different from the teacher's, the challenge is to discover what
readers make of what they read. Rather than answering questions
made by a teacher, Ted, Randy, and Kevin further processed their
initial personal responses through expressive writing and talk. In
the classroom, reading logs or gathering in groups to formulate
questions about the reading also have been found to help learners
make their own connections with what has been read, so that learning proceeds from a personal center (Martin, 1976). Time for peer
discussion can permit students to clarify and enlarge their understanding by sharing diverse perspectives. They can learn to value
one another's contributions instead of assuming that the teacher
possesses the single right answer (Duckworth, 1987). This realiza-
tion brings us to consider some factors that help to account for the
different versions.

VARIED EXPECTATIONS SHAPE THE TEXTS

The three students brought their own complex and diverse expectations, both linguistic and experiential, to their reading. They understood the printed page as the work of an author; when their expectations were unmet, they turned to the author and articulated some of these. For example, one student, angered by "Seals," looked behind the narrative to demand, "Who wrote this anyway?" Meek (1983) suggests that "a quasi-social relationship" with an author is something that "all good readers understand and inexperienced readers scarcely glimpse" (p. 56). Readers response studies of fiction offer evidence that explicit reference to the author is frequent among fluent readers (Dollerup, 1971) and is developed as a natural part of the reading process (Cooper & Petrosky, 1976).

What sort of author expectations did these older children bring to a reading? Their written and spoken comments contained statements about authors as individuals with whom both identification and conflict are possible (Burke, 1969). They considered them to be speech-act partners with claims on their attention as well as responsibilities toward them (Pratt, 1977). They expected them to use the kinds of written discourse conventions and forms they had met in their past reading. In these ways, the students resembled each other. They differed much more in the extent to which they looked to authors as sources of significant knowledge. All of these expectations provided them with multiple frameworks within which to locate and make sense of a text. They understood that "the written utterance transcends the margins of the printed page"; they inferred "contextual realities" that helped to guide their construction of meaning (Iser, 1978, p. 55). In Bruner's phrase (1973), they demonstrated the achievement of adolescence, the ability to "go beyond the information given."

Two sorts of expectations mentioned previously yield the most interesting findings. If we look again at "Ice," we can see that these students had learned from their experience to anticipate that writers will work within certain rules and forms when they shape a piece of writing. When a writer starts in a certain way, they identified the passage as a particular kind of discourse. So Ted recognized "Ice" as history and retold it in strict time order, and the summaries of the other two show their tacit knowledge of other writing conventions.

In the interview, Randy compared and contrasted informal storytelling and history as variations on a single type:

> All of this seemed to me like the person who wrote the story was an old person who, just like my grandmother, told these stories. Perhaps with a little more detail and fact as you see here [pointing

to the text], in an actual form of an article. But it's still the same type of story, thinking about how it was when you were a little kid.

Kevin, in summarizing, identified "Ice" as history. But in his opening written response, he put it into a special category of school texts:

It struck me as a story told in a 3rd grade english book. Kind of interesting just to help you learn to read better.

When I read this response back to him, he elaborated, describing a type of writing that, at least with hindsight, he found lacking in intellectual seriousness:

You know those grammar books, you know, that you read in third grade, that had stories about really big things. But you knew it wasn't really that, because they wanted you to learn about it and memorize and then give you a test on *who* invented ice, *when*, you know, *how* [inaudible] just so you get reading, so you were reading something, just something to read.

These older children's resources clearly were not limited to the expectations for fiction that are highlighted in English classes. In the course of their reading experience, they had become familiar with a range of conventions for nonfiction.

Differences in the ways the three students constructed and responded to the reading passages seem closely related to the degree of their concern to know about the external world, other people, and themselves and to the extent to which they expected authors to serve them as sources of knowledge (Baker, 1982; Berger & Luckmann, 1966). All three, free of the constraints of tests and grades, looked to each reading for some personal significance. Ted complained that "Ice" lacks "anything interesting, for example, about human nature. . . . just fact after fact concerning the role ice has played in our lives." He conceded in the interview that an earlier audience might have cared about the information: "It doesn't matter now, but it probably mattered then. But to me it doesn't matter." Ted's responses indicate that what mattered to him at that time was the quest for his own identity. He could not identify with Tudor, and his complaint about the lack of human interest in "Ice" ignored the fact that fully half of the reading is devoted to a portrait of Tudor.

Randy was more extroverted. The vivid detail of his responses indicates how eagerly he absorbed and integrated information about the world. He came from a family that told stories about the past and about poverty and hardships in former times. His version of "Ice" reflects this perspective, even as Ted's account reflects his accustomed affluence and focuses on how the wealthy lived. Randy, reminded of his grandmother, wrote: "[My grandmother's] family could not afford a decent ice chest. . . . My grandmother had to do without decent milk, just like people did before the icebox." Unlike Ted and Kevin, Randy enjoyed reasoning about the past, and he connected this reading to an issue that intrigued him:

> That's something that I've been asking myself for a long time.
> Everyone talks about the good old days when we didn't have
> TV . . . and cars were a luxury, and we didn't have this or that.
> And I'm thinking: you didn't have TV. What's so good about not
> having TV? As far as I'm concerned, TV is one of the better
> things that they've come up with in the last century.

Of the three, Kevin was the most alienated from school and reading. Although he had developed into a strong reader, his mild learning disability had made learning to read difficult, and he still compared himself unfavorably to others. He was involved in making sense of the external world as it related to him, with a lively interest in understanding the psychological and moral aspects of human behavior. He considered school texts "so boring, and I'm failing history not because I'm so stupid, but because it's just so uninteresting to me." He used three of the readings to pursue his concerns; "Ice" is the reading that most resembles a typical social studies assignment, and so he dismissed it.

The students' responses demonstrate that they added to the textual cues a formidable store of background knowledge and strategies. They also drew on a background of reading and writing experience and knowledge to question credibility or purpose. They knew how to make inferences about the author's unifying attitudes, distinguish their own views and views in the text from those of the author, and engage in dialogue.

The presence of such complex expectations should make it clear that there is no question of teaching isolated skills. In fact, the students' understandings parallel the astonishing achievement of young children, who learn oral language not by direct teaching but in the context of a rich language environment and demonstrations by successful language learners. In the history of these above-average readers, I found evidence of their ample opportunities in school to listen to reading aloud, participate in reflective discussions, and engage in broad reading and writing in many genres. These are factors that other teachers might replicate. We need further research in the middle and high school years to follow the development of expectations when groups of varied abilities and socioeconomic backgrounds experience such holistic approaches.

SPECTATOR RESPONSES ENHANCE
NONFICTION READING

The readers in this study responded to nonfiction in ways that have much in common with what we have learned about response to literature. A general finding of researchers is that in reading literature self-involvement is significant. While exaggerated identification has been found to block analysis of literature, initial self-involvement seems related to effective interpretation. In responses to short stories, for instance, students who were emotionally involved made more literary judgments overall (Squire, 1964). Responses of college freshmen to novels similarly indicated that initial involvement seemed "to catalyze and enrich the analysis which follow[ed]" (Wilson, 1966, p. 40). In a 1969 study (Shirley), students' retrospective look at the works they had read in the recent past indicated that they became as involved with nonfiction as with fiction. The responses of the eighth graders in this study support the application to nonfiction of these findings about involvement. They exemplify Britton's paradoxical distinction between the involvement of a spectator and the distance of a participant.

Britton's (1970, 1975, 1982) spectator–participant distinction corresponds roughly to Rosenblatt's (1978) aesthetic and efferent stances—the aesthetic attends to the lived-through experience, the efferent narrows focus to what will be taken away from the text. Britton describes the spectator as free to be involved at the deeper levels of values, while the participant is caught up in practical and social demands. As spectators involved in the reading experience, the students expressed personal responses to ideas and information and aesthetic responses to the author's language; as participants distancing themselves from the reading experience, they expressed analytic responses to content and rhetorical responses to language. A sampling of what Kevin and Randy said and wrote illustrates these varied responses and how they can enhance the reading of nonfiction. It also contrasts Kevin's style of response with Randy's: the one as the author's opponent, defining himself through conflict of attitudes and ideas; the other as a participant with the author in an ongoing conversation, full of story-swapping, questions, and speculations.

The spectator, as Britton explains the stance, reads for more than information. He "is not concerned simply to perceive and understand, for what he sees engages his feelings and invites him to apply his sense of values" (1975, p. 80). The spectator savors, associates with, and evaluates patterns of feelings and and events as well as the forms of language used (Britton, 1970) and the "dance-like movement of thought" (Britton, 1975, p. 81).

Kevin's involvement with the author's ideas in three of the four readings had a dramatic quality: his savoring and making associations were suffused with the intense moral evaluation that was his dominant personal response. His summary of "The Psychology of Seals" ("Seals") indicates his indignation at the narrator's attitude toward seal hunting: "It's about how you can slaughter seals and this guys no fail techneque [technique]." He was aware of the narrator as author and condemned what he viewed as a trivial rationale for killing: "I don't think people should kill them. Especially some jerk who is just hunting and killing to write a stupid story."

A comparison with Randy's responses shows how Randy companionably matched details of his experience with the author's:

> This [explorer's pretending to be a seal] immediately reminds me of 4 years ago . . . [our guide] jumped in the water, (holding the gun above it, of course) & made the noise a fish makes when splashing. As the bear looked over the side of the barge, to try and catch the "fish," Andy shot him twice between the eyes.

Kevin, instead, returned repeatedly in the interview to the final image of "Seals":

> He absolutely shot it, and made it out be like he was the one who was suffering if he lost it. Whereas the thing is dead. It's just rotting in the bottom of the ocean.

The scene fired Kevin's imagination; he added more detail, imagined the author's motivation, and invented monologues and dialogues in which the author explained himself. In this way, the energy of his evaluation led him to continue elaborating on his version of the text.

Kevin's opposition was accompanied by the awareness that the author shaped his particular version of reality in presenting the event: "The man who wrote this was trying to make it out to be sport." This important understanding allowed Kevin not to accept unquestioningly what he read. Randy shared this sense that what he read was an author's version of how things are, but he did not fight the author. His expectation was that, while "you don't necessarily agree," you learn what you can, raise questions, and develop your own ideas.

Kevin made a wealth of associations with this reading. He referred to what he knew about endangered species, survival of the fittest, funding of scientific projects, and concentration camps; he offered very definite opinions about the treatment of animals, religion, and justifiable hunting; he drew from his lexicon such words as fascination, observant, slaughter, lean-to, phoney, crucify, obnoxiously; he described personal experiences involving family pets and his observation of someone crying over a dead squirrel.

Kevin also connected "Seals" with his past reading: "It could be a newspaper article or an article in the *National Geographic.*" He also spoke of "these comments of a scientist, which I assume he is," giving the text still another framework. His text classifications thus provided criteria for evaluating the text as a piece of writing shaped by an author.

These active and varied spectator responses make for a more solid version of the text, but they do more than this. Even when these readers moved to a participant stance, elements of their initial spectator stance colored what they wrote or said.

The participant responds in terms of practical purposes, including being informed, instructed, or persuaded. Such readers are free to mesh the new ideas that they select from the author with their own knowledge, experience, and interests (Britton, 1975). Sometimes these readers probed the ideas that were significant to them, an analytic perspective; at other times they looked behind the ideas to analyze the author and the author's choices, a rhetorical perspective. For these older children, their varied expressions of a participant response appear to be guided by their spectator stance.

In the first place the three readers bring their knowledge and experience of the world and their sense of values to bear as they analyze and reflect. Secondly, at times they use the idea of the author as a special analytic tool that opens dimensions of the text beyond the actual words; they listen to their own awareness of an author behind the text with underlying attitudes, motivations, levels of expertise, purposes, and social and historical pressures. I have explored this aspect of older children's reading at length (Downing, 1989); here I only briefly illustrate some of these different aspects of a spectator stance in Randy's and Kevin's participant responses.

Randy expanded his personal responses to "Seals" by giving reasons for his opinions. Drawing on similar experiences he shared with the author, he indicated his own views on the issue of killing "another animal." In the course of the interview, he analyzed aspects of the issue: why hunters kill, why hunting is pleasurable; he made an analogy from his personal experience:

> Just being able to outwit an animal, I guess. Because, like, I know when I go fishing, you have to know where the fish like to hang out, what they like to eat. . . . And catching fish is sort of like the climax of the whole thing. All the preparation that goes into it is another part of it. And in hunting I imagine it's much more, because you have to know where to get the animals, you have to know what kind of gun to use, and know how to sneak up on an animal, whatever.

Randy used the idea of the author as a tool to help him speculate about ideas; he did not focus on style. While he, like Kevin, gave the author of "Seals" a negative persona, he did not continue to focus on him, but moved on to the issues his behavior raised. Randy understood that authors shape texts from a variety of motives. This comprehension served him well in building a specific framework for "Seals." Alert to cues in the text, he was the only reader in the study to notice the rhetorical situation mentioned at the beginning:

> It sounds like this article was written also in part because he wanted to prove [to] whoever said that it's ridiculous to hunt seals 'cause it's so hard, he wanted to prove that person wrong. So by trying it out or doing it, he obviously proved him wrong.

Kevin's aesthetic awareness became the starting point for thinking rhetorically. Having analyzed and criticized the author's attitudes vigorously, he acknowledged how the author's writing pulled him into the experience despite himself:

> He talked, put a little bit of facts in about how long it's awake and how long it's asleep. . . . The guy thinks he's a scientist. . . . He's fascinated by animals. . . . I don't want to hear what he has to say, but it's kind of interesting. . . . His observations were very deep. . . . You really think about what he's saying.

These responses suggest that between the poles of efferent and aesthetic reading the reader's transactions with nonfiction texts as well as fiction are enriched in important ways by attention to the "experiential matrix . . . the continuing flow of sensations, feelings, attitudes, ideas" from which meaning emerges (Rosenblatt, 1978, p. 42). These students assumed a spectator stance at many points in their reading of nonfiction. Their personal and aesthetic responses permitted them to stay longer with the author's ideas and to process them more deeply. Further, their spectator responses colored and gave vitality to their analytical and rhetorical comments.

Lastly, the students responded evaluatively. This observation contrasts with the finding of an international study of responses to literature (Purves, 1973, 1981) that students in the United States tend not to make critical judgments and fail to develop evaluative criteria. These students viewed the text as open to critical scrutiny rather than as worthy of unquestioning acceptance. Such rhetorical awareness would seem to be a condition for thoughtful reading and a safeguard against manipulation by the writer.

Rosenblatt asserts that "Much greater concern than is usual should be accorded the 'first step,' the registering or savoring of the literary transaction" (1978, p. 136). This study suggests that fostering this first step of spectator response is vital in reading nonfiction as well. Expressive writing and talk—following the flow of ideas and feelings, relatively unstructured, and sharing with a sympathetic audience one's attitude toward a topic (Britton, 1975)—were the means of inviting and extending responses to nonfiction in this study. Other modes (such as drama, role-playing, the arts) and other genres of writing (like fictional diaries, letters, speeches) have the potential to engage older children's imaginations and sense of values. What such approaches ask for is reconstruction for oneself rather than reproduction for the teacher. These approaches should not be abandoned in the upper grades. Martin observes that "unless we provide many opportunities all over the curriculum for children to use their imaginations more extensively, their knowledge will remain inert" (1976, p. 86).

It might be argued that a study of successful readers from a privileged environment leads to overoptimism. Too often, theory and small-scale research about children's potential collides with evidence of less hopeful realities. The students in this study were developing into fine readers; they enjoyed opportunities for wide and stimulating out-of-school experiences, a challenging academic environment, individual attention from teachers, and high aspirations for the future that had a realistic chance of being realized. Others are less fortunate in these ways. The National Assessment of Educational Progress (1981) found that U.S. students overall are not progressing in the higher levels of reading, not learning to read thoughtfully and critically. It seems important to place the findings of response studies in this broader context.

Clearly, the reasons why so many students fail to develop as readers are complex, and many lie outside the control of the teacher. Rosenblatt (1978), however, points to one factor that does come within the scope of the school. She suggests that readers who have not lost touch with their own responses often begin by paying attention to the thoughts and feelings that accompany their reading. When readers fail to make such connections, the problem may lie in teaching that has failed to maintain "spontaneity and self-respect while at the same time fostering the capacity to undertake rewarding relationships with increasingly demanding texts" (p. 140).

There are political implications in fostering response to nonfiction as well as fiction. One of these deals with the often-stated goal of fostering critical reading. Whom do we as a society want to be able to read and think critically? Instead of thinking of critical reading as analytical in the first place and the province of an elite, we might understand it as starting with the affective, the aesthetic, the evaluative, and as a democratic requirement for all students.

PROFESSIONAL RESOURCES

Baker, C. D. (1982). The adolescent as theorist: An interpretive view. *Journal of Youth and Adolescence, 11*(3), 167–181.

Berger, P. L., & Luckmann, T. (1966). *The social construction of reality: A treatise in the sociology of knowledge.* New York: Doubleday.

Britton, J. N. (1970). *Language and learning.* London: Penguin.

Britton, J. N. (1982). Spectator role and the beginnings of writing. In G. M. Pradl (Ed.), *Prospect and retrospect: Selected essays of James Britton.* Montclair, NJ: Boynton/Cook.

Britton, J. N., Burgess, T., Martin, N., McLeod, A., Rosen, H. (1975). *The development of writing abilities (11–18)* (Schools Council Research Studies). London: Macmillan Education.

Bruner, J. S. (1973). Going beyond the information given. In J. M. Anglin (Ed.), *Beyond the information given.* New York: W. W. Norton.

Burke, K. (1969). *A rhetoric of motives.* Berkeley: University of California Press.

Cooper, C. R., & Petrosky, A. R. (1976). A psycholinguistic view of the fluent reading process. *Journal of Reading* (December), 164–207.

Dollerup, C. (1971). On reading short stories. *Journal of Reading, 14*(7), 445–454.

Downing, M. (1989). *Adolescents respond to nonfiction: Transactions with authors.* Doctoral dissertation, New York University.

Duckworth, E. (1987). The virtues of not knowing. In *The having of wonderful ideas and other essays on teaching and learning,* pp. 64–69. New York: Teachers College Press.

Iser, W. (1978). *The act of reading: A theory of aesthetic response.* Baltimore, MD: Johns Hopkins University Press.

Martin, N. (1976) *Writing and learning across the curriculum.* London: Ward Lock.

Meek, M. (1983). *Achieving literacy: Longitudinal studies of adolescents learning to read.* London: Routledge and Kegan Paul.

National Assessment of Educational Progress (1981). *Reading, thinking, and writing: Results from the 1979–80 national assessment of reading and literature* (report no. 11-R-01). Denver, CO: Educational Commission of the States.

Petrosky, A. R. (1985). Response: A way of knowing. In C. R. Cooper (Ed.), *Researching response to literature and the teaching of literature: Points of departure.* Norwood, NJ: Ablex.

Pratt, M. L. (1977). *Toward a speech act theory of literary discourse.* Bloomington: Indiana University Press.

Purves, A. C. (1973). *Literature education in ten countries: An empirical study.* New York: Wiley.

Purves, A. C. (1981). *Reading and literature: American achievement in international perspective.* Urbana, IL: National Council of Teachers of English.

Rosenblatt, L. (1978). *The reader, the text, the poem: A transactional theory of the literary work.* Carbondale: Southern Illinois University Press.

Shirley, F. L. (1969). The influence of reading on the concepts, attitudes, and behavior of 10th, 11th, and 12th grade students. *Journal of Reading, 13,* 369–372.

Squire, J. (1964). *The responses of adolescents while reading four short stories.* (NCTE research report #2). Champaign, IL: National Council of Teachers of English.

Wilson, J. R. (1966). *Responses of college freshmen to three novels* (NCTE research report #7). Urbana, IL: National Council of Teachers of English.

CHILDREN'S LITERATURE

Boorstin, D. J. (1965). *The Americans: The national experience.* New York: Random House.

Clark, K. (1985). In cities, who is the real mugger? *The New York Times,* Jan. 14, A19.

Lorenz, K. (1970). Man meets dog. In S. Soltaroff (Ed.), *Man in the expository mode: Book 3.* Evanston, IL: McDougal, Littel, pp. 53–57.

Stefansson, V. (1980). My life with the Eskimo. In M. A. Miller (Ed.), *Reading and writing short essays.* New York: Random House.

Part IV

Literary Responses Throughout Childhood

14

The Princess Learns a Lesson: Three Studies of Theme in Individual and Interactive Contexts

Susan Lehr

A growing body of response research has begun to look at how children construct meaning while reading literature (Cochran-Smith, 1984; Cox & Many, 1989; Cullinan, Harwood, & Galda, 1983; Holland & Lehr, in press; Lehr, 1988, 1990, 1991; Liebling, 1989; Many, 1989; McClure, 1989). What makes these studies distinctive from previous studies is the focus on the child's perspective of meaning. Prior to the early 1980s very little research existed that literally considered the young child's developing sense of theme. Furthermore, real books in natural contexts were not used. Rather, constructed materials with contrived or manipulated story structures were typically used to determine whether identifying themes early in stories would improve comprehension, whether children could identify main ideas, how many main idea units a child could spontaneously recall, and so on. The idea of taking a look at the child's sense of theme during book events and resulting discussions had not been tried. Books like *Wally's Stories* by Vivian Paley were really ground breaking in that educators of young children, like Paley, were beginning to listen to their students and record their constructions of meaning.

Paley (1981) found that five year olds are prolific meaning makers during story time. She set up an interactive classroom in which children shared constantly and related book events to real life events. Paley scaffolded book discussions and encouraged her students to explore the meaning in books. Her students argued with each other and with their teacher. They did not hesitate to tell her when she had gone astray in interpreting a story.

Since that time, a number of studies have explored the child's verbalizations of theme with literature. It has been demonstrated that young children are actively constructing meaning and that, while their meaning may differ widely or by degree from adult perspectives, children listen to and process stories and build their own meaning structures based on their own world views. It is worth noting that the child's success is often linked to having age-appropriate materials used during the study. Personal schemas are being formed from the earliest years, and an important part of that networking system is the narrative information that children process and respond to during and after story events.

BUILDING A CONCEPT OF NARRATIVE

We story. From our earliest years, we hear narratives both formally and informally. Young children tell stories from the beginning. They summarize events. They collapse ideas into thematic bits and pieces. The child who hears about dad's bad day on the way home from the day care center and announces to mom that "Daddy's cranky" has heard narrative informally, has understood the main idea of that narrative, and is able to respond to that information with a thematic inference—tacitly, I suspect, but nonetheless accurately and certainly from an egocentric world view. It is facile to assume that because children think simply or focus on certain parts of stories, such as the violence found in the Three Little Pigs, they do not understand or have meaningful reactions to stories. Their logic and concerns are obviously different from those of the adult; however, their processing frequently coincides with information in the story and often includes highly personal responses to that information. Such response is logical given their unique perspectives.

RESPONSE RESEARCH

Over the past eight years I have been involved in response research that has specifically looked at the child's developing sense of theme as a response to literature. The first study, with kindergarten, second- grade, and fourth-grade children was the first of its kind; the second study was conducted with preschool children; a third year-long study explored interactive contexts in a literature-based first-grade classroom. All three studies had one common link: they all considered the child's thematic construction of meaning from the child's perspective. This stance necessarily affects how we as educators respond to the information that children provide to us in classroom contexts. If we are considering the child's perspective of meaning during literature events, the focus no longer becomes one of finding a preconceived answer. Rather, the child's own reasoning and inner logic become the focus. Process, not product. The fact that finite answers are easily measured products, perhaps helps in understanding their long-held popularity in the classroom.

Hickman (1979) and Hepler's (1982) research with literature contexts in the classroom was critical in providing a unique look at children, literature, and classroom responses. Their ethnographic studies showed how children interacted with books in contexts that were anything but traditional. The children in these classrooms read real books, discussed them in an uninhibited fashion, and grew in their ability to respond to literature during the year.

Applebee's (1978) work with children's responses to common sayings or fairy tales was also helpful in providing a look at how children perceive fantasy and fact and how young children develop a concept of story. His categories for response, a logical sequence beginning with the concrete and moving toward the abstract, provided a framework for analyzing children's responses to literature. The flaw in Applebee's research was that he underestimated the abilities of children under the age of 12, particularly those familiar with books and the language of books. This misperception probably resulted from not reading the stories to the children but simply relying on their memories of familiar fairy tales.

RESPONDING TO REALISTIC FICTION AND FOLK TALES

In my first study, I was particularly interested in how children would respond to literature if asked a set of response questions, which were essentially catalysts to encourage divergent thinking (see Figure 14–1). I had no finite answers in mind, and I went in with few preconceptions. Children listened to a series of books in two genres, realistic fiction and folk tales, matched books that they perceived as being thematically similar and then talked about those books from a variety of perspectives. This procedure was done in a systematic fashion with sixty children from three grades. All of the children in the study took the Revised Huck Literature Inventory (Lehr, 1987) and were grouped according to their exposure to literature. I generated 120 interview transcripts for analysis and found certain characteristics of the child's sense of theme, including: providing information that was text-congruent; the ability to summarize the story, beginning in kindergarten; an awareness of character motivation; and the ability to analyze and generalize information from the text, particularly in the second and fourth

1. Match two titles. Why did you choose these two books? What are they both about?
2. Can you tell me what the whole story was about in a few words or in short form?
3. Are these stories similar to any other stories you have read? How?
4. What were the authors trying to teach you when they wrote these stories?
5. What are the most important ideas in these stories?
6. Pick a story. Why did it end like it did?
7. Is there anything you would have changed?
8. Did you like the story? Why or why not?
9. Would you have changed the ending?

Adapted from Goodman and Burke's (1972) retelling guide.

FIGURE 14-1   *Interview questions*

grades. The flaw in my research was that I initially quantified those answers to develop broad categories with which to qualitatively analyze the thematic answers of the children. In subsequent research, I have found that type of a scale less helpful than simply taking an analytical and systematic look at how children respond to literature, both individually and in groups.

Most of the time, children in all three grades, including kindergarten, second, and fourth, were able to identify two books for realistic fiction and folk tales that matched adult choices and that were thematically similar (see Figure 14–2). Folk tales were slightly more difficult than realistic fiction books, probably because the former is less closely linked to the child's life experience, whereas realistic fiction explores themes common to the child's experience, such as having a friend, fighting with a friend, or growing bigger. These findings suggest that the ability to understand theme at a tacit level develops at a young age. Verbalizing that information comes at a later age and is helped when the young child has experience with books.

The majority of the theme statements given by children matched the text but differed from adult perspectives; however, in all three grades statements that were not congruent with the text primarily originated in the groups of children having a low exposure to literature and occurred most frequently with folk tales. These children didn't have the same depth of experience with literature and had more trouble talking about the books from a variety of perspectives that meshed with the text itself.

Realistic Fiction	
Kindergarten books:	
Titch/The Carrot Seed	16
The Carrot Seed/New Blue Shoes	2
Titch/New Blue Shoes	2
Second-grade books:	
Let's Be Enemies/The Hating Book	20
Fourth-grade books:	
Stevie/Thy Friend, Obadiah	20
Folk Tales	
Kindergarten books:	
Three Little Pigs/Three Billy Goats Gruff	7
Three Little Pigs/Gingerbread Boy	12
Three Billy Goats Gruff/Gingerbread Boy	1
Second-grade books:	
Tattercoats/Snow White	12
Tattercoats/The Swineherd	8
Fourth-grade books:	
Dawn/A Japanese Fairy Tale	12
The Stonecutter/Dawn	4
A Japanese Fairy Tale/The Stonecutter	4

FIGURE 14–2   *Children's choices for thematically matched books*

LINKING ART AND LANGUAGE

Children drew pictures about the themes of the books prior to being interviewed. This activity seemed to focus many of the children on the meaning of the books and acted as a catalyst for discussion (Kiefer, 1989; Siegel, 1983). For example, many of the second-grade girls responded to the folk tale selections by focusing on love and marriage. Katy drew three princesses and chose all of the books as being thematically similar (although she missed the point that one of the endings does not end happily). Cary drew the endings of the stories and stated that "the stories are about love." Her drawings show the happy endings of *Snow White* and *Tattercoats;* her view of *The Swineherd,* however, has captions for the prince and princess that read: "You have been bad." "I am sad." She later told me that the "princess learns a lesson." Cary provided additional thematic information that made moral judgments about the princess's behavior and about justice in that specific situation.

David showed the transformation from hut to palace in his drawings about *Tattercoats* and *Snow White* and wrote, "They both were just plain people then they were both princesses." During the interview, he stated that one of the most important ideas in these stories was "not to use other people to get stuff," which all of the antagonists did. He added an admonition to Zwerger's spoiled princess "not to be greedy." Three words answered the question about what the books were about. "Nice. Not nice." Although succinct, David's answers and drawings indicate a high level of interaction with the themes of all three stories and provide a picture of the eight year old's response to folk tales.

Adam's detailed picture of *The Swineherd* shows the prince with a sword holding the reins of his horse and the princess standing on the other side of a tree. His caption states: "The princess and prince live happily ever after." From his perspective, this comment does not mean that they live together, although the prince does get his horse; it simply means happiness is being alive. Adam later said during the interview, after identifying *The Swineherd* and *Tattercoats* as being thematically similar: "They don't get almost killed. Nobody gets hurt. Sort of boring." This fresh perspective links the boring stories through the idea that the characters make it through situations alive and well. Through art and conversation, children in all three grades demonstrated the ability to respond to books at personal levels by talking about how and why characters acted as they did and suggesting consequences for their actions.

PRESCHOOL CHILDREN AND THEME

Taylor (1983) writes that "the children are also learning of reading as an interactive process, for the parents spent much of their story-reading time relating events in the stories to the everyday lives of their children" (p. 70). Books are catalysts. They relate to real life. In her diary of her daughter's quest into literacy, Dorothy White (1954) relates an extraordinary moment when the child saw snow for the first time, having first experienced it in books. Books are still one of the primary sources for new experiences and information about the world, not just for children but for adults as well. We still know very little about how young children process information and what impact a literature program has on building a young child's background information about the world. In my own experience teaching preschool and primary age children, I know that children's ability to sit and listen to stories increases dramatically over the course of a year and that their critical responses become increasingly rich and varied in an accepting environment.

In my work with four-year-old children, I discovered a steady enthusiasm and excitement for books. Books were real friends. Children were entranced with minute details, liked the notion of familiarity, treated characters like friends, and would stop to chat about activities in which the characters were engaged. Unlike kindergarten children, none of the four-year-old children in this second study were able to summarize the story when specifically asked to retell the story in a short form. This limitation may have affected the children's ability to generate a theme statement; however, some children were able to retell a story using the book as a guide. Several of the children told me the story from beginning to end. Others preferred that I tell the story and took the interview session as an opportunity to hear it again.

Meg, when asked why she liked a book she called *The Bumpy Bus Ride,* said: "Because a cow gets on it and pulls [laughs] the bus down." This comment can be seen as an early attempt at a summary statement and clearly shows that Meg is not far from being able to talk about the plot of the story succinctly. Her statement relates her favorite part of the book and explains why it is a favorite. Similarly, after hearing *The Very Hungry Caterpillar* in three sizes—a big book, the standard book, and a small hand-size version—Brian said: "Big books and little books. I'll bring two of my little books, two of my big backyards. He's a green caterpillar and turns into a butterfly." Although he seems to ramble about a variety of topics and talks about Carle's book without directly naming it, Brian encapsulates the book by reducing it to a statement about the transformation of a caterpillar into a butterfly. Both Meg and Brian were responding to the question "What are some stories you like? Why?" on the reading attitude interview given in the second session of the study. Their replies suggest that they are beginning to sort through familiar books and can categorize them with brief statements.

Laura identified *No More Monsters for Me* as a story she liked "because it's good and it's very dark at night." She also elaborated on why she liked *Keep Me in the Zoo:* "It's all about a little girl and a library who have popcorn who says you belong in the circus. It's a very silly book." Thematic information is absent in the first statement but is embedded in the second. Based on the three children's statements, we can conclude that personal response at this age is a mixture of thoughts and feelings related to the setting of the book, the setting of the storytelling, the size of the book, whether it has humor, who it is about, and familiar content—like cows, popcorn, and circuses. Children at this age are learning to mean, and by the time they reach kindergarten some are already able to pull these segmented thoughts into cohesive statements when asked to do so.

Four-year-old children in this study were not able to generate theme statements when probed individually after a reading of the story *Titch* by Pat Hutchins. However, most of the children were able to talk about thematic elements, an early development of sense of theme. Children also considered the internal motivation of characters, and most children related the book experience to life experience, much as the kindergarten children did. When given theme statements from which to choose, the children were able to identify a theme statement. This capability suggests that four-year-old children are busy constructing meaning from the information that surrounds them. They may not have the information clearly organized into hierarchical structures, but they do categorize information and make connections between direct experiences and literature experiences. They can identify main ideas or themes of stories and can begin to talk about some of those components in a general way.

In a group context, the children built on the statements of other children and carried thoughts in new directions by responding to other children's statements. Arguing, a positive catalyst for language development and stimulation, helped two children work out information about the character, Titch, in relation to the concepts of small, medium, and large. The interactive context can become a forum for exploring thematic meaning in narratives. Children naturally discuss what they hear if it interests them and is sufficiently challenging.

INTERACTIVE LITERATURE CONTEXTS

I spent a year as an observer-participant in Sandy's first-grade classroom, where literature was used as the basis of the curriculum. Whole group time occupied an hour each morning and always included two basic components: books and plenty of interaction. A brief description of the kinds of activities in which the children were engaged is helpful in understanding the interactive nature of the book discussions and the tone that Sandy encouraged.

The children consumed hundreds of stories. During this time of reading, writing, speaking, and listening, the children listened to stories; engaged in lively discussions on a variety of topics before, during, and after book time; wrote in several different modes; worked in groups; learned a number of reading strategies; created comparison charts; looked up words in the dictionary; checked information in other books read; analyzed words phonetically; looked for spelling patterns; made word webs; and discussed conventions of writing. This group of six-year-old children was highly literate. They made numerous independent decisions and statements, so that these sessions and the activities of the remainder of the day were constantly linked. The children made connections between what was learned during rug time when they studied themes throughout the year. The skills and reading strategies that they worked on as they explored topics and books during whole group time acted as catalysts for encouraging literacy across the curriculum.

Response to Picture Books

Before reading *Thundercake* by Patricia Polacco to this group of first-grade children, I invited their predictions as to what the story might be about based on the title. Their responses indicated a savvy group, ready to take risks and offer their perspectives of meaning:

'The cake makes the thunder."
'They could be having a picnic and eating cake and then the thunder."
"Maybe the thunder was the cake."
"The cake would be on the table when they were having a picnic and the lightning struck the pieces and all the pieces fly into their face."
"Maybe they're in the house having a cake because it's someone's birthday and the thunder comes down and the cake starts on fire."

The children understand how stories operate. Three of the children begin to tell a lively story based on the limited information provided by the title alone. This response indicates how children search for meaning and logical patterns based on information provided. It also points out the basic ability of children to take on the perspectives of others using their own schema. They know about cakes; they know about thunder. How do you logically connect the two and create a story? These children also are accustomed to having their answers heard and accepted. Rather than saying no to each answer, I invited more predictions. The focus was on constructing logical meaning, expanding critical thinking, and reinforcing a solid reading strategy.

Folk Tales

The children studied and compared many folk tales throughout the course of the year, from *The Fisherman and His Wife* to *The Three Little Pigs*. During the reading of versions with more complex language, it was interesting to watch them figure out new words and relay their understandings to their peers. Sometimes, as Sandy read, one child would say, for example, "What's odious?" and another child would quietly answer "Smelly," and the flow of the story would not be interrupted. At other points, children would engage in lively dialogue to figure out the meaning of a term or what a character's action implied or by closely studying the illustrations, bringing the story to a full halt.

In many versions of *The Fisherman and His Wife*, the illustrators make the sea and sky reflect the increasing rage of the flounder as the wife's demands grow. The clouds and water roil and churn with anger. The children were fascinated with this technique and noticed, perhaps for the first time, how text and illustrations can match in tonal qualities and how emotions can be effectively mirrored in drawings.

As Sandy read, Sarah maintained a quiet running commentary on the sidelines by interjecting all kinds of information about how the stories differed from each other and what events meant. About the refrain in *The Fisherman and His Wife*, she said: "There's something different than the other poem that they said in the other book." About the fisherman's wife: "She's being nicer than she was in the other book. She's not as snotty." Sarah understood the story of *The Fisherman and His Wife*. She knew about difficult characters, and she was able to compare different authors' presentations of the wife and make subtle observations about that character. About the illustrations, she noted: "Miss Debus, they never showed the clouds before." About the type of language used in *The Fisherman and His Wife:* "Miss Debus, they're talking different things in that book instead of that book." One book had simple modern language, and another used older, less familiar language, words such as alas and hark ye. About text sequencing: "In that book they didn't have the houses when she wanted to be something different. [When] she wanted to be something different she losed the house."

Sandy didn't always stop to comment or respond, but she never stopped Sarah, either. Sarah's commentary wasn't a matter of lack of self-control or negligence on the part of Sandy. Rather Sarah verbalized her thoughts out loud as she processed information. Her comments, which were rather sophisticated at times, indicated that she was being challenged at abstract levels. Her processing was distinctly different from that of other children. In this type of classroom, children can grow and learn at different rates. A child like Sarah can remain challenged at a high level. Seeing Sarah, I have to wonder how important it is to keep children focused on our tasks and questions at all times, to insist that they always be good listeners. A child like Sarah would be swallowed up in such a classroom.

The Critical Role of Writing

Sandy's students were engaged in oral discussion. They read a variety of books each day and listened to many stories. Not surprisingly, they perceived themselves as successful readers, from the children who were reading books with several words to the children who were beginning Nate the Great trade books. In addition, these children were engaged in a wide variety of writing tasks. When the children compared and contrasted information in books, Sandy often wrote their dictated words onto butcher block paper. They chose the categories and the responses. As the year progressed, however, the children themselves took turns putting the words on the charts.

When the children wrote stories based on *The Three Little Pigs*, their adventures took on new form and shape. Sandy spent a great deal of time exploring ideas for writing with the children, both in large-group and in individual conferences. The children also spent time in spontaneous drama, reenacting versions of the folk tales read in class. In the beginning, Sandy acted as narrator, but gradually the children took over the reins of inventing stories and scenarios for the pigs and their mother. Children were then ready to write their own stories about pigs, spiders, ants, and wolves having an assortment of adventures. The reading of many stories, the re-reading of favorite stories, the rich discussions, the comparison charts, and the dramatic play were all critical parts of preparation for writing in Sandy's classroom. These children had no paucity of words at the oral or written level.

CONCLUSIONS

Classrooms like Sandy's tell us a great deal about how children can construct meaning interactively, what their agendas are, and how they begin to take ownership of our carefully crafted lesson plans, units, and notions about how and what they are to learn—if we give them some encouragement and freedom to explore. Studies of a child's sense of theme emphasize the quality of the interactions between the child and literature and the teacher's role in eliciting thoughtful responses from children. Acceptance is a given; open response is a must. Oral discussions are critical. As observations in Sandy's room indicate, interactive contexts allow children to construct meaning jointly as they respond to each other. The teacher's role is to facilitate the students' efforts. Obviously, teachers teach and fill in the many gaps, but they also are part of the constructive process and know when to take a back seat and let it happen.

The child's sense of theme does not occur in a vacuum. A classroom that encourages risk taking, has a wide array of high-quality books and reading materials, and promotes student chatter and problem solving offers an environment conducive to exploring meaning in books. The focus is on the process, not on the color of the curtains in Frog and Toad's kitchen.

PROFESSIONAL RESOURCES

Applebee, A. (1978). *The child's concept of story: Ages two to seventeen*. Chicago: University of Chicago Press.

Cochran-Smith, M. (1984). *The making of a reader*. Norwood, NJ: Ablex.

Cox, C., & Many, J. (1989). Reader stance towards a literary work: Applying the transactional theory to children's responses. Paper given at the annual meeting of the American Educational Research Association, San Francisco, CA.

Cullinan, B., Harwood, K., & Galda, L. (1983). The reader and the story: Comprehension and response. *Journal of Research and Development in Education, 16*, 29–38.

Goodman, Y., & Burke, C. (1972). Additional guide questions to aid story retelling. In *Reading miscue inventory manual*. New York: Macmillan.

Hepler, S. (1982). Patterns of response to literature: A one year study of a fifth and sixth grade classroom. Doctoral dissertation, The Ohio State University.

Hickman, J. (1979). Response to literature in a school environment, grades K–5. Doctoral dissertation, The Ohio State University.

Holland, K., & Lehr, S. (in press). Children's response to literature: Isn't it about time we said goodbye to book reports and literal oral book discussions? In D. Bloome, K. Holland, & J. Solsken (Eds.), *Alternative perspectives in assessing children's language and literacy*. Norwood, NJ: Ablex.

Huck, C. (1960). *Huck inventory of literary background*. Boston: Houghton Mifflin.

Huck, C., Hepler, S., & Hickman, J. (1987). *Children's literature in the elementary school* (4th ed). New York: Holt Rinehart and Winston.

Kiefer, B. (1989). Picture books for all the ages. In J. Hickman & B. Cullinan (Eds.), *Children's literature in the classroom: Weaving Charlotte's web*. Needham Heights, MA: Christopher Gordon.

Lehr, S. (1987). Revised Huck Literature Inventory. In M. White (Ed.), *Instructor's manual for children's literature in the elementary school* (4th ed.). New York: Holt, Rinehart and Winston.

Lehr, S. (1988). The child's developing sense of theme as a response to literature. *Reading Research Quarterly, 23*, 337–357.

Lehr, S. (1990). Literature and the construction of meaning: The preschool child's developing sense of theme. *Journal of Research in Childhood Education, 5*, 37–46.

Lehr, S. (1991). *The child's developing sense of theme: Responses to literature*. New York: Teachers College Press.

Liebling, C. (1989). Insight into literature: Learning to interpret inside view and character plans in fiction. Paper given at the annual meeting of the National Reading Conference, Austin, TX.

Many, J. (1989). The effects of stance and age level on children's literary responses. Paper given at the annual meeting of the National Reading Conference, Austin, TX.

McClure, A., Harrison, P., & Reed, P. (1990). *Sunrise and songs*. Portsmouth, NH: Heinemann Educational Books.

Paley, V. (1981). *Wally's stories*. Cambridge, MA: Harvard University Press.

Siegel, M. (1983). Toward an understanding of reading as signification. Research Report ERIC, ED 246 388.

Taylor, D. (1983). *Family literacy.* Portsmouth, NH: Heinemann Educational Books.

White, D. (1954). *Books before five.* Portsmouth, NH: Heinemann Educational Books.

CHILDREN'S LITERATURE

Andersen, H. C. (1982). *The Swineherd.* Illustrated by L. Zwerger. New York: Morrow.

Bang, M. (1983). *Dawn.* New York: Morrow.

Brown, M. (1972). *The three billy goats gruff.* San Diego CA: Harcourt Brace Jovanovich.

Carle, E. (1979). *The very hungry caterpillar.* Cleveland, OH: Collins.

Galdone, P. (1970). *The three little pigs.* Boston: Houghton Mifflin.

Galdone, P. (1975). *The gingerbread boy.* New York: Clarion.

Hutchins, P. (1971). *Titch.* New York: Macmillan.

Heins, P. (1974). *Show White.* Illustrated by T. Hyman. Boston: Little, Brown.

Ike, J., & Zimmerman, B. (1982). *A Japanese fairy tale.* London: Warne.

Krauss, R. (1945). *The carrot seed.* New York: Harper and Row.

Polacco, P. (1990). *Thundercake.* New York: Philomel.

Rice, E. (1975). *New blue shoes.* New York: Macmillan.

Steel, F. (1976). *Tattercoats.* Illustrated by D. Goode. New York: Bradbury Press.

Steptoe, J. (1969). *Stevie.* New York: Harper and Row.

Turkle, B. (1969). *Thy friend, Obadiah.* New York: Viking.

Udry, J. (1961). *Let's be enemies.* Illustrated by M. Sendak. New York: Scholastic.

Zemach, M. (1980). *The fisherman and his wife.* Translated by R. Jarell. New York: Farrar, Straus & Giroux.

Zolotow, C. (1969). *The hating book.* Illustrated by B. Shector. New York: Scholastic.

15

Going up the Beanstalk: Discovering Giant Possibilities for Responding to Literature Through Drama

Brian Edmiston

After reading *Jack and the Beanstalk* with his first-grade class, one teacher pretended to go up the beanstalk with them. They were all in role as neighbors of Jack, and this teacher was using the type of drama I discuss in this chapter. Like Jack, the students were on the lookout for gold, and when some found gold coins, they put them in their pockets. They agreed that they would like to meet the giant, so their teacher pretended to be him and asked them what they had hidden in their pockets. The students were unsure what to say. Some pretended they had no coins; others admitted they had them. When the giant asked them to return the coins, some refused and ran away, while others stayed to negotiate. The students were making up a drama together, but they were also concerned with one theme of the story: taking other people's things. The students had previously drawn pictures showing what they wanted to do with the gold; later, they negotiated for the release of those who had been caught by the giant and then wrote letters to him.

In all of these activities, the students were responding to literature through drama. This use of drama was pioneered in England by Dorothy Heathcote, and it has been used by Heathcote (1980, 1984, 1990), Gavin Bolton (1985), David Booth (1982), Cecily O'Neill (1982, 1983, 1988), myself (1991a, 1991b), and others to enable students to respond thoughtfully and insightfully to literature.

DRAMA, PLAY, AND CREATIVE DRAMATICS

The experiences that young children have as they read or are read to quite naturally lead them into spontaneous dramatic play in which they imagine that they are characters in what can usefully be called the "story world."[1] Trina Schart Hyman (1981, p. 9) has described how, at age 3, the story world of *Little Red Riding Hood* "was so much a part of me that I actually became Little Red Riding Hood" for over a year. She dressed in a red cape and hood made by her mother, and her backyard became a forest, her dog was the wolf, and her father the woodcutter. She was clearly responding to the story in her play just as she did years later in her writing and painting for her version of the folk tale that won the Caldecott Honor. Though the story world is normally an imaginary world that individuals create as they read, when children play together they can, in effect, create a shared imaginary story world. Vivian Gussin Paley (see, especially, Paley, 1986) has given us unequalled rich descriptions of how, as part of their unsupervised dramatic play, children interact with and respond to stories without any adult prompting or involvement.

Using drama in the classroom draws on children's natural ability to play. Teachers of creative dramatics do this when they encourage their students to use puppets or act out a story by improvising characters' actions and dialogue in the dramatization of stories (Ward, 1930, 1957; Siks, 1960). Though children may have significant insights into a piece of literature during a dramatization or afterward in a discussion, children and teacher, unfortunately, are too often more concerned with the details of recreating the plot than with considering meaning.

Rather than using drama to help students act out a story, Dorothy Heathcote advocates that teachers should isolate moments from stories to create dramatic encounters in which students of any age may be challenged into new ways of thinking. Heathcote notes that, "Drama is not stories retold in action. Drama is human beings confronted by situations which change them because of what they must face in dealing with those challenges" (1984, p. 48). In drama you "put yourself into other people's shoes and by using personal experience to help you to understand their point of view you may discover more than you knew when you started" (1984, p. 44).

By stressing attention to a person's point of view or attitude, Heathcote provides a simple but significant solution to the problem

---

1. A reference to "story world" is not meant to imply that drama can only be used with stories. Examples from stories are used in this chapter, but drama can also be used to structure students' responses to novels, poems, and plays.

of how you, as a teacher with a class of thirty or more students, can dramatize an event from a story that has only four or five main characters. Rather than limiting students to imagining that they are the characters in a story, *all* of the students can take on a role that has the same point of view as a character or another person concerned with the events of the story. For example, Jack's neighbors going up the beanstalk will have a perspective parallel to Jack's, and the giant's friends would view missing gold as theft as much as would the giant Jack met. Though police officers or social workers do not appear in any version of the tale, they, too, would have a perspective on Jack's escapades that the teacher might want to explore with the students.

In other words, rather than putting our energies as teachers into getting the story right, we can work with our students to create dramatic situations in which they may all take up perspectives on certain aspects of the story. They may see the story world through the eyes of characters or others, and, in doing so, the students will have experiences from inside the story world. If they reflect on those experiences, they may well discover new insights into the characters, the themes, and themselves.

COMPARING THE EXPERIENCE OF READING WITH DRAMA

Louise Rosenblatt (1968, 1978, 1982) has repeatedly emphasized that response to literature should not be regarded as anything a text may do to the reader but is rather a highly complex ongoing process resulting from each reader's transactions with texts. Rosenblatt (see, especially, 1978, pp. 69–70) has stressed that we need to be aware of the difference between the text (the words on the page), our aesthetic experiences (or "lived-through evocations") as we read, reread, and recall texts, and our reflections on those experiences, which we can organize into what may be labelled an interpretation. She stresses that reading must be seen experientially and that, after an initial reading of a text, as teachers" our initial function is to deepen the experience . . . to return to, relive, savor, the experience" (1982, p. 275). Only after such rich experiences and their reflections on them should we expect students to be ready to make or share any meaningful personal interpretation.

These distinctions are important when discussing responding to literature through drama. The text must be distinguished from students' experiences and reflections. After reading a text, students frequently discuss literature and in doing so continue to experience the events and characters of a story. They also reflect on their experiences, which are then often transformed into speech, writing, and artwork. Janet Hickman (1979) found that, given the opportunity in the classroom primary-age children will engage in dramatic play about literature. In play, the children continue to have experiences with the text if they are paying attention to the characters' concerns and thus the themes and issues in a story. These experiences may well be "lived-through evocations" of their own sense of what the story means for them. In any interactions during and after their play, the children often may be reflecting on these experiences and thus forming interpretations of the story.

Drama can similarly be used with students of all ages.[2] An important difference, however, is that in drama the teacher, along with the students, is structuring the work and is thus affecting both the students' lived-through experiences and their reflections upon them. During dramatic encounters, students may have rich, deep, and extended experiences in which they consider the themes, issues, dilemmas, and implications in literature. Students can also be enabled to reflect on those experiences both during and after dramatic encounters so that they can discover and then shape their interpretations into words, music, drawing, or other ways of sharing a personal response.

STRUCTURING THE WORK SO THAT STUDENTS RESPOND TO LITERATURE

Though students may be interpreting literature without teacher intervention, as in play, or with external structuring, as in creative dramatics, Heathcote (1984) argues that it is the teacher's responsibility to intervene as the drama is unfolding in order to structure the work so that such situations occur.

There are two broad ways in which the teacher structures the work: externally and internally. Externally, the teacher plans and decides what to require or allow the students to do. This position can be very passive when the teacher acts like a facilitator or stage manager of the students' dramatic play, or it can be much more active when the teacher sets tasks and takes on the functions of director and playwright. In any event, the teacher is structuring from outside the drama. If children eagerly ask "Can we go up the beanstalk?" then the teacher's structuring could be to help them work together, listen to each other, and agree on what they find there and what they want to happen. And, provided they are all working productively, the teacher could choose not to intervene if, for example, they find gold coins and put them in their pockets or creep into the giant's closet looking for more gold.

---

2.   Chapter 8 in Purves, Rogers, & Soter (1990) is the only other detailed discussion of drama and response to literature of which I am aware. Using drama with literature is considered in most of O'Neill's illuminating writings, and David Booth's (1982) use of "Story Drama" is always concerned with the themes of literature.

However, to challenge the students in a particular way, the teacher can be more active and, for example, suggest and agree with the students that those who crept into the giant's closet were locked in and could not get out. In this way, the teacher is structuring the dramatic encounter so that the students may be challenged in their thinking and response to the situation. The first-grade children who found and then pocketed gold coins had put themselves in a situation that paralleled Jack's decision to take gold from the giant. However, by running away they did not face any of the consequences of their actions. When some of the children pretended to run into the giant's closet, the teacher, in role as the giant, locked them in. After, the students agreed that this had happened, the teacher talked with them in role as the giant. His actions had structured the drama and put the children in a similar situation to the one they had been in before when they were confronted by the owner of the gold coins. However, this time the children had more need to talk to the giant, and it was harder for them to run away because now they would be leaving their friends. The teacher's structuring had put the students into a situation that required them to think more deeply than they had before about whether or not they should keep the stolen gold in their pockets.

Heathcote is well known for her structuring of interactions by the use of "teacher in role," in which the teacher takes on roles alongside the students and interacts with them. This is how the teacher structures internally. For example, in role as the giant, the teacher could confront the children with having to explain why they had gold coins in their pockets and then require them to negotiate with him over the release of their friends. He was responding to their ideas, but through interactions he was keeping their attention on the circumstances in which they might take, keep, or return the coins they had found.

Structuring needs to be quite meticulous if the teacher wants the students to experience and reflect on a particular situation. I recently worked with fifth-grade students on *The Journey,* a picture book that deals with the internment of Japanese-Americans during World War II. In my own class, I would have spent time with the students selecting situations to explore through drama, but as I had only limited time with these students I chose a passage in the text that I wanted the students to respond to in depth. Sheila Hamanaka writes, "In 1943, all prisoners in the camps over the age of seventeen were ordered to fill out Loyalty Questionnaires. Would they serve in combat wherever sent? they were asked. Old people and women worried they would be drafted. Also asked: Will you forswear allegiance to the Japanese emperor, Hirohito? . . . 263 were sentenced to prison for resisting the draft" (1990, p. 24).

I planned how to structure the drama so that the students would be able to consider this situation in the drama. Externally, I set tasks that helped the students build up a sense of what it meant to have both a Japanese and an American heritage and to be taken away to a camp: students created "photographs" in small groups, in pairs they took friends on tours of their houses, as a whole group they shared family treasures, and in pairs experienced arrest by the FBI. With everyone (including myself) in role as a detainee, I internally structured the drama by telling the group that I had heard we would be offered our freedom if we renounced any allegiance to the emperor. Then I joined in the discussion about whether or not we should sign a renunciation. What followed was a heated debate. Some of the interactions included the following:

"There must be some mistake, we are Americans."

"I don't want to be American if they treat us like this."

"I have to sign, my poor little baby and when she was born in the concentration camp she would die and if I sign I can never speak of my homeland again but my baby will live to tell the truth about the foolish Americans so it won't happen again."

"I want to go back to Japan where I'll be treated equally. I want to be part of bombing these people that have done this disgusting thing to us."

"That will make us just as evil if we do something to them, just as foolish, as cold-blooded as them. How can you see in this way?"

"We can be American on the outside but inside we can't change being Japanese."

With another group, at a similar point, I switched roles and met them as the camp commander. Again, I was structuring the work internally. In this role, I now could set tasks like asking them to say the pledge of allegiance. I could interact with them and tell those who forswore allegiance to the emperor to line up to be drafted and to take arms; I could show those who refused to say the pledge how disappointed the camp commander was that they would not declare their loyalty.

By structuring and interacting in role with the group, I was able to continue to affect their experiences. I was also able to press them to reflect more deeply than they might have without my presence in role. Those who remained silent were pressed to decide whether or not to speak out. One person asked whether they might be sent to fight their family in Japan if they were drafted. I answered that they would be sent to fight the enemies of the United States. Many scoffed in reply and asked me if I would kill my own relations. I reply that I was a soldier and would do my duty, as they should if they were loyal Americans. When they were reciting the pledge of allegiance, one person shouted that it was a lie because it did not guarantee liberty and justice for all. She walked forward, stood in front of the recently armed Japanese-Americans, and dared them to kill her. The atmosphere was electric.

The intensity of these students' feelings and the range of their thoughts did not occur by accident. Just as with all significant moments in classrooms, careful teacher structuring, both externally and internally, in all cases brought the students to situations in which they were challenged in their thinking about aspects of a piece of literature.

In this chapter it is impossible to make more than a brief reference to how teachers might structure work with their own classes. The books and articles noted under "Professional Resources" at the end of this chapter are useful resources, though, of course, only by using drama with our classes can we learn most how to use it.

HOW DRAMA DIFFERS FROM A BOOK DISCUSSION

Before continuing to discuss response to literature through drama in more detail, it is important to note some of the differences between drama and discussion.

As readers, we may go inside a book as we become characters, empathize with them, and critique their actions. However, when we talk about literature, we are always outside our world of the story and are no longer experiencing it except in retrospect. Even if we relive a moment as we share it with a friend, neither of us are inside the story as we talk about it.

Any sharing of responses in the classroom is detached in this way from the previous experiences the readers are describing. This is true whether the students are sharing poems, stories, paintings, enactments, or are discussing their feelings and thoughts about a book.

In drama, however, we can enter the world of the story with others. Our private world of literature can become a drama world, a public shared world of the text in which we can walk around and interact with other people in role. When we interact in role everything we say is significant and related to the story; everything we say and do may be part of an interpretation.

Dorothy Heathcote (1984) uses the phrase "now and imminent time" to describe the feeling that an experience is happening now rather than in the past. In discussion, we stand back and look at events that happened to other people in a different world. In drama, we feel in the middle of events that concern us or are happening to us because in role we are in the same world as the story.

What we say and do within the drama is not just a detached comment about the world of the story. On the contrary, every action and inaction affects that world directly and affects the person we imagine ourselves to be in the drama world. For example, when the students in the role of Japanese-Americans were asked to stand up and recite the pledge of allegiance, whether they stood up became significant and changed what was happening at that moment. The students were not making a detached decision about "what I would do if I were in the camp," this decision had to be made and acted upon by students who were feeling "what will I do now that I am in this camp?" Even inaction affected the situation because those students who stayed seated in effect were saying to the others that they would not say the pledge. Those who did stand were accepting the authority of the commander and were emphasizing the inaction of the others. Thus the students' words and actions, as well as those of the teacher, affect the experiences the students have in the drama world.

Nevertheless, students do stand back to reflect on what is, has been, or may be happening in drama. We can discuss drama work in the same way as we discuss a book, either after or during reading, by sharing our thoughts and feelings about the events that occur or may occur in the drama. We can do this by stopping to talk, just as we do when we pause in reading and when we discuss at the conclusion of a piece of work.

However, in drama, we can also reflect from inside the drama as it is being created. Reflection inside the drama and reflection in an ordinary discussion differ in that when we are in the drama we are not only able to look at the significance of events and interpret them as "ourselves" but we can also do this from the perspective of the person we are pretending to be. This double perspective seems to create the possibility of what Gavin Bolton (1985) calls "a unique subjective/objective relationship with the world" that promotes "the kind of understanding any writer whose subject matter is human life must have in abundance." Clearly, as teachers, we want to promote a similar understanding in our students' readers.

For example, as has been noted, the students' reactions within *The Journey* drama became part of their overall experience of the situation, but this experience then meant that they could continue to reflect, both in role and as themselves, on their own and others' actions. In doing so, they could ponder the significance and thus discover their meaning of the situation.

These two responses to the situation, in and out of role, may be quite different. A student may agree with a statement or action in role, but disagrees with it in actual life (Purves, Rogers, & Soter, 1990, p. 108). This contradiction can increase the awareness that a response to an experience is not automatic but can be a matter of choice. The choice may not be easy. The harder the choice, however, the more dramatic a situation is and, thus, the more thinking a student will do to wrestle with the difficulty. Inevitably, this process must result in more thoughtful responses to literature.

DRAMA AS A SHARED CONTEXT FOR RESPONSE

Response is not static. As Louise Rosenblatt reminds us, it is a dynamic, ongoing experience of our transaction with the text. Response should be responding and continuing to respond as we see more implications in the events of a story, understand more of the feelings and motivations of the characters, and draw more parallels between the world of the book and the experiences of our own lives.

When we read and think about books, we may each create rich, complex, and very realistic imaginary story worlds that we explore and respond to (Enciso Edmiston, 1990). But by pretending to go up the beanstalk together, the teacher and his first-grade students created a shared imaginary drama world that paralleled and drew on the world of the story and in which they were able to share responses. Thus, because everyone was creating the reality of the imaginary world up the beanstalk, each individual's attitudes and responses could affect and be affected by what others, as well as the teacher, said and did.

Drama is a group art; you can only create drama when people interact. When the focus of their interactions is a literature text, then they are collectively responding to that literature. The different responses of participants can result in a deeper consideration of a theme, so that responses may become more complex.

Before meeting the giant, the first-grade students who went up the beanstalk considered the morality of killing him. Their teacher noted that, "Some wanted to kill the giant so nobody would get caught and it would be easy to take his gold. Others said that was murder. What a lively discussion!" Ordinarily a teacher might feel uncomfortable discussing killing, but in considering what they might do to take the gold this option was a seriously argued position of these first-grade students and is clearly an aspect of the original story. Significantly, however, the students, rather than the teacher, eventually convinced each other that it would be wrong to kill the giant.

They also considered whether it was right to take his gold. They challenged each other's ideas and considered when taking money might not be wrong. Their teacher wrote, "Kristen was very adamant that it was all right to take the gold from the giant because they were so poor. Katie was equally strong in her belief that stealing is always wrong. The class was divided. During the discussion Sarah changed her mind about taking things but wanted to go to the giant's castle just to see how big everything would be."

The class was unable to reach consensus on the right action, though Sarah provided them with a way of agreeing to disagree. This solution was sufficient until they discovered that some people had taken gold coins and that the giant had captured some of their friends. Then they had to consider whether they should return the gold, and they had to agree. "Let's only take one gold coin," said Adam, who earlier had argued in favor of taking all the money and now said that they did not have to return it all. Allie, however, responded, "That's still stealing." In the ensuing discussion it was eventually decided, with Adam's consent, to return all the gold coins to the giant in exchange for their friends.

The reality of the drama world allowed these students to discuss and argue about important interpretations of their experiences of this story. Here was a "community of readers" (Hepler & Hickman, 1982) who were sharing their responses and thereby affecting each other's reading of the text. However, because they were interacting with each other and the teacher in an imaginary situation, they could challenge each other in role and do so in the context of situations in which their decision made a difference. Taking money had to be weighed against the lives of their friends, and they had to listen to each other and decide together what to do. Individuals may have changed their attitudes because it was appropriate and protected for these students to share their responses and interpretations with each other in a way that allowed for the possibility of deepening and questioning the initial responses.

STANCES IN DRAMA AND READING

As teachers, we may want students to find out facts, information, or significant ideas as they read, but with literature we also want them to experience the work as a whole so that they will "stir up personal feelings, ideas, and values" (Rosenblatt, 1982, p. 259) and be changed by what they read. Rosenblatt made the significant observation that we take up an efferent stance when we read for information and an aesthetic stance when we read for experience. Our purposes for reading are quite different in each case. Though efferent reading of literature may be important, she argues that aesthetic reading must precede it.

In drama there is always an overall aesthetic stance because students are interacting and thinking about events and actions that happen in an imaginary world. Details and descriptions in a text are all read in the wider context of the drama world. When the drama world is woven from the fabric of a piece of literature, then if the words or images from the text are referred to in the drama they will naturally be interpreted holistically. For example, *The True Story of the Three Little Pigs* was read to a class of fifth-grade students, and as soon as the class agreed to imagine they were the lawyers for the wolf and began to discuss his case, every reference to details of exactly what the wolf said he had done was made in the context of the entire story. This approach was clear from the students' repeated references to the story in their interactions.

In role, the students may take an efferent and/or an aesthetic stance. For example, as lawyers for the wolf, the students were very concerned with some of the particular phrases the wolf gave in his statement. They focused on facts and details but always within the overall stance of their reaction to his statement as a whole. As the drama proceeded, the lawyers decided what the wolf might be charged with, what his defense might be, and if found guilty what his punishment might be. In order to discuss these issues the students needed both an aesthetic stance and an efferent one. They had to see the wolf's actions within the wider context of his relationships with others, but they also needed to consider the specifics of what he said and did. In doing both, the students returned to the text, which had been typed as if it were a statement made by the wolf. As the lawyers interviewed potential witnesses, visited the wolf's home, and went to the police station, the students continued to reread the text as they checked what he had said and how reliable they thought his statement was. For example, most were impressed with his analogy between a wolf eating a pig and humans eating a cheeseburger, but many began to think it implausible that he would go to borrow sugar from *three* pigs, even if they were all neighbors. The students in role as lawyers were paying attention both to the details of the text but also to the text as a whole. Later in the drama when they studied photographs taken by the press (illustrations from the book), the lawyers realized that the police and newspaper reporters were pigs. Then they began to question whether they could believe what had been said or written by the police or reporters any more than what the wolf and his granny had said. Throughout this drama the students were considering one of the central themes of this picture book: the truth of a story depends on who is telling the tale.

In this work, the text had been available for the students' reference. However, though a text can be read as part of the drama, it does not need to be read in role to be the basis of a drama. The interactions in the ensuing drama may still be an ongoing interpretation and response with an aesthetic and/or efferent stance, as they were with all the dramas referred to in this chapter. For example, the fifth-grade students who had read *The Journey*, the picture book about the internment of the Japanese-Americans during World War II, did not reread the text during a two-hour drama session, but they repeatedly made implicit references to the events and experiences of being interned that are so graphically recounted in the text.

DIFFERENT FRAMES OF REFERENCE GIVE DIFFERENT PERSPECTIVES

As well as taking an overall efferent or aesthetic stance in drama, students adopt this stance from a particular perspective. Heathcote has borrowed the term "frame" from sociology (Goffman, 1974) to emphasize that just as a person's perspective on events in everyday life is determined by that person's sociological role, so in drama the role we play gives us a particular frame of reference that implies a certain power and responsibility (Heathcote, 1984, 1990). For example, the lawyers for the wolf have the responsibility to prepare a defense and the power to interview and gain access to people, places, and documents. The police have similar power, but no responsibility to defend the wolf. The wolf's family may want to defend him, but they have little power once he is arrested. Each individual in these roles views the same events differently, and in considering response to the story, each reads the same statement by the wolf in a different way because of the different frame of reference.

When we ask students to respond thoughtfully to literature, we are asking for more than initial ideas. We want readers to consider events from the perspectives of characters, but we also expect them to stand back from the work and critique it. We want more than a bland "I like it" and expect students of all ages to be able to appreciate some of the complexities of a book by seeing it from different points of view. Emyrs Evans (1987, p. 36) argues that "the more viewpoints we are offered . . . the more complex, and so the more thought-provoking and significant, the text and the work become." He is describing how the reader's viewpoint moves during the act of reading a text, but he could equally be describing how, by reframing the class, the teacher can shift the viewpoint of the students during a drama.

One drama with sixth-grade students began with reading *Nettie's Trip South,* which is written in the form of a letter by a young girl describing her impressions during a trip with her journalist brother to the South just before the Civil War. In the drama, the students' frame shifted as they took on the roles of present-day museum curators setting up an exhibit about slavery, newspaper reporters at that time looking at photographs of enslaved people and writing reports, abolitionists meeting to decide what to do about a runaway in their town, museum curators looking at images of the effects of war, and finally as citizens meeting to decide how to advise their senator to vote on the proposal to go to war. Students interacted, wrote, read, pretended they were in photographs, and spent nearly two hours responding to the book. By the time they were in role as citizens, they had transformed themselves from a reticent giggling group who offered no opinions on what they thought about slavery to a group whose talk had to be stopped so that they could go to their next class.

Students had taken up multiple perspectives that included characters in the story but also perspectives on the story world as a whole. From the point of view of an enslaved person, one student wrote, "The pain was unbearable as I was beaten." Another, after visiting the present-day "museum," described a slave auction as a journalist at that time: "The black slave was standing with her son on the stage. My eyes opened wide as people started bidding on the mother. . . . I almost started shouting and crying when two black men came on stage and yanked the two apart. The expression on the mother's face was of pure horror as she started screaming. The boy's shouts were lost in the laughter that followed. And then it went on again, another slave stepping forward as if it was the most natural thing in the world." One student wrote a letter to the newspaper from the perspective of an abolitionist: "We must take action. I have stood by watching slaves being beaten and sold like property long enough. How much longer can we let blacks undergo this torture? How much more pain can they take? We must speak out about our beliefs no matter what the consequences are. God created us equal." When they considered the consequences of war and the possibility of seeing their own children die, many students in role as citizens were less enthusiastic about rushing into conflict. Some vocal boys argued that attacking the plantations was a solution, and some said the slave owners should be killed. However, as one girl said quietly, "We can't kill slave owners because then we would be no better than they were."

At the conclusion of the drama, the same girl, writing as "herself," said: "I never knew slavery was that wrong. I guess I grew up in the wrong generation." Many commented on how they had felt they were really back in the time of slavery. One student concluded, "If only everyone who is prejudiced took this class, I'm sure they would become aware of the wrongness and cruelty slavery brought to our country."

By shifting perspectives and experiencing events from the frame of reference of different people with different concerns, the students had been able to see *Nettie's Trip South* through multiple lenses. They drew on whatever attitudes they had to slavery as they interacted and transformed their responses into words and actions. As the drama continued, they were able to see more and more perspectives, so that the discussion about going to war had multifaceted reasoning as well as being intense and passionate. Some argued that they had to defend the defenseless; others said that it would only make matters worse for everyone. One quietly asked "Would you die for someone else?" in response to a call to attack the South. Some said they could not fight their relations, and others said they did not know what to do.

These students were clearly responding to their many different experiences of the world of *Nettie's Trip South.* They had considered from many perspectives the book's brief but significant reference to the impending war and descriptions of Nettie's reactions to visiting a plantation, having to see a slave auction, and questioning of slavery. This classroom drama took place in May 1991, during the aftermath of the Gulf War and the debate over rescuing the Kurds, so who knows what ideas and feelings about war these students were drawing on and reexamining as they interpreted this story?

MODES OF RESPONSE TO LITERATURE THROUGH DRAMA

Many references have been made in this chapter to students' talk in role. Because drama involves the whole person, it cannot exist without interactions. As has been shown, students can respond deeply and sincerely as they interact and talk with each other and with the teacher.

However, within the drama students can transform their feelings and thoughts in other ways to form interpretations. Some mention has been made of writing in role. For example, first-grade students wrote letters to the giant, and sixth-grade students wrote accounts of what they had seen in the South and newspaper articles and headlines about slavery. The possibilities for writing in role are countless. For example, the lawyers for the wolf could have taken notes as they interviewed or written letters to potential witnesses, and the Japanese-Americans could have written diary entries, haiku, or letters to Congress. Writing in role frequently flows naturally from the drama, and students want to write because they have something to say and someone to write to (Edmiston, Enciso, & King, 1987; Wagner, 1985). Of course, students can write as "themselves" at any time as they stand back from the work and respond to it as a whole.

Similarly, students may want to draw or paint in or out of role. For example, students might draw pictures of the giant's castle or paint the view from inside an internment camp cell. They may draw alone or paint together—for example, by drawing a mural or making a map.

Drama uses more than words; people are continually moving in drama. Movement or dance can easily be part of a drama; for example, students could show the dreams of the Japanese-Americans as they moved to some Japanese music. Less threatening is the use of depictions or tableaux where students represent photographs, statues, portraits, films, or other static or moving images (Heathcote, 1980).

All of these modes of response can be integrated into the drama and form aspects of ongoing and evolving interpretations by the students of their experiences in the drama. They can also form a culmination or concluding response that incorporates individual responses but collectively builds a shared response. For example, students in role as survivors of the Japanese-American internment stood as statues in a memorial. They took up poses as guards, non-Japanese-Americans, and the people who had been interned. Visually they represented a diversity of emotions from anger and resignation to strength and determination. Orally they provided a montage of voices; as they stepped into the statue they spoke messages for all U.S. citizens. These included:

"We're all different and we should be proud of all of our cultures."

"I've been in concentration camps, my sister's died, and my daughter's gone away, but I know one thing after living through all I've gone through: you've got to be good to yourself and when doing that you can't be bad to anyone else. You try to be the best person you can be and in doing that you don't hurt anyone else."

"Nobody needs to know who you are, as long as you know who you are that's all that matters."

"When I was young my mother and father would tell me about it and I wouldn't really care. . . . I didn't know what they were talking about, but now I do I'm going to act on it, I'm going to do something, I'm going to write something, draw something . . . do something to show we care."

"Educate. Tell the truth. Write what actually happened in the social studies textbook."

"Even if it is an opinion, it is the truth, We have to speak out no matter what."

"Nobody can change anybody else, it's that person that has to change themselves. The only way we can help is to say,"This is what's going to happen if you do this.' We can tell them what happened and show them. You need to go by what you believe in."

IMPLICATIONS FOR TEACHERS

To ignore the power of drama in the classroom is to overlook the potential of using the basic human ability of imagination to foster and deepen students' responses to literature. In drama, students can have lived-through interactive experiences inside the worlds of literature in addition to their talk about books. And by reflecting during as well as after their experiences in drama, students have more opportunity to deepen their responses and influence each other as they form their interpretations.

Any literature text can be explored through drama. As teachers, we do not need to develop lengthy or complex dramas in order to tap into the power of drama. Nor do we have to allow students to run around and be destructive. We can start by considering what roles would give students different perspectives on the text as a whole or on the dilemmas or problems faced by characters or narrator. We then can plan to interact in role with our students for a few minutes and use all we already know about learning, grouping, motivation, self-discipline, and our classes as groups in order to have a successful beginning. And, in my experience, students usually beg for more chances to work in drama—a reassuring position for any teacher to be in.

As teachers, we can enjoy playing with texts and exploring with our students different viewpoints on worthy literature. Rosenblatt (1982, p. 276) extoles "the potentialities of literature for aiding us to understand ourselves and others, for widening our horizons, to include temperaments and cultures different from our own, for helping us to clarify our conflicts in values, for illuminating our world." Drama can help us realize these potentialities provided that we are prepared to go up the beanstalk with our students and explore what is there.

PROFESSIONAL RESOURCES

Bolton, G. (1985). Changes in thinking about drama in education. *Theory into Practice, 24*(3), 151–157.

Booth, D., & Haine, G. (1982). Story drama: Access to the world of the reader. In *2D Drama & Dance, 1*(2), 43–49.

Byron, K. (1986). *Drama in the English classroom.* London & New York: Methuen.

Edmiston, B. W. (1991a). *What have you travelled? A teacher-researcher study of structuring drama for reflection.* Unpublished doctoral dissertation, The Ohio State University.

Edmiston, B. W. (1991b). Structuring for reflection: The essential process in every drama. *Drama Contact, 15,* 5–12.

Edmiston, B. W., Enciso, P., & King, M. (1987). Empowering readers and writers through drama. *Language Arts, 64,* 219–229.

Enciso Edmiston, P. (1990). *The nature of engagement in reading: Profiles of three fifth-graders' engagement strategies and stances.* Unpublished doctoral dissertation, The Ohio State University.

Evans, E. (1987). Readers recreating texts. In B. Corcoran & E. Evans (Eds.), *Readers, texts, teachers.* Upper Montclair, NJ: Boynton/Cook.

Goffman, E. (1974). *Frame analysis.* New York: Harper & Row.

Heathcote, D. (1980). Signs and portents. In L. Johnson & C. O'Neill (Eds.), *Dorothy Heathcote: Collected writings on drama and education.* London: Hutchinson.

Heathcote, D. (1984). *Dorothy Heathcote: Collected writings on drama and education,* edited by L. Johnson & C. O'Neill. London: Hutchinson.

Heathcote, D. (1990). Keynote address. In K. Byron (Ed.), *The fight for drama—The fight for education.* Newcastle upon Tyne, Eng.: National Association for Teachers of Drama.

Hepler, S. I., & Hickman, J. G. (1982). "The book was okay. I love you"—social aspects of response to literature. *Theory into Practice, 21*(4), 278–283.

Hickman, J. G. (1979). *Response to literature in a school environment, grades K–5.* Unpublished doctoral dissertation, The Ohio State University.

O'Neill C. (1983). Role play and text. *The English Magazine, 11,* 10–12.

O'Neill, C. (1988). Ways of seeing. *NADIE Journal, 13*(1), 11–17.

O'Neill, C., & Lambert, A. (1982). *Drama structures.* London: Hutchinson.

O'Neill, C., Lambert, A., Linnell, R., & Warr-Wood, J. (1977). *Drama guidelines.* London: Heinemann.

O'Neill, C., & Enciso Edmiston P. (Eds.) (1989). Drama in the classroom: Landscapes for action. *Literacy Matters 1*(2). There is an accompanying Drama Handbook that is distributed by the Martha L. King Language and Literacy Center, The Ohio State University, Columbus.

Paley, V. G. (1986). *Mollie is three.* Chicago: University of Chicago Press.

Rogers, T. (1990). Dramatic response and oral interpretation. In A. Purves, T. Rogers, & A. Soter (Eds.), *How porcupines make love II.* New York and London: Longman.

Rosenblatt, L. (1968). *Literature as exploration* (3rd ed). New York: Modern Language Association.

Rosenblatt, L. (1978). *The reader, the text, the poem: A transactional theory of the literart work.* Carbondale: Southern Illinois Press.

Rosenblatt, L. (1982). The literary transaction: evocation and response. In *Theory into Practice, 21*(4), 268–277.

Siks, G. B. (1960). *Creative dramatics: An art for children.* New York: Harper & Row.

Wagner, B. J. (1985). Elevating the written word through the spoken: Dorothy Heathcote and a group of 9- to 13-year olds as monks. *Theory into Practice, 24*(3), 166–172.

Ward, W. (1930). *Creative dramatics.* New York: Appleton.

Ward, W. (1957). *Playmaking for children.* New York: Appleton-Century Crofts.

CHILDREN'S LITERATURE

Cauley, Lorinda Bryan (1983). *Jack and the beanstalk.* New York: Putnam.

Hamanaka, Sheila (1990). *The journey.* New York: Orchard Books.

Hyman, Trina Schart (1981). *Self-portrait: Trina Schart Hyman.* Reading, MA: Addison-Wesley.

Hyman, Trina Schart (1983). *Little Red Riding Hood.* New York: Holiday.

Scieszka, Jon (1989). *The true story of the three little pigs.* Illustrated by Lane Smith. New York: Viking Kestrel.

Turner, Anne (1987). *Nettie's trip south.* Illustrated by Ronald Himler. New York: Macmillan.

16

Children's Responses to Picture Books: A Developmental Perspective

Barbara Kiefer

Students and colleagues who know of my interest in art and in picture books often ask, "What types of illustrations do children like?" As an art educator and elementary classroom teacher just beginning my doctoral studies some years ago, I also asked this question. But as I reviewed similarly driven preference studies conducted over the course of some sixty years, I realized that the question is both naive and superficial.

First, in efforts to determine children's preferences for style, media, or content of illustrations, many researchers reduced their testing instruments to single pictures or slides that controlled for variables like color, pictorial content, or style and asked children to choose the picture that they liked best (Smerdon, 1976). Such studies (which found, for example, that children prefer color over black and white, realism over abstraction, and familiar content over the fantastic) failed to consider that the picture book is a unique art object, one that is a combination of image and idea in a sequence of turning pages and that can produce in the reader an effect that is greater than the sum of the parts (Bader, 1976; Marantz, 1983).

Moreover, in many of these studies, children's reactions were observed only momentarily. For example, in Smerdon's study, children were asked to look at pairs of slides flashed on a screen at five-second intervals and then to mark their preference for pictorial styles on a checklist. In this fashion not only was the artistic object simplified but also the event of picture viewing. Like Smerdon, other researchers had not taken into account the complex nature of aesthetic response, the fact that it involves affective as well as cognitive understandings, or that it might change over time (Purves & Beach, 1972; Rosenblatt, 1976). Nor had they considered the social and cultural nature of the picture book reading that is part of children's experience with picture books (Heath, 1983; Hickman, 1981). Despite such shortcomings of these preference studies, researchers used their findings to suggest that publishers and book buyers should limit the media, style, form, and content of books published and purchased to those that children liked.

Similarly, when illustrations were the focus of reading comprehension or word recognition studies, researchers often isolated words and pictures from the context of the whole book or story in the way that researchers of children's picture preferences isolated single pictures from the context of the entire book. In one such study, for example, Samuels (1967) presented groups of kindergarteners with four words on index cards, either with pictures or without. When the "no picture group" gave significantly more correct responses to the printed words than to words and pictures, Samuels concluded that pictures interfered with word learning and recommended that books for beginning readers contain no illustrations (1970). Fortunately, researchers have more recently concluded that both listening and reading comprehension are facilitated when illustrations overlap and extend the printed words in books, a characteristic inherent in the definition of the picture book as an art object (Levin, 1981; Schallert, 1980).

Because of these and other problems with previous studies of children and picture books, I determined to enter classrooms where I might find children regularly interacting and responding to picture books and to study and describe the dimensions of their responses. I thus chose first/second-grade classrooms in alternative schools in a suburb of Columbus, Ohio. The classrooms were modeled on the British informal system, which might currently be called "whole language." Children's literature, not textbooks, formed the core of the curriculum, with learning activities organized around themes. There were between 300–500 picture books in the classroom libraries. The teachers read aloud to children and discussed books with them several times a day, and children had opportunities to read alone and with other children, to talk about books with each other, and to respond to books through art, writing, drama, and other avenues.

I entered the classrooms as a participant observer, first for a period of ten weeks and second, the following year, for a period of twelve weeks. Initially my role was mainly observational. I kept a field notebook, noting behaviors and comments during read-aloud sessions and during individual and group work times, and I recorded some sessions on audiotapes. During the second observa-

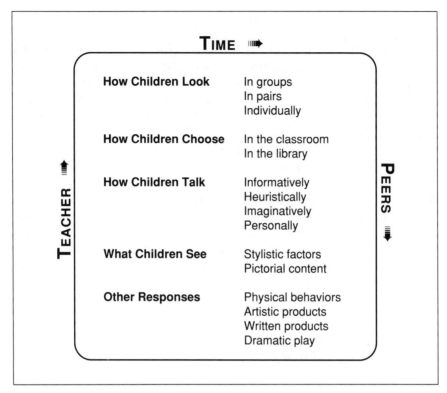

FIGURE 16–1   *Responses to picture books*

tion period, I also conducted and taped interviews with children, both singly and in pairs. In one set of interviews, I presented children with two recently published picture books that differed in style and content and asked them to show me how they liked to look at a new picture book and to talk about each book as they looked through it. In the second group of interviews, I read children a Grimm's fairy tale without showing them the pictures, asking them to try to imagine pictures in their heads. Later I showed pairs of children three versions of the tale illustrated in different styles and media and asked them to talk about their responses to the books.

During my early observations, as field notes and tape transcripts were reviewed, several general themes began to emerge concerning children's responses to picture books. These themes or domains involved the variations in children's responses, the changes in responses over time, and the stylistic and content differences among the picture books. Then, as data gathered from further observations and interviews were reviewed, I developed a descriptive framework for children's responses to picture books (see Figure 16–1).

While children's responses were not quantified within these categories in my research, the categories and subcategories were useful for observations conducted in other settings and with other populations in subsequent years. These further studies were conducted in a third/fourth-grade combination classroom in the same school I had initially visited in suburban Columbus; in a university preschool in Houston, Texas; in a second-grade, urban Houston school with a multicultural population; and in a below grade level multicultural fifth-grade classroom in a suburban Houston school. In all these settings, by using the ethnographic techniques described previously, I was able to describe a variety of possible responses to picture books that reinforce the validity of the descriptive framework. In addition, by looking at children's responses at different ages I also have been able to note developmental differences in children's awareness of stylistic factors relating to the art in picture books. The remainder of this chapter discusses the dimensions of response that teachers might expect or hope to find in their students and the types of aesthetic awareness that also may develop as children have time to respond to picture books as they mature developmentally.

A DESCRIPTIVE FRAMEWORK FOR RESPONSE TO PICTURE BOOKS

Unlike studies of children's preferences for illustrations that sought norms for particular styles, media, or content of books, my studies have identified the wide variation in individual responses. Thus the descriptive framework for children's responses includes the many behaviors that grew out of their contact with picture books, how children chose picture books, how they looked at picture books, how they talked about picture books, and what they said they saw in the illustrations. Moreover, I included the classroom context—that is, the many picture books available, the actions of teachers and peers, and the changes over time in children's responses—as an essential part of this descriptive framework.

When teachers gave children encouragement, opportunity, and time to respond to picture books beyond the group read-aloud or individual reading sessions, children often chose a variety of ways to extend their initial reactions to books. Many chose some form of artistic response, either two-dimensional (paintings, collages, murals) or three-dimensional (dioramas, sculpture, displays). Children often chose to write in response to books in informal journals, in short pieces telling about their personal reaction, in poetry, or in more formal reports. Often these responses involved small groups of children who wanted to work together. Creative drama (puppet shows or plays) was one result of such of group response.

When it came to selecting books, I found that many children chose books that the teacher or librarian had recommended or read to them. Children also used peer recommendations or relationships in choosing books to read. One first-grade boy, for example, explained that he selected his book because it was on the same shelf as the one his friend picked. Often children chose books that were displayed attractively, cover facing forward, or they chose books because they were deeply interested in the topic, such as horses.

In observing children looking at books during read-aloud sessions, I found more variation in behavior. Some children sat close to the teacher, their eyes intent on the pages or moving back and forth between the teacher's face and the book. Other children sat further away and appeared to give less attention to the book. Even these children, however, seemed to note small details in the illustrations, despite their distance from the book, and they often called these details to the attention of their classmates.

Children looking at books on their own also seemed to have idiosyncratic approaches, some looking through the entire book from front to back or back to front before reading and others proceeding directly to the printed text and giving less attention to the pictures. This last approach was found among the more fluent readers; emergent readers tended to preview the illustrations first and then rely on the illustrations on each page before they tackled the printed text.

A third category of response, and the one that provided the most data, was children's verbal responses. As I observed children in all settings, I found an enthusiastic willingness to immerse themselves in the contents of their picture books, and verbal language seemed to give them the tools for understanding this complex art object. Although I considered using several already existing schemes for literary response to organize this wealth of data (Applebee, 1973; Odell & Cooper, 1976), I felt that these did not allow me to detail the full range of responses to picture books that I was finding. In reviewing transcripts of read-aloud sessions and interviews, I noticed that children seemed to employ many different functions of language as they talked about books within the larger social context of each particular classroom. This brought to mind M. A. K. Halliday's (1975) work on language development, *Learning How to Mean.* Because the children I observed seemed to be intent on making meaning regarding picture books, I therefore developed a classification scheme for children's verbal responses to picture books based on four of Halliday's functions of language: informative, heuristic, imaginative, and personal. As data from subsequent studies, particularly with older children, were examined, a taxonomy of functions was further refined and categorized. (See Figure 16–2.) These categories are useful for helping to understand how children *learn how to mean* in the world of the picture book.

Primary Function	Subcategories	Examples
1. *Informative:* Provides information, a pointing or telling function	1.1. Report the contents of the illustration	"There's the witch."
	1.2. Provide information about art styles or techniques	"He used brown."
	1.3. Describe or narrate pictured events	"You just see them sleeping there and the witch leaving and then you see her talking to them."
	1.4. Compare contents of the illustrations to something in the real world	"This looks like wood."
	1.5. Compare one book to another	"This looks like *Jumanji*."
2. *Heuristic:* Problem solving function, includes wondering about as well as offering solutions	2.1. Wonder about the events or contents of the illustrations	"Couldn't they just sell the bed and buy food?"
	2.2. Make inferences about events, the setting, or a character's personality, motives or actions	"This looks deep." "She looks mean."
	2.3. Make inferences about cause and effect or possible outcomes	"If they stepped on a twig they would of got real hurt."
	2.4. Make inferences about the preparation of the illustrations—what the artist did	"It looks like he used a little pencil line to just do little sketches for it."
	2.5. Make inferences about the illustrator's intentions	"He liked to use darker colors."
3. *Imaginative:* Recalling, creating, or participating in an imaginary world	3.1. Enter into the world of the book as a character or onlooker	"The father looks like he's saying, 'Why do we have to leave them?' and she's going, 'Hah hah.' "
	3.2. Create figurative language	"These [leaves] look like tropical birds."
	3.3. Describe mental images	"This doesn't look the same as I thought."

FIGURE 16–2 *Functional categories for children's verbal responses to picture books*

Primary Function	Subcategories	Examples
4. *Personal:* Connecting to individual experience, reporting emotions, stating opinions	4.1. Relate personally to events, setting, or characters	"I wouldn't of went up there with a snake up there." "Here she's yelling. My mom does that."
	4.2. Express feelings or describe personal effects of art elements	"That makes me sad." "Darker colors give you a feeling of being scared."
	4.3. Express opinions or evaluate the illustrations	"He shoulda put a wart on her nose." "The pictures don't look so good here— it looks like he repeated. He just used orange and a grey."

FIGURE 16–2   *continued*

Informative Language

Many children used language to convey information about picture books, often literally pointing to the pictures as they spoke. For example, a first grader looking at Plume's version of the Grimm brothers *The Bremen Town Musicians* pointed to the picture and stated, "Here's the dog and here's the cat and here's the donkey." Other children seemed to use the pictures to retell or reconstruct events in the story. A fifth grader looking at Galdone's version of *Hansel and Gretel* explained, "Here you see the witch looking right through the curtain. You don't even see the witch talking to them. You just see them sleeping there and the witch leaving and then you see her trying to get her [Gretel] to go in."

The informative function also helped children compare the illustrations to the real world or to other books. Comments such as "this looks like wood" or "this reminds me of that other book" were found at all age levels. Children often seemed to use these comparisons as a reality check. First and second graders, for example, looked at Domanska's expressionistic animals in *The Bremen Town Musicians* and stated, "Cats aren't usually pink and orange" or "I never seen a purple donkey."

Children also provided information about the process of illustration as well as the content of the pictures. They talked not only about the elements of art ("He used brown") but also about processes of composition. Two fifth graders, for example, discussed the artist's use of object placement as it affected eye movement in Zwerger's *Hansel and Gretel:*

KRISTEN: Here it looks sort of like a hill—how they've brought the color up.
MARK: Maybe to shift your eyes.
INTERVIEWER: Do they kind of do that for you? Shift your eyes?
KRISTEN: It depends on where the main part of the picture is—
MARK: You see this [a tree] and then you follow there [to the right] and then you see the girl and then you're crazy to turn the page.

Heuristic Language

Wondering about an apparent discrepancy between the parents' poverty mentioned in the verbal story of *Hansel and Gretel* and the rather cheerful setting pictured in one of the illustrated versions, a fifth grader mused: "I don't see why they don't have enough food. It looks like expensive beds. Couldn't they just sell the beds and buy seeds and plant food?" A second grader asked "How could she fly?" of Sendak's heroine in *Outside over There.* "Because it's a magic cloak," replied a classmate. These remarks were typical of children who used the heuristic or problem-solving function to ask questions about the illustrations or to make inferences or predictions about the events in story.

A fifth grader made inferences about a character in Anthony Browne's modern-day version of *Hansel and Gretel* when he stated, "It looks like the mom isn't really responsible because she throws her clothes around," while two fourth graders suggested that a storm at sea pictured through a window in *Outside over There* represents the inner emotions of the heroine. "She has to take care of the baby and that's her responsibility and she feels bad and that's why the storm is there," they argued.

In addition to heuristic language applied to understanding the story, children also seemed interested in understanding art techniques or the illustrator's intentions. A first grader speculated that Bloom had used paint in Chaffin's *We Be Warm 'til Springtime Come* because she could "see the brush strokes coming down." Looking at Galdone's *Hansel and Gretel,* a fifth grader suggested, "It looks like he used a lot of line . . . like he used a pencil line to just do little sketches and then he put a little color in because he thought everything would be white at first and he just took a pencil line and sketched it in."

Imaginative Language

The imaginative function allowed children to participate in an imaginary world created by the author or artist or to create their own mental images. Some children assumed the roles of characters and created imaginary dialogue as they viewed the illustrations. A third grader said, as she looked at the woodsman confronting the wolf in Hyman's *Little Red Riding Hood*, "So here you are, you old sinner. I've been looking for you all this time and this is where I find you." Two fifth graders improvised the following exchange as they looked at a version of *Hansel and Gretel:*

KRISTEN: Right here the expression on his face he says, like, "I know, I'll pick up these rocks and we'll find our way back."
MARK: Yeah, like, "Heh heh, look what I'm gonna do now. They won't lose us."

At times, children described how their own mental images differed from the illustrator's version, as with this fifth grader's comment, "I thought the witch's house would be in a clearing and all you'd see was gingerbread and candy." At other times, children described mental images evoked by the pictures. Two first graders were looking at Diamond's black-and-white illustrations for *The Bremen Town Musicians* when one said it reminded her of Van Allsburg's *Jumanji*, also illustrated in black and white. As they looked at the two books side by side, they stated:

NINA: They look pretty different.
INTERVIEWER: They do, don't they? How are they different?
NINA: Because this [Jumanji] has a little bit more colors in it—like—
INTERVIEWER: Colors?
NINA: See—the game board—
AMANDA: It looks like different colors, doesn't it?
INTERVIEWER: Uh-huh.
NINA: And, like, when you just turn it and you can see white—and you can see a little bit red.

Since the illustrations were only in black and white, these statements clearly described mental images rather than what the children saw on the page.

The imaginative function also allowed children, particularly young children, to use verbal imagery in formulating unusual comparisons. A first grader, for example, looked at ripples behind a boat in Shulevitz's *Dawn*. "That's like whipped cream that men put on to shave," he explained. On another occasion, first and second graders described de Paola's distinctive clouds as "pumpy or "like mashed potatoes."

Personal Language

On many occasions, children connected personally to books, either relating the books to something in their own lives or discussing feelings or opinions about the books. These connections were similar to what Cochran-Smith (1984) called text-to-life interactions. A story event or illustration often triggered a personal connection that might seem to have little relation to the book itself. "We got bathroom wallpaper colored like that," reported a first grader. The dog character in *The Bremen Town Musicians* reminded another first grader that "I love dogs. They're so cute. We were going to get one, but my grandma had to come [live with us] because she kept messing up the [her] house." A fifth grader pointed to a picture of the stepmother in *Hansel and Gretel* and observed, "Here she's yelling. My mom does that."

The pictures also evoked expressions of emotion. As they looked at a close-up of a dog's face filled with porcupine quills in Carrick's *Ben and the Porcupine*, first and second graders exclaimed, "Don't show that picture. It makes me so sad." Third, fourth, and fifth graders recognized the effects of color on their emotions and reported that bright green made them feel happy or that browns and greys made them feel sad or scared.

At all grade levels I found children willing to express opinions about books and to evaluate their quality. As Applebee (1978) found in studying children's responses to stories, the younger children whom I observed evaluated books based on their own subjective responses rather than on some objective quality in the book itself. For example, when asked to explain why she had stated that Domanska's *What Do You See?* was a good book, a first grader replied, "Because I liked it." In observing third through fifth graders, however, I found children more apt to back up their subjective reactions to a book with objective criteria. Looking at one of the versions of *Hansel and Gretel*, a fifth grader, for example, complained that Galdone, "didn't take her [sic] time with this book. She used too much of this brownish stuff and it doesn't look good." Later he came back to the book and said, "I didn't like that one. It didn't look good. The pictures, she coulda took her time with it." A fourth grader comparing two illustrated versions of an old Japanese tale wrote:

> I really notice the difference in the language and the illustrations of the two books. In *The Wave* the language is very exquisite and very delicate—the words carefully picked one by one and in *The Burning Rice Fields* the words are slopped on the page. The illustrations in *The Wave* is cardboard cuts carefully cutted to resemble objects in the story and in *The Burning Rice Fields* the pictures are done in a child's version of crayon drawings. Unfortunately I like *The Burning Rice Fields* better because its in more detail.

Detail was a criteria that other children used to judge a book's quality. Two fifth graders looking at Zelinsky's version of *Hansel and Gretel* remarked,

PATRICK: I like the end pages in this one. I think from the end pages that I'm going like it better than the two I've read so far.
INTERVIEWER: What makes you feel that way?
RHONDA: Clouds.
PATRICK: Yeah, it looks bright . . . and it's got some dark, but not as dark as that whole thing [Anthony Browne's version] and I like books where they're like happy.
RHONDA: And this looks like you're really standing outside, standing outside and seeing birds and clouds.
PATRICK: I think the illustrator did a good job because I like realistic illustrations.
INTERVIEWER: And you don't think the others were realistic, huh?
RHONDA: Not that much.
INTERVIEWER: What is the difference?
RHONDA: The details and the colors.
PATRICK: And they look really poor because look at his pants. They're all torn. . . . He used a lot of detail because the walls are cracked.
RHONDA: And look at their faces.

Such exchanges show how fluid and dynamic all these functions of language were—one function quickly giving rise to another, one child supporting or extending the understanding of another, all in the context of making meaning through picture books.

WHAT CHILDREN SEE IN PICTURE BOOKS

As I examined these verbal responses to picture books in a variety of classroom contexts and as I began to articulate a theory of style in picture books (Kiefer 1982, 1988), I began to note developmental differences in children's awareness of stylistic factors relating to the art in picture books. I noted first that children seem to see small details in picture books that adults miss. Indeed, studies of visual perception have found that children's eye movements within a pictorial plane are quite different from adults. Children, for example, have many more and longer eye fixations. This tendency may not be a factor of immaturity as much as it is a learning function, as Coles, Sigman, and Chessel (1977) have suggested. It seems that, as children pour over the pages of their picture books, they find the many small details that many illustrators include in their pictures and that we adults may over look. The rewards of sharing what one teacher called "secrets" with the illustrator may in turn help children become more sensitive to the artistic qualities in picture books.

Indeed, as I observed children at different grade levels responding to picture books in many different ways, I found that they developed more critical thinking not only about cognitive factors but also about aesthetic factors and that this awareness was different depending on the age of the child. The differences in stylistic awareness may be tied to factors of cognitive development, as Applebee (1978) has suggested.

One change that I noted at different ages related to the children's awareness of the artist behind the book. I found that some younger children were confused about who created the pictures. Some thought that machines made the pictures rather than an artist who created an original work that was then photographed and printed by machines. Other young children were unsure about variations in individual styles or the stylistic choices made by artists in the process of illustration. Often their attention to stylistic qualities was idiosyncratic. One first grader argued that *Mother, Mother, I Want Another* (Polushkin) was illustrated by the same artist who did *I Saw a Ship A Sailing* (Domanska). When pressed to explain why he thought two books that differed greatly in style were by the same artist, he explained, "the words." Both books had been printed in Abbott Old Style, a rather distinctive typeface. This first grader had overgeneralized the form of the printed letters to the entire artwork. On another occasion, a first grader supported his contention that three different artists had illustrated the three versions of *The Bremen Town Musicians* by pointing to the copyright page. "This one is from New York, this one from the United States, and this one is made in New York, New York," he stated.

Older children seemed to know that a real person lay behind the creation of the pictures, although when they discussed the pictures the illustrator was sometimes referred to as "they," as when a fifth grader stated, "they shoulda made some dust or something instead of all this money—you know, to show he's really poor, that he doesn't have any money." Many older children were aware that the artist existed in the real world and could be the subject of dialogue or study. Looking at Chris Van Allsburg's *The Wreck of the Zephyr*, a third grader suggested, "Those are nice pictures. We ought to write to Van Allsburg." A fifth grader remarked that he had decided to do a study of Van Allsburg "because he does black and white in some of his books and I like the way he puts his details in with black and white, like making it light or dark."

The differences in stylistic awareness among the ages also extended to the elements of art that are the artist's means of expression. All children seemed to be familiar with elements like lines, shapes, and colors, although they didn't always have the correct nomenclature. Kindergartners and first and second graders talked about squiggly lines, twisty lines, or construction paper shapes (those with sharp edges). Many of these youngsters confused bright colors (in intensity) with light colors (light in value) and used the term "light" to indicate brightness. Children of all ages referred to the element of texture by using terms like rough or smooth. And although even the older children rarely used the term "value," they seemed to be aware of the presence of this element by talking about dark pictures or an artist's use of "sunlight."

Unlike the younger children, children in grades three and above seemed to be aware not only of the elements of art but also that the artist chose these elements in order to convey some meaning to the viewer. These children talked about an artist's role in evoking emotional responses through the elements of art, and they commented on technical choices relating to book production. A fourth grader stated of Galdone's *Hansel and Gretel,* "The lines sorta make it look detailed and the detail makes it look scary." Looking at Maruki's *Hiroshima No Pika,* a third grader remarked, "The pictures look sad. They don't have a certain shape to them." Other older children mentioned such technical choices as end pages, page layout, and choice of original media. A fourth-grade boy examined the rust-colored end pages as he opened Zwerger's version of *Hansel and Gretel:* "They look reddish brown, like somebody's put something there and just forgot about it and never got it up again. They put it in the forest and left it there forever." Many of the third, fourth, and fifth graders who looked at Zwerger's book speculated about what seemed to be an abrupt cut-off of several of the illustrations that left large areas of white at the edge of the page.

MATT: Maybe he did this while he was on a trip or something. He saw those people that looked like his characters and he had a special size of paper and he couldn't blow it up.

JASON: They shoulda put something there [in the margin], a bird or something.

A third grader's remarks about the illustrations and page layout in *Hiroshima No Pika* is indicative of how children seemed to grow in understanding the meaning-making power of visual art. Maggie had been looking at the small vignettes and single-page illustrations in the first part of the book and remarking on the rather cheerful colors. Then she turned the page at the point in the story where the atomic bomb is dropped, a double-page spread in tones of red, rust, and black. "It gives me the impression that the illustrator's just seen the bomb happen and she just choked and doesn't want to talk about it and she'll show you a picture of what happened," she stated. Maggie seemed to recognize the unique ability of visual art to convey deep emotion as well as to deepen understanding.

Books that engendered such deep emotions rather than those the children "liked" were the ones around which the longest-lasting response grew and deepened (Kiefer, 1985). It often seemed that when a book was puzzling rather than pretty, children talked more about it, argued more about it, wrote more about it, and created more art or dramas in response to it. One such book was Van Allsburg's *Jumanji,* a book that some preference studies suggested children would not like because it had black and white illustrations rather than color. When I asked first and second graders how they felt about black and white illustrations, Steve replied, "Pictures don't have to be in color. . . . It's harder when its in black and white. It takes more time and you don't just whip through the book." He pointed to the cover of *Jumanji* and explained that the monkeys hiding in the closet would have been easy to see if the book had been in color. But, he explained, "You like to take time." Older children also seemed to agree that an important criteria for a picture book was not to make it "easy for you to find things" but to "make us think more."

CONCLUSIONS

While it is difficult to generalize the responses of children in these classrooms to all classroom situations, the variety of children's responses to picture books described here show what is possible rather than probable when children have the time and opportunity to interact with picture books. Practical recommendations that grow out of these observations are tied to the contexts in which these responses occurred. The descriptive framework for the children's responses (Figure 16–1) would not, I believe, hold together were it not for such crucial factors as access to books and teachers who give children time to respond to books in a classroom community of readers (Hepler & Hickman, 1982).

Teachers who wish to explore the meaning-making potential of picture books with their students will want to begin by building a good classroom library, supplemented by books from school and municipal libraries. Such a collection should include a variety of different styles and types of picture books (see Huck, Hepler, & Hickman, 1987, or Kiefer, 1988, for a discussion of styles in picture books). Teachers should plan to use picture books across the curriculum at all ages, not just in the primary grades, and they also might plan special experiences such as illustrator studies or a mock Caldecott Award process.

Collaborating with the school art teacher to help children deepen their understanding of a variety of art forms both in and out of museums also may help teachers foster their students' critical awareness. But more important may be the mutual exploration of picture books by teachers and students in the classroom. Here children do not need art experts as much as they need teachers who enjoy picture books and read them regularly, sometimes several times a day. Children also need time to talk about picture books, with the teacher in large group settings or more informally in small discussion groups or with another friend. They need time to chose books that interest or intrigue them, time to read, and the time and encouragement to respond to books through a variety of means other than talk—especially through art, writing, and creative dramatics. In contexts such as these, children can move beyond mere preferences and deepen their understanding of the rich worlds of images and ideas found between the covers of picture books.

PROFESSIONAL RESOURCES

Applebee, A. N. (1973). *The spectator role: Theoretical and developmental studies of ideas about and responses to literature, with special reference to four age levels.* Doctoral dissertation, University of London.

Applebee, A. N. (1978). *The child's concept of story.* Chicago: University of Chicago Press.

Bader, B. (1976). *American picture books: From Noah's ark to the beast within.* New York: Macmillan.

Cochran-Smith, M. (1984). *The making of a reader.* Norwood, NJ: Ablex.

Coles, P., Sigman, M., & Chessel, K. (1977). Scanning strategies of children and adults. In G. Butterworth (Ed.), *The child's representation of the world.* New York: Plenum Press.

Halliday, M. (1975). *Learning how to mean: Explorations in the development of language.* London: Longman.

Heath, S. (1983). *Ways with words: Language, life, and work in communities and classrooms.* Cambridge, Eng.: Cambridge University Press.

Hepler, S., & Hickman, J. (1982). "The book was okay. I love you": Social aspects of response to literature. *Theory into Practice, 21,* 278–283.

Hickman, J. (1981). A new perspective on response to literature. *Research in the Teaching of English, 15,* 343–354.

Huck, C., Hepler, S., & Hickman, J. (1987). *Children's literature in the elementary school* (4th ed.). New York: Holt Rinehart Winston.

Kiefer, B. (1982). *The response of primary children to picture books.* Unpublished doctoral dissertation, The Ohio State University.

Kiefer, B. (1985). Looking beyond picture book preferences. *The Horn Book Magazine, 61,* 705–713.

Kiefer, B. (1988). Picture books as contexts for literary, aesthetic and real world understandings. *Language Arts, 65,* 260–271.

Levin, J. (1981). On functions of pictures in prose. In F. Pirozzolo & M. Wittrock (Eds.), *Neuropsychological and cognitive processes in reading.* New York: Academic Press.

Marantz, K. (1983). The picture book as art object: A call for balanced reviewing. In R. Bator (Ed.), *Signposts to criticism of children's literature,* pp. 152–155. Chicago: American Library Association.

Odell, L., & Cooper, C. (1976). Describing responses to works of fiction. *Research in the Teaching of English, 10,* 203–225.

Purves, A., & Beach, R. (1972). *Literature and the reader: Research in response to literature, reading interests, and the teaching of literature.* Urbana, IL: National Council of Teachers of English.

Rosenblatt, L. (1976). *Literature as exploration* (3rd. Ed.). New York: Noble and Noble.

Samuels, S. J. (1967). Effects of pictures on learning to read: Comprehension and attitudes. *Review of Educational Research, 40,* 397–408.

Samuels, S. J. (1970). Effects of pictures on learning to read, comprehension and attitudes. *Review of Educational Research, 40,* 397–408.

Schallert, D. L. (1980). The role of illustrations in reading comprehension. In R. Spiro, B. C. Bruce, & W. F. Brewer (Eds.), *Theoretical issues in reading comprehension: Perspectives from cognitive psychology, linguistics, artficial intelligence, and education.* Hillsdale, NJ: Lawrence Erlbaum.

Smerdon, G. (1976). Children's preferences in illustration. *Children's Literature in Education, 20,* 97–131.

CHILDREN'S LITERATURE

Bryant, S. (1963). *The burning rice fields.* Illustrated by M. Funai. New York: Holt Rinehart.

Carrick, C. (1981). *Ben and the porcupine.* Illustrated by D. Carrick. New York: Clarion.

Chaffin, L. (1980). *We be warm 'til springtime come.* Illustrated by L. Bloom. New York: Macmillan.

Domanska, J. (1971). *I saw a ship a sailing.* New York: Macmillan.

Domanska, J. (1974). *What do you see?* New York: Collier Macmillan.

Grimm Brothers (1980). *The Bremen town musicians.* Illustrated by I. Plume. New York: Doubleday.

Grimm Brothers (1980). *The Bremen town musicians.* Translated by E. Shubb; illustrated by J. Domanska. New York: Greenwillow.

Grimm Brothers (1981). *The Bremen town musicians.* Illustrated by D. Diamond. New York: Delacorte.

Grimm Brothers (1976). *Hansel and Gretel.* Illustrated by P. Galdone. New York: McGraw-Hill.

Grimm Brothers (1979). *Hansel and Gretel.* Translated by E. Crawford; illustrated by L. Zwerger. New York: Morrow.

Grimm Brothers (1981). *Hansel and Gretel.* Illustrated by A. Browne. London: Julia MacRae Books.

Grimm Brothers (1984). *Hansel and Gretel.* Retold by R. Lesser; illustrated by P. Zelinsky. New York: Dodd Mead.

Hodges, M. (1964). *The wave.* Illustrated by B. Lent. Boston: Houghton Mifflin.

Hyman, T. (1983). *Little Red Riding Hood.* New York: Holiday.

Maruki, T. (1980). *Hiroshima no pika.* New York: Lothrop Lee and Shepard.

Polushkin, M. (1978). *Mother, mother, I want another*. New York: Crown.
Sendak, M. (1991). *Outside over there*. New York: Harper and Row.
Shulevitz, U. (1974). *Dawn*. New York: Farrar, Straus & Giroux.
Van Allsburg, C. (1981). *Jumanji*. Boston: Houghton Mifflin.
Van Allsburg, C. (1983). *The wreck of the Zephyr*. Boston: Houghton Mifflin.

17

Making Connections
Across Literature
and Life

Kathy G. Short

In their daily lives, learners constantly make connections across past and present experiences in order to construct their understandings of themselves and their world. In fact, learning can be defined as a process of making connections, of searching for patterns that connect so that we can make sense of our world (Harste, Woodward, & Burke, 1984). We learn something new when we are able to make connections between what we are currently experiencing and something we already know. When we make few or no connections, learning within these experiences is difficult and easily forgotten. On the other hand, if we stay too close to what we already know, we are not pushed as learners into new understandings. For all learners, the most productive learning situation is one in which we stand within sight of what we already know as we push into new territory. Vygotsky (1978) argues that this zone of optimal learning is what we are able to learn with the support of other learners, not what we already are able to do alone.

In the classroom, teachers are currently looking for ways to support learners in making these connections between the new and the known. While the search for connections is a natural part of learning, students' experiences in schools have led many to expect fragmentation and lack of connection in what they are learning. Educators have responded to this fragmentation by emphasizing background experiences. Teachers are encouraged to ask students questions about their experiences or provide some type of prior experience before students read. The problem with this focus on background experience is that the teacher provides connections for students instead of helping students develop strategies for making their own connections. The teacher (or the teacher's manual) does the critical thinking about meaning. Thus students often are forced to try to make sense of someone else's thinking and connections (Short, 1985).

When the focus is on how to prepare readers for reading experiences, the reading event itself, as an experience, is overlooked. Educators forget that a reader can read one text to prepare for reading and understanding a second text (Crafton, 1981). Instead of focusing only on what readers have to do to get ready to read, educators need to consider what happens when readers read one text to facilitate their understanding of other, related texts.

Fragmentation also has occurred because traditional reading tests, instruction, and research have treated reading as an isolated instance and comprehension as the act of understanding a single passage. This isolated view of reading is so imbedded in how educators think that they disregard their own reading processes. Proficient readers understand as they read by connecting ideas to previous reading experiences (Hartman, 1990). In life, reading is an open transactive process, not a process of reading one text in isolation from life. Readers make multiple connections across texts, ideas, and experiences. These connections keep changing over time with each new experience and text.

This isolated view of reading raises the need for curricular strategies such as Text Sets that highlight the process of searching for connections and using one book to facilitate understandings of other books and issues (Harste, Short, & Burke, 1988). Text Sets are collections of conceptually related books that are used by a small group of students for discussion and comparison. Within the group, each student usually reads several books and shares these books with the rest of the group. Together they spend time exploring comparisons and connections across their books and lives. Readers are encouraged to first share their "lived through" aesthetic responses (Rosenblatt, 1978) with other readers and then to reflect on and analyze their responses and connections.

My interest in Text Sets grew out of classroom-based research on literature circles where students met in small groups to read and discuss their personal responses to and differing interpretations of literature (Short, 1986; Short & Pierce, 1990). While these literature circles typically involved the use of multiple copies of a single title for each group, some groups began using Text Sets organized around a theme, author, genre, or topic. As students participated in these discussions, I noted interesting differences between their dialogue about Text Sets and shared pieces of literature. When the group read and discussed the same piece of literature, they had a shared experience and so tended to focus in depth on their different interpretations of that book. In contrast, their discussions of Text Sets involved more retellings and searches for connections across their books. Students searched widely across the books and their own experiences within and outside of school to look for connections and issues that cut across the books in their set. Text Sets highlight intertextuality, the process of making meaning through connections across present and past texts and life experiences (Beaugrande, 1980).

BEGINNING THE INQUIRY

To explore further the meaning-making processes within the Text Set discussions, Gloria Kauffman, Kaylene Yoder, and I put together a number of Text Sets related to the interests of a group of third- and sixth-grade students. These sets were introduced to students, who chose the group to which they wanted to belong. Field notes were taken as they read, discussed, and presented their sets to the class, and the literature discussions were either audio- or videotaped. We also collected charts, webs, literature log entries, and any other written artifacts produced during the discussions.

Gloria and Kaylene were involved with me in designing, implementing, and completing the initial analysis of the study. We were interested in exploring the type of dialogue that occurred in Text Set discussions and how Text Sets facilitated children's search for connections in meaning making. We also wanted to examine the kinds of strategies children used to support their search for connections across literature and life and the kinds of intertextual connections they made during this search.

Gloria, Kaylene, and I functioned as teacher-researchers during the study. There were always two of us present in the classroom during the discussions, so that one person could take field notes and record the groups while the other interacted with students in discussion groups. After I completed an analysis of the data through the constant comparative method (Glaser & Strauss, 1967), Gloria and Kaylene responded to the analysis; I made needed changes.

The Text Sets used in this study were developed by brainstorming possible topics for the sets with the children. The different sets were not connected to each other by a broad theme because we wanted to explore a wide variety of types of sets. We then pulled together sets that had a range of kinds of literature and reading materials, levels of difficulty, and perspectives on the topic of the set. Students signed up for the group they wanted to join and started exploring their set. Each group contained four or five students. The Text Sets read and discussed by the groups were:

Third grade:

1. Magic pot set: folk tales with the motif of a magic pot that provides the owner with wealth and/or food.
2. Pig set: fictional picture books, poetry, and information books with pigs as the main characters.
3. Eric Carle set: picture books by this author.
4. Anne McGovern set: informational books by this author.
5. Caldecott set: picture books that won the Caldecott Medal.

Sixth grade:

1. Betsy Byars set: realistic fiction books by this author.
2. Chris Van Allsburg set: picture books by this author.
3. Japanese set: folklore, poetry, and informational books on Japan.
4. Dragon set: legends and folklore on dragons.
5. Plains Indians set: legends and historical information books.
6. War and Peace set: fictional and informational picture books dealing with the theme of war and living at peace with others.
7. Cinderella set: cultural variants from around the world.

All of the sets except for the Betsy Byars set consisted of different kinds of picture books. Most contained a variety of genres, as in the Pig set, which contained poetry, folklore, informational books, fantasy, and informational brochures from the Pork Society. Sets also contained materials aimed at students who differed in reading proficiency, background, and familiarity with the topic.

While the students in these two classrooms had been involved in many literature circles in their classrooms, they had not previously used Text Sets. To get them started, we suggested that they each read one or two books within their sets. The groups then came together, and students shared their books with each other, continued reading other books in the sets, and began to compare and contrast their books. As students continued discussing their sets, differences in dialogue across the groups became apparent. These differences were not influenced by grade level but by the readers' background experiences, the focus of the specific set, the types of connections explored, and the strategies used by the group to read and compare their books.

STRATEGIES TO SUPPORT A SEARCH FOR CONNECTIONS

As the groups began to talk and explore, they faced the problem of finding ways to deal with a number of different books and an overload of responses, ideas, and information. Each group found strategies that seemed to fit their members and the type of set with which they were dealing. These strategies included different ways of handling how the books were read, shared, and compared. Groups also explored strategies for focusing the discussions on particular connections to be explored in depth by the group. To facilitate the development and awareness of these strategies, a short sharing time often was held after students had met in their literature circles. We encouraged them to share the strategies they were using in their groups, pointed out strategies we had seen groups using, and together brainstormed other ideas for handling the discussions and comparisons.

Strategies for Reading, Sharing, and Comparing Books

The first differences that emerged across groups concerned the number of books read by group members and how the groups handled the initial sharing and comparing of books. As students began reading books in the sets, they were encouraged to write about their initial aesthetic responses in literature logs. The first group discussions were sharing sessions as students talked about the books and their responses with each other. These discussions were not focused on analysis or comparison but on enjoyment of literature. Groups differed, however, in how they continued the reading and discussing of connections across their books.

In some groups, students became experts on one or two books. Each day the group would discuss in depth a particular connection they saw across their books. Then each group member would relate that connection to the book on which he or she was the authority. Often group members had read several other books in the set, but during discussions they primarily referred to the one or two books that they had read first. They were considered the experts on these books. When the Magic Pot group discussed the ways in which the pot was magic, the members each described how the pot was magic in their specific book. As a group, they then looked for similarities and differences across their books based on their sharing. Group members had to collaboratively build connections and closely listen to each other because of the limited knowledge each group member had of the other books in the set.

In other groups, group members became interested in other books and continued reading throughout the discussions as a result of the initial sharing of books. By the end of their discussions, they had read most or all of the books in the set. Instead of talking about a particular part of one book in their group discussions, individual members talked about several books in comparison to each other.

Their initial discussions focused on sharing connections rather than on group members sharing and retelling stories. When the Cinderella group discussed stepsisters, each group member already had made a list of connections in their literature logs because they each were familiar with most of the books. Their discussions consisted of sharing and then comparing their connections across the books as they listened to each other's insights. Groups collaboratively used these insights to further develop the connections.

The group that discussed the war and peace books developed a different strategy. After several days, they decided to all read and discuss only one book from the set each day. Their books consisted of picture books that dealt with difficult issues related to war and peace, and they needed the collaborative reading and discussion of one book at a time. As they read and discussed each book separately, they made connections back to previous books, but, unlike the other groups, these connections were not the main focus of their discussions. This group primarily focused on their personal connections and aesthetic responses to each book. They were not ready to go beyond those responses to analyzing their responses.

Another group, the Japan group, divided their books into subsets and dealt with one subset a day. They used genre as the deciding factor and broke their books into poetry, information books, folklore, and other. Each day, group members read different books from one particular subset and then discussed the books and looked for connections within the subset. Near the end of their discussions, they began to connect these subsets to the broader topic of Japanese culture.

During their first discussions, the groups tended to spend the majority of time sharing and retelling. Because each person had read a different text, they all had something to share, and they had real reasons for retelling their book to someone else. In most classrooms, students are asked to retell a story to others who already know the book, and so they view the retelling as an exercise or quiz to see if they have read the book. In the Text Set discussions, students knew that most of the others had not read the book and needed to understand it to make comparisons. Thus, their retellings did not come from an efferent stance of looking for specific information but took the form of sharing their enjoyment of the story with someone who had not yet read the book. This type of sharing frequently led to children grabbing books they wanted to read before the next group meeting. In addition, students often started making comparisons during the retellings as they saw similarities between the book being shared and the book they had read. Many of the conversations freely moved back and forth between retellings and comparisons.

Strategies for Focusing on Connections

Initially, the discussions on the Text Sets ranged across a wide variety of topics and tended to be unfocused. Many ideas were mentioned but not explored in depth by the group. To an adult, these conversations might appear to be unproductive because they often consisted of false starts and rambling comments, without anyone developing or building on those ideas. These discussions, however, initially allowed readers to draw on their feelings for a book and to enjoy participating in another's vision of the world. The students' primary concern was not to analyze the books but to talk about what the books meant to them and share their own lived-through experiences with those books (Rosenblatt, 1978).

Having time to explore broadly without focusing the discussion also seemed to be critical in helping students develop a broader range of ideas to be considered by the group and to find the issues that most interested them for in-depth discussion. Gradually, each of the groups developed different ways to focus their discussions so that they could talk together about topics or issues in common among their set of books. Most of the groups used a specific strategy such as a web or list of possible comparisons, literature log entries, or the physical sorting of books to help them focus their discussions and connections.

Several groups brainstormed a list or web of possible comparisons and connections. One group brainstormed a list of questions about their set. These lists represented the range of connections, similarities, and differences that they might discuss. The groups then chose what they wanted to discuss each day from this list. Not everything on the list was discussed and new topics arose, but the brainstorming gave them a sense of what they could focus on in their discussions. The Betsy Byars group used this brainstorming strategy. Each group member read a different chapter book by Byars. After sharing their books with each other, they brainstormed a list of similar characteristics across their books. Their list contained topics such as "the kinds of problems kids have, types of solutions to kids' problems, enemies that cause problems, parents who are a problem, endings where things are better but not perfect, kids having adventures, and stories about everyday life." At the end of each day's discussion, the group would decide what they wanted to discuss from their list the following day, and group members prepared for their next discussion by thinking about the topic, rereading in their books, and/or writing about the topic in their journals.

Another strategy used by groups was to sort books physically. The Cinderella group frequently sorted their books into different piles as they discussed the different kinds of princes, the ball or festival, how Cinderella was illustrated, or the endings. The Caldecott group spent several days putting together pairs of books that they saw as related in some way. From these pairings, they went on to stack the books to develop their own broad categories for what they believed made a book a Caldecott Medal winner.

Many of the groups used different kinds of category systems or lists of characteristics as they focused their discussions. The relationship between broad categories and specific lists of characteristics was interesting to trace within the groups. Some groups began with broad categories and then listed characteristics from their different books. The Dragon group came up with several different category systems within which they searched for characteristics. They looked at categories for types of dragons (cartoon, real, and fairy tale) and the category of dragon as compared to dinosaur. Within these categories, they spent time listing characteristics from the different books they were reading.

Other groups listed characteristics and then sorted these characteristics into categories. The Caldecott group made lists of the characteristics of their books and then sorted these into five main categories that they saw as representing their major criteria for winning the award. These categories included illustrations (bright colors, action, imagination, etc.), characters (people, animals, birds, etc.), writing (details, title, exciting action, unusual words, etc.), solving problems (running away, thinking, asking for help, etc.), and how the book related to other books (kind of characters, use of borders, type of illustrations, etc.).

Other groups did not focus on categories or characteristics but explored a theme or question that cut across their books. Sometimes these groups began with a broad insight or theme that focused their entire discussion, while other times they began by listing many smaller details that gradually led to a broad insight. The Pig group focused their discussions on the question of why authors use pigs as main characters so frequently in their books. "What is it about pigs?" they asked. They discussed reasons, such as that pigs are more popular and cute than people, they are funnier and look better, that they make a book more exciting and fun, and that authors can write about pigs without hurting anyone's feelings, as might happen if they wrote about people.

On the other hand, the Chris Van Allsburg group spent a great deal of time pouring over his pictures looking for anything that he used in several books, such as a specific boy, dog, chair, wall covering, or style of porch. They began to wonder about his life, so we added several articles on Van Allsburg to their set. Their focus on details then moved to a larger perspective as they considered these details in relation to his life and home and to how his life influences his illustrating.

In examining the discussions, we found that often a particular book caused the group to take another perspective on their topic. This book was usually one that did not seem to quite fit with the rest of the books in the set and so the group was forced to reconsider the connections they were making in their set. *The Funny Little Woman* (Mosel, 1972) in the Magic Pot set raised questions because it was the one book in which there was no pot, only a spoon. *Emma's Dragon Hunt* (Stock, 1984) in which a modern Chinese child hunts for dragons with her grandfather raised the issue of whether dragons were real and not just part of legends. *Yeh-Shen* (Louie, 1982), a Chinese variant of Cinderella, was an older tale than the more familiar French variant, and this observation raised many questions about the story's origin and how it spread to other countries. *Bang, Bang, You're Dead* (Fitzhugh, 1969) brought the issue of war into the everyday lives of the boys reading the war and peace books. When the McGovern group listened to the tape of Anne McGovern discussing her work, they reread her books and then listened several more times to the tape as they discussed her books in more depth. In each case, these texts caused the group to rethink the connections they had been making and often resulted in the group making more complex connections across the books and their lives; this process, in turn, gave them a new perspective on the set and the issues being discussed.

In other experiences with Text Sets, groups have used tools such as comparison charts and time lines to help them organize and think through their connections. These tools, however, work best when used after a group has had time to talk and share their responses with each other. In one instance, a folk tale group moved to a comparison chart too early in the process, and their discussion became an activity focusing on details and filling in the blanks on the chart instead of a dialogue among readers. Students need the range of the possible before they begin organizing their connections. Then, whether they focus on a question, theme, characteristic, category, or book, they still consider these within the broader framework of their set. Readers need the support of discussion strategies that encourage them to explore broadly as well as to focus on specific intertextual connections.

EXPLORING INTERTEXTUAL CONNECTIONS

Just as the groups varied in how they went about searching for connections, there were interesting differences in what they discussed and the types of connections they made across texts and with their experiences. Intertextual connections that were frequently discussed were characters, themes, plot, illustrations, the response of the reader, the life of the author, and their own experiences.

Connections to Elements of the Story

The groups frequently discussed connections to particular kinds of characters, plot elements, and themes across their books. The Pig group focused on the character of pigs in books. The McGovern book focused on genre and theme. The Byars group looked closely at character and plot. The War and Peace group discussed symbolism in their books and how this symbolism related to larger themes about the impact of war on ordinary people's lives. They particularly talked about how innocent people and animals suffer in war. Sometimes the group focused on looking for connections across all literary elements to define what books fell within a particular set. The Magic Pot group spent their time figuring out the kind of plot, characters, and themes that made a book a "magic pot" book as compared to other folk tales.

While groups often discussed literary elements such as character and theme, they considered these in terms of the impact on the reader and decisions by the author. The Pig group looked closely at the character of pigs, but they did so from the perspective of why authors and illustrators choose them and why readers like pigs in books. The McGovern group spent the majority of their time talking about why they thought McGovern wrote about the theme of danger and how the concept of danger related to their lives as readers. They also talked about her decision to write information books and the reasons why they found certain kinds of genres easier or more difficult in their own writing.

Connections to Illustrations

Illustrations were frequently a topic of discussion as students made connections across illustrations, between illustrations and the text, and to the illustrator or readers. The Caldecott group discussed how illustrations and printed text work together in a story. They decided that it was impossible to give the award for just the illustrations without also considering the printed text. The Cinderella group spent a day discussing the way Cinderella was portrayed in the illustrations. They considered the illustrations so important to the story that they decided to draw their own illustrations of Cinderella for several short stories that had none. Illustrations became important to the Dragon group as a source of information about their hypothesis that dragon legends came from dinosaurs. They used the illustrations to list the physical characteristics of dragons and dinosaurs.

The Eric Carle group focused their discussions on why Eric Carle's books appeal to so many age levels. They were especially interested in the ways he engages readers through the unusual formats and bright colors of his illustrations. Other groups did not focus specifically on the illustrations in their discussions but used the illustrations as part of the story context for the comparisons they were discussing.

Connections to the Lives of Authors and Illustrators

The discussions on Text Sets based around authors and illustrators evolved naturally into an interest in the author and the relationship of authors' lives to the books they wrote and illustrated. Information on their lives was made available as the groups expressed interest. The McGovern group used a taped interview of McGovern to help them make connections between her life and her books. The Van Allsburg group focused on the details of his life and the items and people in his environment that they felt he continuously pulled from when illustrating his books. Only the Byars group showed little interest in the authors' life, perhaps because they found exploring the connections to their own life experiences more productive.

The groups tended to focus on authors and illustrators in relation to the children's own lives as readers and writers. The Eric Carle group focused on the impact of his books on readers and on the different ways in which readers of different ages use his books for a variety of insights. As noted earlier, the Pig group discussed their responses as readers and authors to the use of pigs in books. Groups often talked about why they felt authors or illustrators had made particular choices and what impact that decision had on them as readers. They also made connections to their writing and how they made similar decisions or had gained new writing and illustrating strategies.

Connections to Life Experiences and Previous Texts

Children's own life experiences were brought into the discussions when they seemed related to the issues or connections being considered. The Byars group was one group that focused primarily on connecting their personal experiences to the books they were reading. They felt a close connection between their lives and the kinds of problems with parents and friends faced by characters in Byars's books. Several of the children in the pig group came from farms and used their experiences with pigs to help the group compare real pigs with the talking pigs used in many stories. The McGovern group had a long discussion on their personal definitions of danger and their control over whether situations in their lives become dangerous.

Readers' past experiences also involve literary interactions with books. The Magic Pot group brought in other folk tales with similar characters or plot elements. The Pig group often made connections to *Charlotte's Web* (White, 1952), which had been read aloud to them earlier that year. The Cinderella group used their past experience with the Disney movie and book as the basis for all of their comparisons of their books. The literature children used for comparisons included their own writing and published books. One of the girls in the Magic Pot group had written a book in which a family went from poor to rich, and this book was often referred to in the group's discussions.

Connections to New Experiences

Sometimes groups realized that they needed to do additional research beyond the books in their set and their own experiences to build the background knowledge necessary to understand their Text Set or to explore particular issues. When the Dragon group began debating whether dragons were real, fantasy, or legends based on dinosaurs, they checked out many books on dinosaurs. The Eric Carle group found they needed more information to answer their questions about why his books appeal to so many age levels, and so they went to various classrooms and interviewed children and adults about why they liked Eric Carle books. The War and Peace group checked out additional books on World War II. The Plains Indians group read informational books and encyclopedias to find out more about how different tribes of Plains Indians communicated with each other.

What a particular group discussed was affected, of course, by the type of set that we had put together. It makes sense that the Eric Carle group focused on him as an illustrator or that the Cinderella group focused on how the different variants were alike and different. While the type of set highlighted a certain category of connections, the specific connections made by a group varied because of the past experiences with life and literature that each member brought to the group and because of the strategies the group chose to deal with their set. The war and peace group had a different type of discussion because of their decision to look at one book at a time. The focus of the Eric Carle group on reader appeal grew out of their interactions with a visiting adult who commented on how much she liked his books. The Dragon group focused on legend and fact because one group member's experiences led him to believe in the possibility that dragons are real.

PRESENTING INTERTEXTUAL CONNECTIONS TO OTHERS

The content focus of the different groups was highlighted as they finished their discussions and began to think about what they wanted to share with the rest of the class. Most of the groups spent around two weeks reading and discussing their books before moving into working on presentations. Some groups took only a day or two to prepare and give their presentations, while other groups worked on their presentations for a week. As each group finished, they gave their presentation and then went back to free choice, independent reading while the other groups continued working.

When a group was ready to work on a presentation, we asked them first to think as a group about what they wanted the class to understand about their set and about the ideas and connections they had discussed. They then brainstormed different ways they might be able to present those understandings effectively to others. Students previously had done presentations as part of other literature groups, and so they had many ideas for ways to present. Because the students valued the ideas and connections they had developed with each other, they worked hard to create ways to communicate some of these to other class members. During their work on these presentations, new ideas often were introduced and previous connections were considered from a new perspective. Students faced the task of conveying ideas discussed in language through another communication system such as art or drama, and so they had to reconsider those ideas and what they wanted to communicate (Siegel, 1984).

Most of the groups focused on the intertextual connections, which they had made through their dialogue with each other, rather than on presenting the books themselves. They seemed to use the presentations as an opportunity to think through and present the connections that had been most central to their group process. The Magic Pot group took the characteristics of magic pot stories that they had developed in their discussions and presented their own original magic pot story through drama. In contrast, the Cinderella group wanted others to see the differences across cultures in their stories. They wrote a reader's theatre in which one of the group members began reading the Disney variant and, as she read, she was constantly interrupted by others who told her she had the story wrong. Each person would interrupt to give her variant of Cinderella's name or where she went, only to be interrupted by another person.

The author groups combined their understandings of the author and the books in their presentations. The Eric Carle group took the information they had gathered through interviews and presented a radio show in which they played the roles of children and adults of different ages being interviewed about their responses to Eric Carle's books. The Anne McGovern group felt that their author was being ignored by other class members and deserved more popularity. They created posters describing the characters in her books, the theme of danger, and information on McGovern and the places she wrote about. They wore these as sandwich advertisement boards and paraded up and down the classroom. The Chris Van Allsburg group made a mural of what they thought his house must look like based on his illustrations and their reading about his life.

Several groups planned experiences so that the class would be actively involved in thinking about some of the issues with them and making their own connections. The Caldecott group developed a learning center where they listed their five categories and had class members sort Caldecott books based on those criteria. The War and Peace group presented a skit about the effects of war and engaged the class in a discussion about war and living in peace with others. The Pig group brought a real pig to the classroom for the morning and had class members take observational notes that they later compared to the pigs presented in literature. The Betsy Byars group wrote "Dear Abby" letters about the problems of their main characters. They posted the letters on a board for class members to respond to by giving advice on how to deal with that problem. The Native American group involved the class in several experiences using communication systems developed by Plains Indians. The Dragon group made a poster about dragons and one about dinosaurs. After presenting these posters, they asked classmates whether they thought the legends of dragons could be based on dinosaurs. The Japanese group borrowed nature slides and showed the slides as they read their favorite haiku poetry and served tea to class members.

These presentations were well received by class members, and students spend the next several weeks reading widely from books in other sets. What impressed us as teachers was the way these presentations reflected the discussions in the groups and the intertextual connections that had been most influential in their thinking about their sets. The process of thinking through and putting on the presentations seemed to help the groups step back and pull together what had been most significant about their experiences with the set. Their presentations were not just plot summaries or surface connections between the books. Rather, they were thoughtful presentations of critical intertextual connections that emerged from their dialogue.

AN ENVIRONMENT THAT SUPPORTS CHOICE AND STRATEGIES FOR LEARNING

In reflecting on this experience as educators, we found a number of implications for classroom learning environments. The role of choice and purpose in learning was especially evident. Students were given many choices as participants in these discussions. They had input into the choice of topics for the sets. They could choose which group to join, which books to read within the group, the strategies they used within their groups for reading and discussing their books, and the connections they discussed in depth. These choices helped them to feel a sense of ownership and responsibility in the group process because the decisions were not forced upon them. Because they made the decisions, they took more active roles.

Having choices in the content and process of the reading and group discussions allowed students to connect more easily with their own life experiences. Students could choose what books to read from their sets, and so they could pick books in which they had a greater interest and background for the topic and which were at a comfortable level of difficulty. Because these students saw themselves as active readers and writers, they drew from their life experiences as they searched for connections and discussed authors and elements of stories. They did not consider literature in isolation from themselves but always in connection with themselves, the world, and other literature in that world.

The brainstorming and discussion of connections came from the students. They chose how to respond. Thus they could respond in ways that connected with their own thinking rather than trying to figure out how the teacher wanted them to connect. The result was a much greater diversity of strategies and connections than if teachers had tightly controlled the process.

While there was a great deal of choice and student involvement in this strategy, there was also a supportive structure within which students made their choices. As teachers, we were responsible for establishing broad structures that would support the students' decision making. We established processes for choosing topics for the sets and signing up for the groups, got the groups started with reading and discussing, suggested strategies they might use in their groups, set aside a reflection time when groups could share their strategies with each other, and provided materials and time for presentations. Often we joined groups during brainstorming and suggested additional ideas and connections that the group might consider in their discussions. Some groups invited us to join them because they were having difficulty, either with the group dynamics or with a particular issue.

As teachers, we were a resource and had a definite influence on the groups, but we were not the sole determinant of the direction of the group. We suggested, for example, the strategy of reading several books, sharing those books, and then brainstorming some possible topics for comparison. This suggestion supported the groups in beginning their discussions but allowed them plenty of room for developing their own strategies to support the discussions. We did not expect the diversity of strategies that emerged from these groups and were quite surprised by what the groups developed. The structures we established gave students the support they needed to make choices. Without that support, there would have been confusion. But with restrictive structures, there would have been passivity and sameness. We continuously struggled to create structures that supported choice so that we could build curriculum collaboratively with students.

Another key construct was the social nature of learning and the power of dialogue in changing the thinking of learners. The Text Sets highlighted the contributions of each member of the group dialogue. Since each person had read something different from others in the group, each had something unique to contribute to the group process. Students were valued regardless of their reading proficiency or life experiences because they each had something to offer. The group had to work hard at dialogue and at critically listening and building from what others had to say as they searched for connections that would bring new understandings about their set. Through their interactions with each other and the books in their set, they considered new perspectives and intertextual connections.

This experience with Text Sets allowed us, as teachers, to see how we could provide experiences in the classroom that highlight important learning strategies in ways that are meaningful for students. In their discussions, students were involved with ideas and connections that were meaningful and important to them. They were not engaged in a lesson to practice making connections. Because the search for connections was essential to their discussions of these sets, it was natural for the class to spend time sharing their strategies for making these connections. In later experiences, we realized that the connection making was enhanced if the different Text Set groups all related to a broader theme, such as change or culture. When this broader theme was present, teachers could carefully choose read-aloud books to provide a broader context for discussions and connections. The groups also did more informal sharing with each other during the discussions.

These strategies and the focus on searching for connections became a conscious part of how students and teachers thought in other situations. We specifically noticed students making a more conscious search for connections in later discussions and bringing in broader connections when everyone in the group had read the same book. We also observed them using some of the strategies developed during the Text Set discussions in math and science experiences where they were working with large amounts of data.

What students first experienced through dialogue with others became part of the thinking they brought to later experiences. The focus on learning as a search for connections was a general perspective they began to bring to a variety of learning situations in their classrooms. They were more aware of the need for connections and the ways they could go about searching for these connections. Instead of passively responding to the ideas of powerful others, these learners were actively and critically searching to make sense of their worlds and their own learning processes. They were part of a strong community of learners focused on creating these understandings together.

PROFESSIONAL RESOURCES

Beaugrande, R. (1980). *Text, discourse, and process.* Norwood, NJ: Ablex.

Crafton, L. (1981). *Reading and writing as transactional processes.* Unpublished doctoral dissertation, Indiana University.

Glaser, B., & Strauss, A. (1967). *The discovery of grounded theory.* New York: Aldine.

Harste, J., Short, K., & Burke, C. (1988). *Creating classrooms for authors.* Portsmouth, NH: Heinemann Educational Books.

Harste, J., Woodward, V., & Burke, C. (1984). *Language stories and literacy lessons.* Portsmouth, NH: Heinemann Educational Books.

Hartman, D. (1990). Eight readers reading: The intertextual links of able readers using multiple passages. Unpublished doctoral dissertation, University of Illinois, Champaign-Urbana.

Rosenblatt, L. (1978). *The reader, the text, the poem: A transactional theory of the literary work.* Carbondale: Southern Illinois University Press.

Short, K. (1985). A new lens for reading comprehension: Comprehension processes as critical thinking. In A. Crismore (Ed.), *Landscapes: State of the art assessment of reading comprehension.* Bloomington, IN: Language Education Department, Indiana University.

Short, K. (1986). *Literacy as a collabortive experience.* Unpublished doctoral dissertation, Indiana University.

Short, K., & Pierce, K. (1990). *Talking about books: Creating literate communities.* Portsmouth, NH: Heinemann Educational Books.

Siegel, M. (1984). *Reading as signification.* Unpublished doctoral dissertation, Indiana University.

Vygotsky, L. (1978). *Mind in society.* Cambridge, MA: Harvard University Press.

CHILDREN'S LITERATURE

Fitzhugh, L. (1969). *Bang, bang, you're dead*. New York: Harper.
Louie, A. (1982). *Yeh-Shen*. New York: Philomel.
Mosel, A. (1972). *The funny little woman*. New York: Dutton.
Stock, C. (1984). *Emma's dragon hunt*. New York: Lothrop.
White, E. B. (1952). *Charlotte's web*. New York: Harper.

18

How Preferences and Expectations Influence Evaluative Responses to Literature

Lee Galda

Those of us who love to read want other people to experience the same joys. We read pieces of books aloud to spouses or friends, we read to our children and talk about books with them, we join book discussion groups, we take time out of our busy schedules and go to the library or the bookstore to look for new books or to revisit old favorites. One of the reasons that we like to read so much is the pleasure it gives us. Connecting with books can bring immense pleasure to any reader. We connect with narratives, whether realistic or fantasy, by becoming involved with and caring about the characters, by being engrossed in the events of a story, by feeling like we are there in the story world. A young girl once told me that she liked to read because she liked to be "inhaled by books"—a metaphor that perfectly sums up the single-minded absorption that connecting with a book can provide. It is opportunities for this kind of connection with books that schooling so effectively has denied to so many children for so many years and that new initiatives toward a literature-based curriculum seek to address.

The author would like to thank the faculty and students of Athens Academy for their cheerful cooperation. This research was supported by grants from the University of Georgia Research Foundation, the International Reading Association–Elva Knight Grant Program, and the National Council of Teachers of English Research Foundation. All views expressed in this chapter are solely those of the author.

FROM PLEASURE TO APPRECIATION

To encourage this connection between readers and texts, teachers now provide time to read, books to choose among, and, in the best circumstances, opportunities to talk about books with a variety of people in collaborative ways. We do so because we assume "that literature works by affecting readers and that teaching literature works if the student connects with the text" (Willinsky, 1990, p. 98). In this view, connecting with literature is not the end result that we are working toward, but rather a necessary condition for the end result, which is learning to love to read and to appreciate literature. Thirty years ago Early (1960) wrote about young readers moving from unconscious pleasure toward conscious delight and appreciation. It is this movement that I have been studying for the past twenty years, as both a teacher and a researcher.

Rosenblatt (1982) characterizes the pleasure of reading literature when she describes the aesthetic stance. An aesthetic reading of a text involves linking past experience with the world, with language, and with other texts to the text we are reading. As we do so, we construct our individual story. As we read aesthetically, we are aware of the sound and feeling of the text as well as of the experience that we are having as we identify with characters, "shar[ing] their conflicts and their feelings" (p. 270). To read aesthetically, we must "learn to draw on more of the experiential matrix. Instead of looking outwardly mainly to the public referents, the reader must include the personal, the qualitative, kinesthetic, sensuous inner resonances of the words" (p. 217).

Rosenblatt suggests that children quite naturally read (or listen) aesthetically when they are young, but soon learn to read "efferently" rather than aesthetically as they confront school reading tasks. Thus school reading can work against establishing the aesthetic stance that allows for a full, rich evocation of a story or poem.

What Rosenblatt describes as the aesthetic stance, Britton (1970) calls the "spectator stance." Although not identical concepts, these two ideas have much in common. (For a comparison of these two ideas, see Rosenblatt, 1985, and Britton, 1984.) Basing his description on Harding's (1937) idea of the role of the onlooker, Britton describes how we can emotionally participate in a story and contrasts that participation with real life, in which we are physically involved as well. The spectator stance, Britton argues, gives us the emotional space in which to evaluate the feelings, actions, and decisions of the story world and thus construct our personal values. It would seem, then, that an aesthetic or spectator stance is necessary if readers are to give themselves over to the potential emotional experience of reading a literary text.

SOCIAL AND INDIVIDUAL RESPONSE

When we have rich experiences with texts, we often want to talk about them. Yes, we generally read as individuals (although there are certainly wonderful ways to read socially, such as paired reading and reading aloud), but one of the most natural and compelling responses when we have finished reading a particularly good book is to tell someone about it. That's why we join book discussion groups and know which of our friends like to talk about the same kinds of books that we like. The social dimensions of response in elementary school classrooms have been explored by a number of studies, among them Hepler (1982), Hepler and Hickman (1982), Hickman (1981, 1983), and Kiefer (1983). They have found that children naturally share their reading with their peers when the classroom context allows them to do so. Further, this sharing of responses often helps children to explore and expand upon their initial responses. In order to talk about a book, a reader must move beyond unconscious pleasure and toward conscious delight and appreciation as they articulate both their opinions and the reasons behind those opinions.

Another thing that we readers do as we read is develop a concept of story (Applebee, 1978), a set of expectations for different genres, strong likes and dislikes, and a critical stance that enables us to appreciate or evaluate a story on at least two levels. First, we certainly respond on a personal, idiosyncratic level. I remember throwing Paterson's (1980) *Jacob Have I Loved* across the room because I was so upset by the ending. But we also learn to respond with a more detached evaluative stance. And thus I picked up the book, read it again, and, although I still don't like the ending, I can now appreciate why Paterson ended her story as she did.

THE STUDY

My interest in this movement from unconscious pleasure to appreciation that led me to a study of children in fourth, sixth, and eighth grade as they read and discussed realistic and fantasy juvenile novels in a school setting. My general research questions were: How do conscious delight and appreciation, as evidenced by evaluative responses to books, vary across grade levels? How do these responses vary according to genre? And, how are these responses linked to personal preferences (such as for genre) and expectations?

In order to explore these questions, I first observed in the classrooms during reading and language arts time and interviewed the teachers about their reading and literature programs. I then interviewed thirty-six students, six boys and six girls each in grades four, six, and eight, about their concepts of story, reading habits, preferences, and expectations. All of these students were reading at or above grade level, identified themselves as "liking to read," and were judged by their teachers as avid readers who would feel comfortable participating in this study. They were interviewed in an often-used conference room in their school, the middle-grades block of a kindergarten through twelfth-grade private school in a small southeastern American city. Generally, students in this school were academically successful and went on to college upon graduation.

After the interviews were completed, I or a research assistant (who had been a classroom teacher for a number of years) tape-recorded same-sex, same-grade groups of three as they discussed two juvenile novels, Betsy Byars's (1970) *The Summer of the Swans* and Madeleine L'Engle's (1973) *A Wind in the Door.* The order in which the books were read and discussed was counterbalanced across grades and groups. The discussions took place over a four-week period and were held in the same conference room. They were led by the researchers using open-ended questions and non-directive prompts such as "Tell me about the book," "So you thought . . . ," and "What do you think of what *X* said?" There was little need for adult intervention once the discussion began, as the groups quite freely discussed the books among themselves.

The books that they were discussing were selected because of their literary quality, age appropriateness, and genre differences: *The Summer of the Swans* is contemporary realistic fiction, *A Wind in the Door* is fantasy.

This research was part of a larger four-year study that has been reported elsewhere (Galda, 1990, in press). The following discussion is drawn from the transcripts of interviews and discussions and the information from classroom observations from the first year of the study only.

THE FOURTH GRADE

Classroom observations and interviews with the classroom teachers revealed that the reading program in the fourth grade was a basal program, with students reading aloud to the teacher, supplemented by daily reading aloud by the teacher and daily opportunities for independent reading by the students, who were encouraged to read for fun. The teachers also selected books for reading aloud with pleasure as the criterion and consistently selected books that they were sure the children would like—many of them humorous—rather than books that might introduce new genres, authors, or stylistic techniques. During the study they were reading Judy Blume's (1980) *Superfudge,* a book that all but one of the students had previously read on their own, passing it around the classroom.

Not surprisingly, six of the fourth-grade readers in this study preferred humorous stories, and most read a steady diet of funny, light fiction that dealt with problems and events that these students themselves might encounter or had experienced. Three readers mentioned liking stories with contemporary settings, problems, and characters. These young readers all listed what they expected in a book with words that described their own potential responses: They wanted books that were "exciting" and "interesting."

During the small group discussions, all of these readers spontaneously evaluated the books they read for this study, often comparing them with other books. There was, however, little demonstrated consciousness of the influence of their own preferences and expectations on their evaluation of the books. The fourth-grade readers' opinions of *The Summer of the Swans* were mixed, with no one expressing intense enjoyment and one group of boys dubbing it "a girl's book" and "boring." Generally, the boys reacted negatively to the "lack of excitement" in *The Summer of the Swans* by saying that "it needed more action." They had stated preferences for humor and excitement and the lack of both in *The Summer of the Swans* contributed to its negative evaluation by the boys. The girls were more positive in their evaluations, saying that they thought that the book was "sort of boring" but that it "got better in the middle." As they had said in their interviews, these girls enjoyed reading about "people our own age doing daily kinds of things." The boys, wanting excitement, pigeonholed this book as a boring, girl's book. The girls, wanting excitement and true-to-life characters, found it boring as well, but enjoyed the main character.

Although they were all reading well above grade level, basic comprehension was a problem for these readers when they read the fantasy text, *A Wind in the Door.* Half of these readers had previously discussed "knowing and correctly pronouncing all of the words" as the hallmark of a good reader, and this concern for the surface features of the text made this book difficult to read. All but two of these readers were stopped by the dense dialogue and, most of all, the difficult names. They spent their time trying to pronounce words rather than simply reading over them. As one reader put it, "I was doing okay, then I tried to figure out the names and got all mixed up." Only two of these readers reported that they "replaced" the hard words and "tried to figure out [the meaning] by context." They were still reading orally in reading groups in their classrooms, and for many of them their concern for correct pronunciation, an appropriate concern if one is reading aloud, was inappropriately applied to independent silent reading, with the result that they were unable to get beyond their difficulties with the proper nouns in the text.

In spite of their difficulties with comprehension and their preference for realistic books, however, the consensus among the group was that *A Wind in the Door* was a "better" book than *The Summer of the Swans*. It was confusing, comprehension was often lacking, and it certainly wasn't realistic, but it was a good adventure. As one said, "I didn't understand it, but the big words didn't make me not like it. I didn't want to put it down because it was getting so interesting and had all the adventure and it was fun." The entertaining nature of adventure clearly outweighed the lure of realism without adventure. The adventurous plot of *A Wind in the Door* met their stated preferences for action and excitement and thus it was judged a good book.

There were other indications that these readers focused primarily on plot. During all of the discussions, these fourth graders commented about the "details" in the texts, and these comments were further indications that most of these readers were responding primarily to the plot. For example, all but one boy thought there were a lot of "unnecessary details" in *The Summer of the Swans*. They felt that the minor characters "weren't really necessary" as they didn't do much to move the plot forward. Some of the girls, however, enjoyed the details and the book, saying, "those kind of little things make it funny and interesting" and "little things are important." Judgments about the importance of details in *A Wind in the Door* were also mixed. A few felt that the details "made the story interesting," but most complained of the "unnecessary parts just stuck in there," referring to anything not essential to the forward movement of the plot, whether dialogue or minor characters. This focus on plot was consistent with their expectations for literature; they wanted excitement and focused on the plot, which delivered it.

THE SIXTH GRADE

In the sixth-grade classroom, instruction in reading was based on a basal series. In addition, the classroom teacher had a daily read-aloud program in which she sought to "introduce students to good literature." She read from a variety of books that had been written for children and that were generally considered to be of good literary quality; many of the selections were Newbery winners or honor books. The read-aloud program was not accompanied by any systematic literature instruction. The students rarely read orally themselves, but were required to read at least two books per month and to report on them in some fashion. Reporting options included the traditional written book report, book talks, and card files. The students made regular visits to the school library and were allowed to visit the library during their free time as well.

In the sixth grade, reading preferences were clearly split according to gender: half of the girls had found fiction and romance, and the boys were reading science fiction and fantasy. These readers generally preferred adventure, excitement, and a "fast pace" in the books they read. Five of them talked about books that would absorb them or get them "away from the real world." They listed identification with characters, reading about relationships, and escape as sources of pleasure in their reading.

The sixth-grade readers' evaluations of *The Summer of the Swans* were similar to those of the fourth-grade readers: not enough action and excitement. The girls also felt that more "romance" would have improved the book, reflecting their stated preference for romances. With one exception, the girls did not like *A Wind in the Door* at all. The difficult vocabulary and the imaginative science fiction fantasy genre were not appreciated. The boys, unlike the girls, enjoyed the "weird" and "scientific" nature of the book. The boys had indicated preferences for science fiction or fantasy during the interviews, and this was evident in their evaluations. One boy was enthusiastic about it, and the other five expressed enjoyment despite their problems with the vocabulary and the dense style. However, these readers persevered and did come away with an understanding of and liking for the story, perhaps in part because they didn't stop to worry about the correct pronunciation of the proper nouns. As one boy stated, he "got it from the context a lot of the time." Thus, although the vocabulary was difficult, it was not the major problem for these readers that it was for the fourth graders. These readers did little oral reading in their classroom.

Both negative and positive evaluative comments on these books generally indicated that these readers knew that their evaluations were the result of an interaction between the kind of book it was and their own personal taste. They commented: "This kind of book I like a lot." "I liked *A Wind in the Door* better because I like stuff that's far-fetched." "I think I liked this book better because this is the type of book I like." Some specifically mentioned the genre as the reason behind their evaluation: "I liked it because it was science fiction." "[To understand it], you have to be used to science fiction and know what to expect." "I don't like science fiction. It's not my type of book." These readers seemed to recognize that there was a connection between what they preferred and how they responded to what they read. This idea of self-awareness in reading was also mentioned during the interviews as an attribute of a good reader. Knowing what one enjoys and selecting accordingly were things that these readers tried to do.

These readers also seemed to recognize that literature is not a unitary construct. During the interviews, most of them talked about stories as a range of possibilities, and they continued to do so during the discussions, saying things such as, "There are scary and exciting books and this kind of gentle, caring, touching book." Comments like this indicate that these readers were not only aware of how their own preferences influenced their responses but also of the fact that there are differences in books that do not necessarily detract from quality.

Interestingly, these readers, while cognizant of the influence of their own preferences on their responses and of the multiple possibilities inherent in fiction, were not consistent in their perceptions of the books they read as depictions of possible realities. Indeed, the realism of *The Summer of the Swans* was a negative element for some. They complained of the lack of fit with their own worlds: The characters were "kind of like us," but "they don't act like we act at my house," "they don't fight like real brothers and sisters."

Some of these sixth-grade readers drew on their real-world experience to criticize characters' actions, while some used that same knowledge to explain characters' actions. For example, when one reader remarked that Sara was "a bit too calm" about Charlie's disappearance, another commented, "Well, some people do react that way." Thus, while some of these readers could treat the world of the text as a possible reality, others insisted on directly comparing it with their own world and responding negatively to the differences. *A Wind in the Door* was not discussed in this way, perhaps because the fantasy ensured that these readers would not find correspondences with their own worlds. Interestingly, only one of these readers mentioned comparing herself to the characters, even though they discussed identification with characters as a source of pleasure in their reading.

THE EIGHTH GRADE

The eighth-grade teacher used a traditional English literature text for instruction but also emphasized the value of personal response to reading. The literature that his students were required to read was, in his words, "the classics," but he encouraged students to "read, think, and respond in an individual fashion." The eighth-grade readers read, discussed, and analyzed a wide variety of literature in their classroom as they learned to use the techniques and terminology of literary criticism.

An eclectic group of preferences and a strong move toward adult novels typified the eighth-grade readers. Some readers were rather specific in their preferences, citing genres such as "historical fiction of the thirties and forties," while others were more general, preferring "stories that you can really live," and "that change you." Identification with characters was paramount; they wanted "characters you can relate to so you'd know how to feel in the same situation." Further, these readers were aware of their own responses to the books they read as they read them.

Like the fourth- and sixth-grade readers, the eighth-grade readers noted the lack of action in *The Summer of the Swans* and the imaginative nature of *A Wind in the Door,* but their evaluations of these attributes were quite different from those of the younger readers. The eighth-grade readers agreed that *The Summer of the Swans* was "too easy" for eighth grade (although many teachers would disagree with them) and would be enjoyed more by younger readers. In spite of this, they could appreciate why the book won a Newbery Award; only one reader expressed negative reactions, complaining about the "simplicity of the plot." The general consensus was summed up in one reader's response: "It was a good story but it could have evolved more."

The imaginativeness of *A Wind in the Door* was less distancing for these readers than it was for the younger readers. They found the human characters of the novel believable enough that one "kinda got involved with them." The book was "written believably" and one could "almost see oneself doing those things." They discussed how L'Engle's style blurred the distinction between real and not real: "I don't think this could possibly happen, but the way she writes it sounds believable to me." Another added, "The conversations are real enough." One boy remarked that the author "tried to set all these situations into language that was more realistic to us." Able to see the truth behind the fantasy, these readers could enjoy the book in spite of the demands imposed by the genre. Unlike the fourth-grade readers, they were not bothered by the difficult vocabulary. Indeed, these readers spoke of the necessity for a special vocabulary, saying that ordinary names for unusual characters "would have ruined the story," "would have taken away from it." One reader went on the explain why "imaginary names" were important: "You don't have a concept of your own to stick on to it. . . . Your own feelings about a word don't affect this particular case."

When these readers evaluated the books, they seemed more objective than the younger readers. Rather than dismissing parts of stories that they found extraneous, as the younger readers did, these eighth graders could go beyond their personal reactions to see how parts functioned in the story as a whole. They were able to work in the realm of "conscious appreciation." Indeed, they were learning how to do this in their classroom, as they read, discussed, and analyzed a wide variety of literature.

These readers were also aware of how their own preferences influenced their responses. Commentary on their own and others' responses was frequent. Comparing *The Summer of the Swans* and *A Wind in the Door,* one reader explained his preference for the latter by saying that he didn't mean that *The Summer of the Swans* was a bad book but that he "just liked books that are solid action" and he "liked unrealistic books." These readers also talked about stance;

one remarked, for example, that you "have to read it as fiction." Some cited genre preferences to explain or elaborate on their evaluations: "I was surprised because I usually don't like that kind of book very much and I enjoyed this one." Another added, "Me, too. I usually like books about people." And a third said, "I wouldn't have picked this book. I don't like science fictions [sic]. But I thought it was good." More elastic in their expectations for story, these readers were able to appreciate, if not always enjoy, books that were not their usual fare.

DISCUSSION

Generally, preferences and expectations differed across the grades, moving from global to differentiated, general to relatively specific. Identifying with characters and creating a virtual experience while reading were more important to the older readers than to the younger readers. Appreciation of these books, as evidenced by evaluative responses, differed with age as well. The older readers were more able to articulate the interaction between their preferences and their responses. They were less likely than the younger readers to judge a book as bad simply because it did not reflect their favorite kind of reading material. There was a greater understanding of the interrelatedness of literary elements in the older readers than there was in the younger readers and, along with this, a diminishing tendency to judge a book according to its fit with their own perceptions of reality. Thus, even fantasy came to be understood as being about recognizable people with familiar problems, as containing the possibility of truth even if not reality.

The preferences of the older readers were both more specific and more articulated than those of the younger readers. At the same time, their ability to approach a variety of literature with an open mind; to appreciate a wide variety of characters, styles, and genres, regardless of specific preferences; and to assume a spectator stance (Britton, 1970) enabled the older readers to better utilize literature as virtual experience (Langer, 1957). That is, they could enter into the world of the story and live through the events of the story, even if the story was not a preferred genre or concerned with familiar problems. Because the tendency to insist on a real-world analogue for fictional characters and events was less strong for the eighth-grade readers than for the fourth-grade readers, the older students were able to get involved with the stories they were reading regardless of character age, gender, or type and in spite of fantasy settings. Their interest in characters rather than plot also contributed to their growing ability to live the stories as they were reading.

The influence of preferences and expectations on response was markedly different across the grades. The preferences and expectations of these readers moved from a focus on action, or plot, to a demand for intriguing characters. The fourth-graders preferred the more difficult fantasy text because it was more adventurous, one of their stated preferences. The sixth-grade girls also showed a marked influence of preference; they looked for romance, and not finding it hampered positive responses. The sixth-grade boys, however, were able to appreciate texts that were outside of their personal preferences, as were the eighth-grade readers.

Further, the way in which these readers evaluated the books was different across the grades. The fourth-grade readers tended to categorize rather than analyze by judging texts in terms of general attributes that related to their own stated preferences. Sixth-grade readers were evenly split according to gender: the girls evaluated categorically, relying on their own stated preferences, while the boys were more flexible in their appreciation of variety in literature and also responded with more analytic evaluations. The eighth-grade readers analyzed the books, rising above their own preferences to appreciate the craft of the author. This progression of evaluative behaviors parallels that noted in other research (Applebee, 1978; Galda, 1983, in press).

These differences in responses across grades also reflect the differences in the classroom contexts across grades. The fourth-grade readers participated in oral basal lessons and were encouraged to read independently for pleasure. They were steered toward books that would entertain them. They were not asked to do much more with literature than read it and tell others what a book was about. The older readers, on the other hand, were expected to read widely and were learning to analyze and appreciate a wide variety of texts. As Hickman (1981) has pointed out, what the teacher does in the classroom strongly influences student response.

It would be easy to state that fourth-grade readers can't analyze and can't rise above their own preferences to appreciate an author's craft, but it would also be erroneous. The results of this study arise from interactions among individual readers, two very distinct texts, and three classroom contexts and are understandable only in terms of these factors. The classroom contexts certainly influenced the way in which these readers approached the texts, with the youngest readers encouraged to read for their own pleasure and the oldest encouraged to read critically. Reader factors also contributed to the differences in response across the grades, with cognitive growth increasing the ability and the ease with which readers responded analytically to the books. The texts made a difference, too, with the younger readers responding quite differently to the fantasy text than to the realistic text.

This interplay of context, reader, and text factors is a crucial consideration for teachers of literature interested in moving their students forward from unconscious pleasure to articulated appreciation. First of all, as Rosenblatt (1982) has argued, pleasure is the necessary first step. Certainly the fourth-grade teachers involved in this study were concerned with their students' attitudes toward reading. They sought to read aloud to their students books that would entertain. In doing so, they affirmed for their students the idea that reading is fun. However, by selecting only lighthearted, often humorous, contemporary fiction, they may have unnecessarily limited their students' experiences with books. One of our goals as teachers is to stretch our students by helping them work just beyond themselves with our support. Thus we must systematically build a read-aloud program that includes not only pleasurable experiences with light fiction, but also pleasurable experiences with literature that expands our emotional knowledge. In other words, it is important to remember that humor is not the only source of pleasure. Read-aloud programs that include a variety of genres and authors and that are planned to stretch as well as to entertain are important.

Along with this, we need to ensure that our students are encouraged to read independently from a variety of genres and authors, while still being allowed to make their own selections. This encouragement does not mean that we should force children to read the books we want them to read during their independent reading. It does mean that we can tell them about other books, perhaps through book talks, that we can encourage them to talk with particular peers who are reading different kinds of books, and that we can make sure that our classroom collection is full of books that can offer rich emotional experiences to our students. The older readers in this study were exposed to a wide variety of texts, and this experience helped them develop an appreciation for books that were different from their usual fare. They were more able to aesthetically enjoy a wider variety of books.

We also need to look at the opportunities that we present to our students for sharing and extending their responses to the books they read. Are they encouraged to respond in a variety of modes, such as drama, art, and media, as well as the more traditional modes of writing and discussion? Exploring books through a variety of response activities often helps students develop a greater understanding of and appreciation for what they read. Further, the opportunities for response that we provide ought to help them become more aware of their own responses, of how the story that they have created is a function both of their own experiences and of the text that they read. Thus their responses will differ, in part, from the responses of their friends. Being able to talk with others about the stories that they have constructed can help students learn to trust their own responses and to expand those responses by sharing them with others.

Students also need to be encouraged to refer to the text as they respond. Linking response to elements of the text as well as to personal experience is a necessary condition for developing an appreciation of the way literature works. All of the readers in this study were able to identify both problematic and especially enjoyable parts of the texts they read. Greater experience with literature and with talking about books made the older readers more able to link their own responses to the author's craft.

Britton has suggested that assuming a spectator stance allows readers "to evaluate more broadly, to savor feelings, and to contemplate forms" (1970, p. 121). The responses of intermediate readers that are discussed here document the evolution of that stance. So, too, do they document the growth toward conscious delight in and appreciation (Early, 1960) of the craft of the author, regardless of personal preferences and expectations. Finally, these responses show us young readers in the act of building a conscious critical ability on the foundation of their pleasure in books.

PROFESSIONAL RESOURCES

Applebee, A. N. (1978). *The child's concept of story.* Chicago: University of Chicago Press.

Britton, J. (1970). *Language and learning.* London: Allen Lane, The Penguin Press.

Britton, J. (1984). Viewpoints.: The distinction between participant and spectator role language in research and practice. *Research in the Teaching of English, 18,* 320–331.

Early, M. (1960). Stages of growth in literary appreciation. *English Journal, 49,* 161–167.

Galda, L. (1983). Research in response to literature. In H. Agee, & L. Galda (Eds.), *Response to literature: Theoretical and empirical studies (Journal of Research and Development in Education), 16*(3), 1–7.

Galda, L. (1990). A longitudinal study of the spectator stance as a function of age and genre. *Research in the Teaching of English, 24,* 261–278.

Galda, L. (in press). Evaluation as a spectator: Changes across time and genre. In J. Many, & C. Cox (Eds.), *Reader stance and literary understanding: Exploring the theories, research, and practice.* Norwood, NJ: Ablex.

Harding, D. W. (1937). The role of the onlooker. *Scrutiny, 6,* 247–258.

Hepler, S. I. (1982). Patterns of response to literature: A one-year study of a fifth and sixth grade classroom. *Dissertation Abstracts International, 43,* 1419-A. (University Microfilms no. 82-22100).

Hepler, S., & Hickman, J. (1982). "The book was okay. I love you."—Social aspects of response to literature. *Theory into Practice, 21*(4), 278–283.

Hickman, J. (1981). A new perspective on response to literature: Research in an elementary school setting. *Research in the Teaching of English, 15,* 343–354.

Hickman, J. (1983). Everything considered: Response to literature in an elementary school setting. In H. Agee, & L. Galda (Eds.), *Response to literature:*

Theoretical and empirical studies (Journal of Research and Development in Education), 16(3), 8–13.

Kiefer, B. (1983). The responses of children in a combination first/second-grade classroom to picture books in a variety of artistic styles. In H. Agree, & L. Galda (Eds.), *Response to literature: Theoretical and empirical studies (Journal of Research and Development in Education), 16*(3), 14–20.

Langer, S. K. (1957). *Philosophy in a new key.* Cambridge, MA: Harvard University Press.

Rosenblatt, L. M. (1982). The literary transaction: Evocation and response. *Theory into Practice, 21*(4), 268–277.

Rosenblatt, L. M. (1985). Transaction versus interaction—A terminological rescue operation. *Research in the Teaching of English, 19,* 96–107.

Willinsky, J. (1990). *The new literacy: Redefining reading and writing in the schools.* New York: Chapman and Hall.

CHILDREN'S LITERATURE

Blume, J. (1980). *Superfudge.* New York: Dell.

Byars, B. (1970). *The summer of the swans.* New York: Viking.

L'Engle, M. (1973). *A wind in the door.* New York: Farrar, Straus & Giroux.

Paterson, K. (1980). *Jacob have I loved.* New York: Avon.

Commentary on Research: Response to Literature

Bernice E. Cullinan

We take all sorts of journeys. By air we see a broad landscape from a distance. As train riders we hurtle across the land by day and night to see villages and countryside close, but at high speed. When we drive a car we follow road maps and choose to speed or to linger awhile. On motor boats we plough the water, and on sailboats we drift with the wind. As bicyclists and walkers we meander close to nature along forest paths or city streets.

As travelers we can see engaging vistas along the way and stop to savor them, or we can hurry on to new sights. In this volume, researchers in children's response to literature take us on research journeys. Since this field of inquiry is relatively new, many of the paths are exploratory. Others are well trodden. However, all provide exciting views. My comments include a brief look at where we have been, where we are now, and where we might probe in the future.

THE PAST: WHERE WE HAVE BEEN

Rosenblatt (1968, 1978) helped researchers take major strides when she clarified the distinction between *efferent* reading, where the reader's attention is focused primarily on the knowledge that will remain after the reading (1978, p. 23), and *aesthetic* reading, where the reader's attention is centered directly on the experience that is lived through during a relationship with a particular text (1978, p. 25). Although Rosenblatt has since clarified aesthetic and efferent as two poles on a continuum, the concepts serve to distinguish among reading events.

Rosenblatt and schema theorists support the notion that meaning is not something that resides in a text to be extracted by a reader; instead, meaning is created by a reader in transaction with a text. That is, meaning is shaped by what a reader brings to a text as well as what an author puts into it. As we have seen in the preceding chapters, the interpretation or the meaning created by interaction with a text, then, varies depending upon the reader's life experience and literary experience. Several readers reading the same text each many create different meanings because they bring diverse experiences and levels of understanding to the text. Similarly, the same reader reading the same text at different times will create different meanings depending upon changes in life and literary experiences.

All readings are not equally valid, however. The text constrains the number of possible meanings that can be taken from it; lively discussions ensue about what in the text supports an interpretation. The meanings obtained represent a delicate balance between possible meanings and the interpretations, images, and memories brought by each reader. This balance produces the aesthetic object, or the "poem," according to Rosenblatt. Accepting such a position contradicts the "one right answer" model (sometimes called the inquisition model) teachers have historically used to lead literature discussions.

In the recent past, literature has been adopted as a central unifying element in school curriculum. As a major thrust of the whole language movement, literature becomes the heart of school learning. While this approach has been widely successful, some now caution that we need to protect literature from misuse and abuse.

THE PRESENT: WHAT WE NOW KNOW

The body of research Holland, Hungerford, and Ernst present provides convincing evidence of the power of a teacher and the power of literature. Both sources of power are multiplied exponentially when teachers are researchers who reflect upon their experiences and the literature they use. Similarly, when the literature represents high-quality writing, is freely chosen by students, and reflects their lives in some way, the power is even more potent.

As we have seen in these studies, the role of the teacher in eliciting children's rich responses to literature is crucial. In each case, the teacher creates a literacy environment and establishes the conditions for students to respond. Is there a choice in what students read? Is there a choice in how students respond to what they read? Is there an opportunity to create a community of readers and responders? The answers to these questions establish the conditions for response and alter the support and freedom for responding.

This book expands our understanding of the types of research methodologies and the membership of collaborative research teams appropriate to study response to literature. Case studies, interviews, participant observation, experimental and descriptive methods, and numerous ethnographic techniques were successfully used to add new insights to our knowledge of how children respond to literature. University faculty, classroom teachers, library media specialists, students in teacher training programs, and children constitute the various collaborative research teams. Further, a variety of response modes were invited from students. Verbal, artistic, dramatic, written, and visual responses were elicited in various settings. All have added new information about response patterns and possibilities.

The vantage point for initiating response research differs. We saw how Hungerford's colleagues used children's passion for Star Wars videos and books to develop literary understanding. Teachers here redirected day care students' self-initiated role playing from the rough and tumble of fighting toward group-directed role playing. One teacher wrote down the names of Star Wars characters, scrambled them up, and asked children to take turns playing different roles. This activity required the children to explore the ideas and behaviors of characters other than their particular favorites and to learn about different aspects of space travel. Children created Star Wars books by dictating group stories. They turned their own stories into scripts for dramatic presentations.

Another study shows the value of reusing familiar material and inviting students' active participation. Jacque found that repeated readings of the same stories led to a wider range and depth of responses, which included children taking over the reading and making the teacher feel she was no longer needed as the reader. During repeated readings, students made more predictions, picked up new vocabulary words, made more active responses, and became more active participants.

Kristo showed the value of documenting the ways individual teachers work with literature and talk with students about books. In this case, a university researcher and a talented first-grade teacher worked together in a classroom where read-aloud time was the centerpiece from which all other curriculum flowed. The teacher showed her students that she was a reader who appreciated literature by, among other things, asking students what they noticed about a text and sharing what she herself noticed, such as dedication pages and information about the author or illustrator. Kristo noted that the talk about books helped children to become aware of how they made choices about what to read, to see connections between books they read, and to recognize universals across literature. Books became the glue that bound the classroom community into a network of readers.

Wilson Keenan found ways to deepen the literary experience by helping readers return to a text to relive and savor the experience (Rosenblatt, 1982, p. 275). Through modeling, she supported responses that went beyond talk—for example, the literary letter, following techniques used in *The Jolly Postman*. Students used functional spelling to write wonderful letters to characters. Their letters show that art and writing develop in a reciprocal and mutually supportive way.

McClure showed that students' love of poetry depends on exposure to a variety of poetic forms and on their teacher's enthusiasm for poetry. She documented strategies that inspire a love of poetry and introduced the idea of poetry cycles. McClure identified the conditions needed to create a love of poetry: (1) immersion in poetry through hearing it read aloud, reading it, and writing it, (2) responding personally, aesthetically, before any efferent response is solicited. In a study with nonfiction books, Holland and Shaw found that a sensitive teacher can help students switch back and forth between efferent and aesthetic stances.

Golden and Handloff demonstrate the value of modeling and expand our view of responding to literature through journal writing. Handloff used her own journal entries and those of previous students to model appropriate ways to respond beyond plot retellings. Golden analyzed response types and found them to be mostly narrational responses, literary judgment, and plot retellings.

Anzul's comprehensive study validates Rosenblatt's theories, expands her concepts, and makes them applicable to classroom practice. Notably, it demonstrates the value of an extended period of interaction between a librarian and a group of readers. We see a classroom where literature became the arena for a linkage with the world of the student; it is through literature that such linkages occur. Anzul's students spoke for themselves to reveal their understanding as they moved to higher levels of thinking. We eavesdrop on their conversation as they probe the metaphorical use of language in a discussion of a meadow perceived as a mother figure to a character. Fertile discussions grew out of emotional tension, and students were moved to moments of passion when a sense of joy, playfulness, or sudden thoughtfulness and quiet overcame them.

Short examined text sets. She defined text sets as a collection of conceptually related books organized around a theme, author, genre, or topic, and discussed them as a strategy teachers can use to engage students in reading and talking. Students read several books from the set and together explored comparisons and connections across the books and their lives. Text sets highlight intertextuality, the process of making meaning through connections across present and past texts and life experience. Students learn to search for connections not only in their literature text sets but in other learning situations in the classroom.

THE FUTURE: WHERE DO WE NEED TO GO?

Over the past ten to fifteen years, we have learned tremendous amounts about children's responses to literature. Holland and her colleagues have added significantly to that body of knowledge, both quantitatively and qualitatively. It would be comforting to think that the teachers described in these pages are representative of the caliber of teachers available today. Although we may not trust that this is entirely true, we do know there has been a burst of teacher enthusiasm for whole language and literature, so that now, perhaps, is a time to solidify, absorb, and incorporate what we have learned. It is certainly a time to support teachers in their active search for personal meaning and in the right to make decisions such as the ones exemplified by the studies here.

Many studies remain to be done. One needs to trace changes in the way teachers lead literature discussion groups in their classrooms before and after they participate as members of a book discussion group themselves. Through personal experience as a participant in a book discussion group, I recognize changes that I subsequently made in leading my classroom discussions about literature. I changed from a grand inquisitor to a dialogue participant. Perhaps others do, too.

Another area begging to be researched centers on culturally diverse populations and literature. How do specific ethnic and racial groups respond to literature that purports to represent them? Do Latinos identify with characters who are Cuban, Mexican, Puerto Rican, and Caribbean? Do the levels of aesthetic response change when students read about a character from the same (or different) ethnic group? What literary factors, if any, superseded ethnic identification of characters? For example, do students respond to a well-written book regardless of the ethnic identity of the character?

We need more studies of responses to various genres. For example, do developmental and gender trends persist when students are exposed to a variety of good literature by an enthusiastic guide? Do girls choose realistic romance novels at ages 11 to 13 if a teacher or librarian who is an avid science fiction reader immerses them in science fiction? Do boys turn to fantasy and science fiction if they are exposed to strong realistic writers such as Gary Paulsen, Katherine Paterson, Cynthia Voigt, Lois Lowry, and Richard Peck?

Who are the fantasy readers and what characteristics of fantasy appeal to them? What effect does performing poetry have on readers' attitude toward it? How does historical fiction expand students' understanding of historical periods?

I resist the idea that we need to develop ways to evaluate response, especially aesthetic response, to literature. The reality, however, is that what gets measured gets taught or is given room in the curriculum. Our society seems to value only what we can measure—or we measure what we value. Regardless of the reasons, we need to find new ways to appropriately assess response to literature.

Journeying among children responding to literature is a pleasant voyage filled with bright moments and sudden insights. Teachers and librarians who take the journey will have moments of passion as they discover an idea to take to their classroom tomorrow. Researchers on the journey will see new ways to conduct inquiry and be stimulated to ask new questions. University teachers who take the journey will shape their classroom practices to savor aesthetic responses from participants. Together we can all celebrate the beauty of literature and share in the joy of others who read it.

PROFESSIONAL RESOURCES

Rosenblatt, L. (1968). *Literature as exploration* (3rd ed). New York: Modern Language Association.

Rosenblatt, L. (1978). *The reader, the text, the poem: A transactional theory of the literart work*. Carbondale: Southern Illinois Press.

Rosenblatt,L. (1982). The literary transaction: evocation and response. In *Theory into Practice, 21*(4), 268–277.

Index

Index prepared by Alex Hartmann, March 1993.